To Jim

CONTENTS

ACKNOWLEDGEMENTS

WRITING A BOOK CAN BE AN ISOLATING EXPERIENCE, AND I AM honored to acknowledge the following friends, families, and colleagues, who made the process bearable.

I owe a great debt to two scholars: Sue Armitage, my advisor at Washington State University, and Beverly Beeton, formerly of the University of Alaska. I am particularly honored that both continued to share a great interest in my project as it has evolved. I am also grateful to LeRoy and Mary Ashby for their friendship and for providing encouragement and support as I navigated the difficult publication process.

For their financial assistance, I thank Thomas S. Foley, Edward and Margery Bennett, the Washington State University Graduate School, and the Charles Redd Center for Western Studies. I also owe particular thanks to Peter and Kim Nazzal; Sue Paras-Sacchi; my late grandfather, Vincent Ross; and Kathy and John Gartland, who graciously let me stay at their homes so that I could conduct my research.

Suzanne Julin deserves credit for putting me in touch with Nancy Tystad Koupal, editor of *South Dakota History*, who helped me track down Emma's correspondence at the South Dakota State Historical Society in Pierre. Colleen Smith, a librarian at the Huron Public Library, happily helped me track down information about the DeVoes. Without the assistance of the interlibrary loan staff at Washington State University and the University of Houston, I would not have been able to use so many of the sources found in this book.

Archivists and librarians from Washington to Massachusetts helped in immeasurable ways, and I wish to thank the following institutions for their aid: the Bancroft Library, the Colorado Historical Society, the Eastern Washington Historical Society/Northwest Museum of Arts and Culture, the Huntington Library, the Huron Public Library, the Idaho State Historical Society, the Illinois State Library, the Kansas State Historical Society, the Library of Congress, the Montana Historical Society, the Tacoma Public Library, the Schlesinger Library, the Sophia Smith Collection, the University of the Pacific Holt-Atherton Special Collections, the University of Oregon Special Collections and University Archives, the University of South Dakota Archives and Special Collections, the University of Utah Manuscripts Division, the University of Washington Libraries Special Collections Division, and the Washington State Archives. A special thanks goes to the staff of the South Dakota State Historical Society, who always went above and beyond my requests, offering to work weekends so that I could do research, and once scheduling a personal tour of the Pickler Mansion in Faulkton. And, I owe a special debt of gratitude to the librarians at the Washington State Library, who lugged out Emma's boxes more times than I can count and answered numerous questions about the collection. I also wish to recognize employees of the courts and the register of deeds in Beadle and Faulk counties for their cheerful assistance.

During the revision of my manuscript, I attended a week-long seminar at the Schlesinger Library, where I had the opportunity to share my project with other scholars. There, I was fortunate to have met Melanie Gustafson, and I would like to thank her for her sunny outlook and encouragement over the years.

Other scholars shaped the manuscript in different ways. Karen Blair read the manuscript twice, and I benefitted from her advice and comments. Shanna Stevenson of the Washington Women's History Consortium provided a boost of confidence, when she called out of the blue and asked where she could find my book. Paula Nelson of the University of Wisconsin-Platteville and John Miller, professor emeritus of South Dakota State University, offered suggestions and needed guidance on my Huron chapter.

Many colleagues, friends, and family took an interest in my work over the past nine years and I thank them for their continual support and interest in my book: Kim Weathers, Jane Odom, Kelly Swickard, Sara

McCoy, Bill and Laura Skehan, Andy and Debbie Nazzal, Peter and Kim Nazzal, Scott and Carrie Ross, and Troy and Theresa Wesson. Rebecca Wright and Sandra Johnson have been the most encouraging colleagues I could have hoped for, and I wish to thank them for their assistance and friendship.

Marianne Keddington-Lang of the University of Washington Press helped usher the book from manuscript to book form. I thank her and Mary Ribesky for their close reading of the manuscript as well as for their guidance and assistance with publication.

Rachael Levay deserves credit for finding new and innovative ways to publicize the book, and I sincerely thank and acknowledge the remaining staff who assisted with this book.

As I finished my manuscript and awaited a positive review, I was fortunate to meet Cheryl and Dave Teifke, the owners of the DeVoe Mansion in Tacoma. To my delight, they opened their home to me and shared an interest in seeing this book come to fruition. I was also fortunate to have met Jim and Susan Welch, descendants of the DeVoes, who kindly shared their family records with me and let me spend a weekend at their home in Modesto as we sorted through letters and photographs.

Finally, I wish to thank my parents and in-laws for their support. I also thank my husband, Jim, for his encouragement, especially during the days when it seemed that the project would never end. More than once we combined vacations with research trips, where we spent hours combing collections and scanning newspapers for tidbits about Emma. Thank you for your patience and support!

A NOTE ABOUT NAMES

SOME MAY QUESTION WHY I HAVE NOT REFERRED TO EMMA SMITH DeVoe by her last name throughout the text. She is known as Emma to avoid any confusion with her husband, John Henry DeVoe, who is mentioned frequently throughout the book. He is referred to as Henry. I refer to Emma's colleagues and friends by their last names, as is conventional in historical writing.

LIST OF ABBREVIATIONS

AWSA	American Woman Suffrage Association
ESA	Equal Suffrage Association
FSA	Federal Suffrage Association
GAR	Grand Army of the Republic
GFWC	General Federation of Women's Clubs
IESA	Illinois Equal Suffrage Association
IWSA	Iowa Woman Suffrage Association
KESA	Kansas Equal Suffrage Association
NAWSA	National American Woman Suffrage Association
NCWV	National Council of Women Voters
NWA	National Woman's Alliance
NWP	National Woman's Party
NWSA	National Woman Suffrage Association
PEL	Political Equality League
SDESA	South Dakota Equal Suffrage Association
WCTU	Woman's Christian Temperance Union
WSPU	Women's Social and Political Union

WINNING THE WEST FOR WOMEN

INTRODUCTION

TRAVELING THROUGH ILLINOIS IN 1856, SUSAN B. ANTHONY stopped in the small town of Roseville, where she addressed community members who had crowded in the opera house to hear her speak. At the end of her speech, the women's rights advocate asked all those in favor of woman suffrage to rise. Eight-year-old Emma Smith was the only one to stand. She later remembered, "Everyone looked at me and laughed." Emma added, "I was embarrassed and red with the conspicuousness of it, and though my older sister was mortified to death, and tugged at my skirt to make me sit down, I held my ground." After some time, a few adults rose. Anthony then said to the audience, "A little child shall lead them." When her father heard of the incident, Emma recalled, "He drew me to him and said that he was glad his daughter had the courage to stand up for what she believed." He told her that she should continue to stand up for her convictions, regardless of what others might think.[1]

Following her father's advice, Emma dedicated much of her life to securing votes for women across the United States. Although she committed herself to the cause at an early age, she did not begin working for woman suffrage until she was in her forties, after her father had passed away and she had married. She remained doggedly determined to secure woman suffrage from 1889 until the ratification of the Nineteenth Amendment in 1920, after which she became a member of the Republican Party.

What follows is an exploration of the suffrage movement and partisan politics through the perspective of Emma Smith DeVoe, an overlooked suffragist, beginning with her move to Dakota Territory as a newlywed in 1881 and ending with her death in 1927. This is the first full-length study of her suffrage career and her years in the Republican Party. Details of Emma's childhood and life prior to her marriage have been extremely difficult to track down, as she left behind no diaries or journals. Although she kept many letters and scrapbooks that document her role in the suffrage movement and are now housed at the Washington State Library, no materials in the collection date prior to 1880. Very few letters are from John Henry DeVoe, her husband, affectionately called Henry by friends and family. Only a few family letters, some in the hands of descendants, survive.[2] Details of her private life are virtually unknown.[3]

Gaps in her collection had to be filled by suffrage papers scattered across the country. I scoured archives and historical societies from Massachusetts to Washington and searched hundreds of reels of microfilmed collections. In addition, I combed reels of newspapers, when available, for information about Emma.[4] Her maiden name, Smith, often complicated searches.

Certain facts about Emma's childhood and early life—found in several short autobiographical sketches she composed in the 1890s, and the few local newspapers preserved by the Illinois Newspaper Project—hint at her activities prior to matrimony. Emma was born in Roseville, Illinois, in 1848, the same year that women held the first women's rights conference in Seneca Falls, New York. Her parents, Birdsey and Delia Smith, were Baptists and raised their children in a strict, religious home. Emma's father was an abolitionist.[5] Early on, her parents recognized that she was musically inclined, and they encouraged her talent. Eventually she attended college, although it is unknown where.[6]

In 1870, Emma became head of the department of music at Eureka College, a religious institution, where she taught for only one academic year.[7] At the end of the term, she chose to return home to Washington, Illinois, about seventy-five miles north of Springfield. Reasons for her break with Eureka College are unclear, but in the following year Emma began a private enterprise, offering music lessons to the townspeople of Washington. Over the next ten years, she held music classes in a room over a dry goods store and lived with her parents.[8] Emma sang in the town's choir, the Washington Choral Union, and directed a number of pageants, including the Washington Guard's Company D 7th Regiment festival.[9]

While singing in the choir, Emma met her husband, John Henry

DeVoe. Originally from New York State, Henry was a veteran of the Civil War. In 1865, at age eighteen, he mustered out of the army and returned home to attend school. Two years later, his family moved to Illinois, where Henry continued to attend school and work on the family farm. In 1869, he graduated from Grand Prairie Seminary. After graduation, he chose to attend the University of Michigan before going to teach at Blandville College in Kentucky.[10] Henry eventually moved to Washington, Illinois, from Chicago to work as an agent for the Chicago and Alton Railroad Company. Like Emma, he became an active member of the Washington community and was also a musician. In January 1880, Henry and Emma wed.[11] Nine years later she began working for woman suffrage, and the couple was frequently apart as Emma traveled across the United States, stumping for the cause.

Given the lack of correspondence between the two, it is difficult to determine the quality of their marriage, but one family member recalled that their union was strong. Jim Welch, one of Emma's descendants, remembered that his mother had once told him, "Henry was really ahead of his time in his feelings toward Emma. Not only was she the love of his life, but he fully supported her work in the suffrage movement. This of course included travel and a lot of time away from home at a time when this just wasn't accepted behavior for the wives of respected gentlemen."[12]

Although they were not always together, Emma loved her husband. For several years, she gave up working to care for him while he was ill, and she later urged him to move west to improve his health. Henry adored his wife and devoted himself to trying to take care of her as best he could; given his dabbling in investments—shoe stores, an orchard in Florida, and the automobile industry—it is apparent that he hoped to provide luxuries for his wife and maintain their middle-class standing. He may have been motivated by his knowledge of his mother-in-law's fate upon her husband's death. When Birdsey died, there was not enough money to pay his creditors, and all of his personal property had to be sold to meet those obligations. In the end, Delia signed away all claims to the estate to pay the administrative fees and debts.[13] For their first nine years of marriage, Henry succeeded, but when a massive depression hit South Dakota, the couple lost nearly everything. The couple had moved to Huron during the height of the Dakota boom, when Henry accepted a railroad position in 1881. More often than not, Henry's schemes failed, and Emma turned to organizing and lecturing on the suffrage circuit to help pay their debts.

Emma's career provides a unique lens through which to understand the suffrage reform movement. Beginning as assistant state organizer for the South Dakota Equal Suffrage Association (SDESA) in 1889, she witnessed the unification of two separate national suffrage organizations into the National American Woman Suffrage Association (NAWSA), participated in numerous state campaigns, helped to implement new strategies, led the successful 1910 Washington State campaign, and worked to secure passage of the Nineteenth Amendment. In short, Emma's career is a microcosm of women's struggle to achieve the vote.

Emma's experience as a state and national organizer, lecturer, and president of a state suffrage organization helps to answer important questions historians still have about the suffrage movement. For instance, how did local and state organizations "scattered across the nation" relate to NAWSA? How did suffragists raise money, and how did they spend it? How did suffragists accomplish the difficult task of "persuading those who held the power to share it"?[14]

Her example complicates the narrative presented in the "official record" of the movement—*The History of Woman Suffrage*,[15] which fails to mention the very real conflicts faced within NAWSA over tactics and leadership. Unity prevails in the pages of *History of Woman Suffrage*, but the reality was quite different. As early as 1890, when suffragists established NAWSA, Anthony silenced those who supported radical issues while the "association presented a façade of harmony."[16] The 1894 conflict between national and Kansas leaders never appeared in the pages of the history, nor did the fight between Emma and May Arkwright Hutton. In 1911, suffragist Reverend Olympia Brown questioned the unity that the suffragists fostered, calling such "shallow false talk of love excellence harmony &c &c . . . so false that it makes me vomit."[17] Emma's experience suggests that there was no such concord among suffragists; contrary to the belief that opposition to suffrage "nurtured a sense of sisterhood" among reformers, Emma's career highlights the matters over which suffragists clashed.[18]

The issue over who would lead state and national suffrage organizations frequently provoked dissent among suffrage advocates. Sometimes Emma was at the center of the debate, as in the case of her election to the presidency of the National Council of Women Voters (NCWV). Internal politics frequently provoked rifts, and sometimes suffragists split into separate camps because they stood in opposition to the woman who occupied the presidency.

Money was another major issue, and suffragists frequently fought over how it would be spent and who would control it. Heated debates in the correspondence of state officers, organizers, and national leaders centered upon the difficulty of raising funds and the unwillingness of national leaders to part with the money unless state leaders submitted to the demands of NAWSA. In the 1890 South Dakota and 1894 Kansas campaigns, for instance, Anthony refused to release any funds until the states' leadership agreed to her instructions about how the money should be spent. These were not isolated cases; the national leadership frequently wielded its control over the states through the power of the purse.

Money was a two-edged sword for Emma. Organizing for NAWSA helped pay her bills and keep a roof over her head, but it also led some to question her morals and commitment to suffrage. Some state suffrage associations hired Emma based on her fundraising abilities, while others saw her as a liability because of her need for a paycheck.[19]

Aside from money, Emma's career also illustrates how tactics often divided suffragists. Over the years, established leaders questioned new tactics employed by younger women. When Emma visited Montana in 1895 and organized clubs, Anthony wondered why she was there. As militant suffragist Alice Paul rose to power in 1913, older activists split with Paul over how best to secure suffrage. Solidarity among suffragists was, at least in Emma's case, less common than conflict, which popped up in nearly every campaign battle and among the closest of friends.[20] Suffragists had their own agendas, and many became rivals or opponents even though they favored the enfranchisement of women.

Emma, for instance, preferred to use a feminine approach in winning allies, believing it was important to use sweetness to appeal to male voters. Over the years, many believed her conciliatory approach was effective, although some disagreed. After her successful campaign in Washington, detractors followed her into states where campaigns were pending, telling leaders that Emma's ladylike tactics never helped win suffrage in any state. The issue was not necessarily about strategy, but about politics. Her adversaries branded her as an enemy of suffrage, "a tramp politician, working for the dollar and not the cause," someone who cared more for herself than the votes for women campaign.[21] They urged organizers to drop her at once and to avoid the use of any tactics that she endorsed.

Some historians of women have been critical of the approach used by Emma, which they believe served to only strengthen traditional, stereotypical views of women.[22] Over the years, historians have questioned whether reformers who embraced conservative tactics can even be considered feminists.[23]

The use of feminine methods in the late nineteenth century was, however, necessary, and it proved to be a beneficial technique. As writer Sara Willis Parton explained, "Better policy to play possum, and wear the mask of submission. No use in rousing any unnecessary antagonism . . . I shall reach the goal just as quick in my velvet shoes, as if I tramped on roughshod as they do with their Woman's Rights Convention brogans."[24] As doubts about democracy emerged in the 1890s, suffragists slowly began to abandon their natural rights arguments. Coming directly out of the political culture women had crafted as municipal housekeepers, they began using expediency arguments, focusing on the benefits that woman suffrage would bring to society;[25] these new methods are reflected in Emma's feminine techniques.

Her experience emphasizes the importance of using the feminine approach to win allies in the West.[26] Recent studies of western woman suffrage tend to downplay the importance of the approach employed by Emma and other western women, calling the "still hunt" (persuading influential voters through personal contacts instead of parades or rallies) "of little use in mobilizing volunteers or persuading voters."[27] Although this method did not secure any victories until the Washington State campaign in 1910, the tactics were important in building alliances and winning converts over the years. The techniques Emma endorsed brought respectability to the movement and laid the groundwork for victory in Washington State and eventually the passage of the Nineteenth Amendment.

In 1910, Washington women employed what Emma called "*partly* speech making and partly *still-hunting*" methods, combining some of the newer, more youthful tactics with older, more conservative methods.[28] They avoided the issue of temperance altogether, preferring instead to put their "enemies to sleep and arouse" their "friends to action."[29] Dr. Cora Smith King, treasurer of the Washington Equal Suffrage Association and author of the Washington State chapter in the final volume of *History of Woman Suffrage*, explained that absent the use of "spectacular methods," the women of her state placed an important emphasis on "personal intensive work on the part of the wives, mothers and sisters of the men who were to decide the issue at the polls."[30] Women used a nonconfrontational approach as they sought the assistance of family members and of the men they knew where they shopped or did business. In essence, their victory was partially built upon the women's personal contacts across the state. As Emma explained to Lucy B. Johnston of Kansas, "We did *not fight* for suffrage, we *worked* for it."[31]

Throughout her career, Emma avoided radical techniques and paid a great deal of attention to her presentation, appearance, and arguments, highlighting the difference between men and women. Her consideration of these details helped win supporters for the cause, including governors, ministers, newspaper editors, and other leading citizens, and proved to be particularly helpful in acquiring paid work. For example, in 1893, Carrie Catt Chapman encouraged Colorado state leaders to employ Emma, whom she described as "young, goodlooking, extremely [pleasing] in her manners, . . . everybody likes her."[32]

Emma, who had been mentored by Susan B. Anthony, learned a great deal from older suffragists and applied their lessons to methods she used throughout her career. Recalling the adverse effects of working for controversial programs such as divorce reform or temperance, Emma focused solely on women's enfranchisement. She never argued with opponents, preferring to suggest change rather than insist upon it. In the case of Washington, Emma recalled that suffragists "waited till we got on the platform when [the audience] could not 'sass back.'"[33] As she explained to a reporter for the *Spokane Chronicle*, she and other Washington suffragists sought the ballot in a "womanly way." She distinguished the work of Washington suffragists then working for enfranchisement from earlier advocates whom voters had reviled, but thanked them for their efforts "even though it has evoked much adverse criticism and has caused some to look on all women suffragists as unpleasant people."[34]

Although Emma supported feminine tactics throughout her suffrage career, and the press in every state she visited praised her for her beauty, femininity, and sweet singing voice, her public actions often contradicted her private efforts. Many of her colleagues whispered that she was envious and wanted to be in charge of the campaigns upon which she worked. These whisperings began in the 1890 South Dakota campaign and continued until 1909, when tensions between Emma and her detractors exploded at the state convention of the Washington Equal Suffrage Association. There, Emma used forceful and questionable measures to remain president of the association, and many believed her actions were overtly political and contrary to the ideals of the women's political culture she espoused.

Female leaders, unlike men, were supposed to be above politics and to avoid acting in their own interest. Most women in the Progressive Era believed that men wanted economic and political power for themselves and that women were more likely to work for the betterment of society. Unlike men, they were not motivated by selfishness or ambition.[35] Following her efforts in 1909 to remain president of the Washington campaign, Emma's ladylike reputation was stained, but she persevered in spite of detractors, working with many leading politicians to secure woman suffrage. Once victory had been achieved, she became the Northwest's leading female politician and later—after the passage of the Nineteenth Amendment—played a prominent role in the Republican Party.

As this book illustrates, the West played a particularly important role in the suffrage movement, and Emma dedicated most of her time working in the western half of the United States. Under Catt's leadership in the 1890s, she organized local clubs, lectured on suffrage, and offered advice and training to supporters. For years NAWSA dedicated the organization's meager resources and workers to a region suffragists believed was more liberal and more likely to enfranchise women than the East or South. As Catt told Mary Smith Heyward of Nebraska, "I can not help but feel all the time that our best policy is to put our money on the West and get those States in as fast as possible."[36]

East/West relations were problematic, however. Time and again, eastern women offended their western sisters by organizing in western states. They were rarely welcomed, and their actions brought about splits within the suffrage movement. Women from the East often meddled in state business or decisions, which angered western women, who blamed them for the state defeats they suffered. Interestingly enough, although Emma was a representative of NAWSA, the women of these western states never blamed her for their losses.[37] Eventually, after witnessing numerous failures, Emma came to side with the home workers—noting that outsiders taking control and managing state campaigns only led to defeat.

After the passage of woman suffrage in Washington, Emma refused to work in any state unless a state association extended an invitation to her. She explained to the president of the Kansas Equal Suffrage Association that her National Council of Women Voters preferred "not [to] intrude ourselves upon women in other states, especially during a campaign, for we have seen so much trouble and often defeat where such a course has been followed."[38]

Following the Washington victory, Emma established the National Council of Women Voters. Her council, an often overlooked suffrage organization, complicates the story of the battle for the Nineteenth Amendment.[39] Formed in 1911, women from the five equal suffrage states of Wyoming, Colorado, Utah, Idaho, and Washington initially composed the organization. The council was a nonpartisan interest group and had three goals: to provide encouragement and assistance to other states battling for the ballot; to improve conditions in the states of Washington, Wyoming, Colorado, Utah, and Idaho for men, women, children, and the home; and to help women obtain justice in the political, social, and economic worlds. In its nine-year history, Emma served as the only president of the council, which was headquartered in Tacoma, Washington.

The history of this organization has largely been forgotten, although historians occasionally mention the council in books and articles. Those who do so often refer to the organization as an early prototype of the League of Women Voters, which is correct. Many historians, however, have failed to understand just how important the council's leadership was to the passage of the Nineteenth Amendment. Emma believed that western women, who were "*qualified voters*," had important roles to play in "working for the freedom of women." This was work "that *no other* women" could do because eastern and southern women did not have the ballot and, presumably, the knowledge of how to secure the passage of a suffrage amendment. Consequently, Emma concluded that without the assistance of western women voters, the cause would be greatly hindered.[40] The council was thus more than an educational organization for women voters. It was a pressure group involved in the passage of the Nineteenth Amendment. This history is contrary to the narrative of the suffrage movement, which tends to focus heavily upon eastern activists and their tactics.

Carrie Chapman Catt, president of NAWSA, and Alice Paul, leader of the militant Congressional Union (CU) and the National Woman's Party (NWP), are the women most often associated with the final push for the Anthony Amendment. Western women are absent from these studies, even though they remained active in the suffrage movement after they won the right to vote. Emma and the National Council of Women Voters actively worked with Paul to reinvigorate the push for the amendment to the Constitution, and they later switched their support to Catt's Winning Plan. After Congress passed the amendment, Emma chaired the

Washington committee that pushed for the ratification of the Nineteenth Amendment in the Evergreen State.

The inclusion of the NCWV in the history of this effort illustrates how regionalism played a significant role in the campaign for a federal amendment to the U.S. Constitution. Western women of the council formed an organization that utilized the tactics that led to victories in the West; their leader, a particularly successful and popular suffragist well into the nineteen teens, used tested western methods—those that appealed to the voters of their region—and avoided or discouraged the utilization of strategies that men in the West opposed, namely militancy. The students of the West were finally able to offer advice to their eastern sisters, who had tutored them all these years on organization and securing the ballot. But, women from the East continued to come into the West, which angered the women voters. Eastern militants appealed to western women to band together to vote against the Democrats then holding up a constitutional amendment to enfranchise all American women. With the help of western women and their regional techniques, American women became U.S. citizens in 1920.

Emma's greatest accomplishment was the passage of woman suffrage in the Evergreen State. Although few recognize her name today, she was one of the country's most celebrated suffragists of her time. Many wanted to learn how she had secured the first suffrage victory after fourteen years of drought "with so little noise."⁴¹ The win in Washington was only one of several outstanding achievements in her lifetime. Her predecessors, most notably Anthony and Elizabeth Cady Stanton, promoted women's rights across the country, but it was women like Emma and her contemporaries who secured the passage of the Nineteenth Amendment to the U.S. Constitution. Extending the vote to women doubled the electorate and transformed the political landscape. American women were finally free to affect public policy and politics through the ballot box.

Tintype of Henry DeVoe taken at Meade's Station, behind Union lines at Petersburg, Virginia, March 1865. Photograph courtesy of Tom Welch.

An 1870 portrait of Henry taken in Ann Arbor, Michigan. Photograph courtesy of Jim and Susan Welch.

Henry's song "A Soldier's Tribute to Woman" proved to be extremely popular with audiences across the West. Photograph courtesy of Tom Welch.

A portrait of Emma, taken around the time she began organizing and speaking for suffrage in South Dakota. Photograph courtesy of the Carrie Chapman Catt Collection, Bryn Mawr College Library (Catt 3.10.2e.tif).

Helen M. Barker, president of the South Dakota WCTU, also
served as state organizer for the South Dakota Equal Suffrage
Association in 1890. Photograph courtesy of the Frances E. Willard Memorial Library and Archives, Evanston, Illinois.

Anna Howard Shaw, who worked closely with Emma in South Dakota and Oregon, sported short hair around 1870, when long hair symbolized femininity. Photograph courtesy of The Schlesinger Library, Radcliffe Institute, Harvard University (PC1–147a-8).

In December 1889, Susan B. Anthony mailed this portrait to Emma with her "love and admiration." Photograph courtesy of Jim and Susan Welch.

Emma became close friends with Reverend Olympia Brown in South Dakota and worked closely with the minister in later years. Photograph courtesy of Jim and Susan Welch.

Mrs. C. Holt Flint became Emma's Iowa mother after touring the state in 1892. Photograph courtesy of Jim and Susan Welch.

Emma F. Bates's calling card, presented to Emma in 1895, when she visited North Dakota. Photograph courtesy of Jim and Susan Welch.

Emma shared Populist sympathies with Ella Knowles Haskell, Montana's assistant attorney general. Photograph courtesy of Jim and Susan Welch.

Portrait of Emma taken in Peoria, Illinois. Photograph courtesy of Jim and Susan Welch.

Portrait of Emma in costume, photographed by S. W. Sawyer
Photographic Parlors in Chicago. Photograph courtesy of Jim
and Susan Welch.

NAWSA leader Carrie Chapman Catt frequently called on Emma's organizing and fundraising skills as women fought for the franchise. Photograph courtesy of The Schlesinger Library, Radcliffe Institute, Harvard University (PCI–43–10).

Henry (bottom left with papers on his knee) and Emma (left of the marker) visit Tijuana, Mexico, after the San Francisco earthquake of 1906. Photograph courtesy of Jim and Susan Welch.

The flamboyant May Arkwright Hutton opposed Emma's reelection as president of the Washington Equal Suffrage Association in 1909. Photograph courtesy of Northwest Museum of Arts and Culture/Eastern Washington Historical Society, Spokane, Washington (L-93–66–212.jpg).

Mrs. Emma Smith DeVoe's Principles for Guidance in Suffrage Campaigns.

1—Keep the issue single. Be for nothing but suffrage; against nothing but anti-suffrage.

2—Pin your faith to the justice of your cause. It carries conviction.

3—Rely upon facts rather than arguments.

4—Plead affirmative arguments always. Put your opponents on the defensive.

5—Convert the indifferent; there are thousands of them. Let the incorrigible alone; there are only a few.

6—Avoid big meetings; they arouse your enemies.

7—Avoid antagonizing big business, but get the labor vote quietly.

8—Be confident of winning.

9—Try to have every voter in the state asked by some woman to vote for the amendment; this will carry it.

10—Always be good natured and cheerful.

OFFICE AND HEADQUARTERS, 605-606 PERKINS BLDG.
TACOMA, WASHINGTON

Emma printed and shared these core beliefs with other suffragists. Photograph courtesy of Jim and Susan Welch.

Alice Paul and Emma became brief allies in the early years of the final fight for a federal woman suffrage amendment to the U.S. Constitution. Photograph courtesy of the Alice Paul Institute, Inc.

Henry and Emma pose with their Dodge sedan outside of their Tacoma home, Villa DeVoe. Photograph courtesy of Jim and Susan Welch.

Even in her older years, Emma remained beautiful. Photograph courtesy of Jim and Susan Welch.

1

MORAL REFORM AND STATEHOOD

IN 1848, THE YEAR OF EMMA'S BIRTH, REVOLUTIONS SPREAD LIKE wildfire throughout Europe. Another simmered on the North American continent when women gathered for a tea party and drafted a call for a women's rights convention to be held in Seneca Falls, New York, at the Wesleyan Chapel. Using Thomas Jefferson's Declaration of Independence as a model, they drew up a list of grievances suffered by women, which sixty-eight women and thirty-two men eventually signed. Delegates to the meeting debated the issue of women's rights and passed a number of resolutions, including the controversial decision to secure the franchise for women.

The women's rights movement, which emerged from the meeting, grew out of a number of reform movements that involved women, especially abolitionism. Many of these women actively worked for woman suffrage for the rest of their lives, but only one woman who signed the Declaration of Sentiments lived long enough to witness the ratification of the Nineteenth Amendment in 1920.[1]

Securing the passage of a federal amendment rested upon the shoulders of the second and third generations of suffragists. The women from the second group were born from around the time of the New York meeting to more than a decade later. They became active in the movement in the 1880s in their thirties and forties, and many came to the suffrage movement from the Woman's Christian Temperance Union (WCTU).

Like many women's rights leaders of her generation, Emma followed a similar path into the cause, but her decision to become active in the battle for the ballot was more complicated. Temperance was only one factor that brought her into the suffrage fold. The frontier environment in which she lived probably served as the catalyst that sparked her interest in securing the franchise for women. Sorrow over her mother's death pushed Emma to labor as hard as she could to ease her grief and deepened her involvement in the 1890 South Dakota woman suffrage campaign, which eventually led to a lifelong commitment to the enfranchisement of all American women. Her dedication to the cause, first inspired by her hearing a Susan B. Anthony address, flowered in the wild western territory of Dakota.

Dakota Territory was booming in 1881, when Emma and her husband moved there from Washington, Illinois. Huron had sprung up from the wild prairie in the James River Valley the previous spring, becoming a division point for the Chicago and Northwestern Railroad. Settlers flocked to the region to make their fortunes. Many came on the promise of free, fertile land in central Dakota. The DeVoes came because Henry had accepted a position with the railroad in March, but the harsh winter of 1881 closed the tracks into Huron until May.[2]

When they arrived, Emma and Henry must have been disappointed with what they found. City boosters had encouraged men and women to pack their bags and relocate to central Dakota, but local newspapers chose not to report on Huron's lawlessness and vice, fearing this might discourage financiers from investing in the youthful city.[3] Huron, affectionately called the "Gem of the Jim," lost much of its sparkle when seen in person.

The town, recalled one former resident, was just as wild as Deadwood or Dodge City in the 1880s. Gambling dens and saloons thrived in the town, and men frequently discharged their revolvers in the city limits and fought in drunken brawls.[4] Women filed complaints against men who had seduced them with promises of marriage, but then refused to marry them. Houses of prostitution operated on the main thoroughfares, and a father charged a Huron man with abducting his teenage daughter to make her a concubine.[5] Emma and Henry would have considered such acts scandalous, but they chose to stay, and they made Huron their home for almost ten years.

Both were devout Baptists, and to their dismay, no house of worship had been built in town when they arrived. Instead, the Baptists held services wherever space could be had—the railroad depot or the schoolhouse—every other week, and the minister tended to both the Huron and Pierre congregations. Shanties, land offices, hotels, and saloons dotted the landscape. Given the lack of hotel space and available boarding rooms, many of the town's new inhabitants boarded in restaurants, while others began putting up homes. Living conditions in town were crude, as they were in many less established western communities. Ash, garbage, and animal droppings littered the streets and alleys.

The main streets of town were frequently muddy. There were few sidewalks, leaving pedestrians to trudge through the muck. Thomas F. Nicholl, a member of Huron's board of trustees (the town's first city government) and superintendent of the Dakota Central Railroad, encouraged residents to "improve and beautify" the town. He discouraged Huronites from wallowing "literally in the mud" and encouraged them to connect the patchwork of sidewalks in front of the town's businesses so that a pedestrian "may not be in dread of breaking his neck at every step or falling headlong into a mud hole."[6]

Living conditions were not ideal, but Henry began scouting out land on which to build a home. He purchased a lot on Kansas Street and began erecting the house. The decision to build such a structure seemed preferable when given the choice of sleeping in a restaurant or in a boarding house. The home was not fancy, when compared to Superintendent Nicholl's residence, but it met the couple's needs and cost only $800 to build. The timber structure was similar to other homes in the area. By today's standards, the home was small, a mere 600 square feet, but cozy.[7] Later, in the winter of 1882, Henry purchased 160 acres outside of town for a farm.[8]

In the fall of 1881, construction efforts for the First Baptist Church began. The erection of the church was a cooperative effort, and Emma worked to raise money along with the other female congregants for the church building fund. The Chicago and Northwestern Railroad contributed $500 for the lot and transportation of freight. Many others gave donations of cash or equipment, including an organ worth $125. When the work was complete, the DeVoes participated in the dedication ceremony led by Reverend George A. Cressey. Emma played the organ and acted as the choirmistress, and Henry played other instruments. The entire religious community of Huron, including the Episcopalians, who held a shorter service that day, attended the dedication and participated in the services that Sunday.[9]

The DeVoes' affiliation with the Baptist church shaped their views about their new community and the reforms to which they were committed over the next ten years. Baptists supported temperance, and every year the territorial association pledged their support, votes, and influence to eliminate the sale of liquor in the territory. Huron's Baptist ministers frequently led the charge against drink. Reverend Cressey chaired the executive committee for the Prohibition Home Protection Party of Dakota in 1883, and later, Reverend Elisha English, who identified "the legalized sale of intoxicating liquors" as the nation's primary peril, led the local option campaign in Beadle County (which included Huron, the county seat).[10]

Given their interest in prohibition, ties between the South Dakota Baptist Convention and the WCTU were solid. Many leading members of the union were practicing Baptists, including Helen M. Barker, who served as president of the Territorial WCTU. Union members frequently gave presentations at the yearly conventions and in return received support from the Baptist denomination for their work. The South Dakota Baptist Convention noted the power the WCTU had to stir up support for prohibition, and the ministers pledged "to these Christian women our earnest sympathies, fervent prayers and our hearty cooperation in every way possible in driving the traffic in strong drink from our beloved territory."[11]

Over the next few years, the DeVoes served as Christian soldiers and strove to create a city dedicated to the social mores to which they subscribed: prohibition and the elimination of gambling halls, saloons, and brothels. They clashed with elected officials, who licensed saloons and breweries, and worked to tame the rowdy town to secure law and order in Huron. These moral reform efforts opened the door and paved the way for Emma to become involved with other, broader political campaigns in the Dakota Territory.

Emma and Henry helped to establish many of Huron's voluntary groups, including the literary association. Joining this organization were likeminded reformers such as Edwin G. Wheeler, the owner of a drugstore and deacon of the First Baptist Church; I. J. Mouser, register of deeds for Beadle County and a member of the First Methodist Episcopal Church; and Dr. A. J. Dickinson, a physician and surgeon. They and other Huronites established the literary association for the purpose of keeping "young people away from the haunts whose influence destroys mind, body, and soul," in other words, away from working-class forms of leisure, such as frequenting bars, billiard rooms, and gambling dens.[12] The DeVoes and other middle-class members of the club preferred different types of entertainment, as illustrated by the last meeting of the year at their home on Kansas Street in December 1882.

Held just a few days before Christmas, the DeVoes opened the meeting with a violin and piano duet. Following their introduction, the association had a thoughtful discussion, "fine music," a play, and other entertainment that reflected the value the DeVoes and other middle-class Huronites placed on music and literature. The highlight of the night was a lecture given by Dr. Dickinson, who, with a stereopticon, explained the transit of Venus.[13]

After Christmas, the editors of the *Dakota Huronite* reported that Henry and another Huronite, identified only as Kellogg, planned to establish a new community in Faulk County.[14] By the year's end, the DeVoes had moved to the fledgling town of DeVoe, named after Henry, in anticipation that the coming of the Chicago and Northwestern Railroad would bring more people and opportunities to the area. For a short time, they homesteaded in Faulk County, but the railroad never came into DeVoe. By the end of 1883, the couple's speculative plans had apparently fallen through, and they moved back to Huron. Although they no longer lived in the DeVoe area, they maintained property there, and in 1885, the couple deeded a section of their farm to the Methodist Episcopalian Church for $1. Today, that church no longer stands, and DeVoe is a ghost town.[15]

Upon returning to their home on Kansas Street, the DeVoes continued their efforts to reshape the community of Huron by ridding the town of alcohol and those associated with it. Henry joined the Order of Good Templars, a teetotaler organization, and Emma became a member of the local WCTU. The union sought by "quiet, but devoted womanly efforts to throw social and religious influences around young men to keep them from drink; to turn or rescue young women from ruin; to educate youth in temperance principles; to build up temperance chastity and morality as a public sentiment."[16] In Huron, the WCTU and Young Men's Christian Association maintained a free reading room for the city, hoping to keep the young men away from saloons and billiard halls. The *Dakota Huronite*, whose editors supported prohibition, praised the organizations for their efforts, saying, "It will at least remove the excuse of those who spend their time in places of ill repute, that there is no place else to go."[17]

Emma's decision to join the WCTU and work for its broad agenda was part of a trend among women called "Political Motherhood" or "Municipal Housekeeping," which became increasingly popular in the Progressive Era. Municipal housekeeping was the extension of women's work into the public sphere—in essence, the ability of women to improve societal ills through their "special moral qualities."[18] Countering objections from opponents, municipal housekeepers developed a maternalistic agenda that did not contradict women's prescribed roles but merely extended women's duties from the home outward.[19] Social housekeeping by women represented a significant change in American public policy. "The 'womanhood' identified with 'mothering' was becoming less a biological fact—giving birth to children—and more a political role with new ideological dimensions. The traditional word *motherhood* was being reshaped so as to justify women's assuming new ever-more-public responsibilities."[20] No longer did women's sphere limit women from entering politics. Women could now challenge corrupt politicians and provide new solutions to age-old problems without their husbands by their sides. Having no children of her own, Emma may have decided to dedicate her life to such reforms.

In 1885, Henry was drawn into the fight brewing between middle-class reformers and the city government. Selected to serve on a grand jury in Huron, he heard testimony against Madame Kelly, who was charged with running a bawdy house.[21] During the case, he learned that the police were rounding up prostitutes and owners of gambling joints each month and collecting fines and court fees that amounted to $7.50 per head. The grand jury indicted her, but a jury of her peers acquitted her.[22]

Outraged by what they had heard from the city attorney, the jury censured the city council and mayor for their actions. A supporter of temperance and an opponent of licensing, Henry concluded that the "assessment amounts to nothing short of a license."[23] Jurors believed that the policy did not punish gambling houses and prostitutes, but instead aided and encouraged vice.

Published only a few weeks prior to the city election, the censure reflected the tensions between reformers and those who supported taxing vice. Henry wrote, "We view such officials' conduct with mingled pity and shame, believing the carrying out of such a policy by the Mayor tends to debauch the youth of the city and smirches the good name of Huron, and we believe all moral people will look upon such official action with deserved censure."[24] Frank Ketchum, one of the editors of the *Dakota Huronite* and then a candidate for mayor, agreed with the jury's findings and printed their resolutions in the newspaper, hoping to secure the support of the middle class. He also published letters from those who were dissatisfied with the current administration. An unidentified Huronite, who wrote a number of letters to the editor, believed it was time for a change in leadership: "Now, it is not the best way to have our city governed by one element, and that is the one being administered at present [the saloon element]. There are more than one and the others should have at least the benefit of a chance to try."[25]

Liquor dealers and brewers, however, swept the election. The editors of the *Huronite* concluded that "the citizens of Huron are a queer people in some respects." The outcome of the election made no sense. "Ministers preach and large congregations listen to sermons on morality month after month and year after year business men grumble at taxes paid for money loosely spent; yet on election day—the one and only time in a whole year when any reformation can be accomplished—a handful of saloon keepers have more influence and carry more weight than all these combined."[26]

Emma and Henry must have been disappointed with the outcome of the election. Huron bore no resemblance to the community in which they hoped to live, and their efforts to bring culture and civilization to the city had not succeeded as well as they had hoped. Their attempts to defeat the incumbents and reform city government had failed. Brothels and gambling houses continued to operate openly on the streets of Huron. Two years later, moral issues again became the focus of the city's election.

Reformers ran on the "law and order" ticket which, interestingly enough, included Harvey J. Rice for mayor. In the 1885 election, Rice had been the choice of saloon keepers. The incumbent mayor was popular with reformers for his support of "the rigid enforcement of law and the prompt punishment of all offenders" and for his pledge to support "LAW AND ORDER at all times and in all places" by moving "unsavory hordes" out of town.[27]

Support for the law and order candidates doubled when Huronites learned that saloon owners had sold liquor to a thirteen-year-old girl. The newspaper editors reported that the marshal arrested two women in a drunken brawl and placed the women in jail for a day. At their hearing, the judge heard testimony from a girl, one of the drunken women's daughters. She admitted to the judge that she had purchased the liquor for her mother in the town's saloons and told him that she sometimes got drunk herself.

The news incensed reformers, who learned that the saloons had violated the city ordinances by selling liquor to minors. Newspaper editors Augustine Davis and Frank Ketchum asked readers, "Isn't it about time for the saloon to go?"[28] The day before the election, the editors advised subscribers to think before they cast their ballot. Remember the imprisoned women and the innocent and helpless child before you decide whom you will support, they wrote. Children have suffered at the hands of Huron's saloon keepers "who for a few cents' profit will furnish an innocent child with the means of forever destroying its own physical and moral life. . . . Think that these very men, tomorrow, will be most active on the streets in attempting to elect a government that will overlook *their* violations of the law, and think whether you will assist them in their attempt."[29]

Temperance supporters like the DeVoes won the day as all law and order candidates defeated their opponents in Huron and across the territory in Yankton, Pierre, and Aberdeen. The newly elected Huron officials were moral reformers, and they ordered all gamblers and prostitutes to pack their belongings and leave town.[30] The act had little effect, however, and later that summer, the town marshal and some council members raided houses of ill repute, for which they received praise from the press for not forgetting their campaign promises.[31] Shortly thereafter, the mayor and council unanimously passed an act to suppress houses of ill fame in Huron, making it unlawful to keep a bawdy house in the city limits.[32]

Moral reform campaigns like those waged by the people of Huron were common in the American West in the 1880s. A Kansas cattle town, Caldwell, once tolerant of prostitutes, became more conservative in 1881 when residents signed a petition calling for the closure of brothels. A year later, they closed the Red Light dance house.[33] Similar campaigns appeared in the Rocky Mountain West. In 1885, Helena, Montana, city councilmen began a moral reform program, and the following year they drafted an act to ban prostitution from the city.[34]

Not everyone sided with those who believed that saloons, brothels, and gambling halls increased crime, poverty, and violence. Those in favor of these establishments argued that they contributed to the commercial development of the city and that their taxes helped to support town and county budgets. When Huron council officials invaded these "nests of vice," owners and supporters complained, "You'll hurt Huron!"[35] Henry, who had recently purchased a shoe and boot store in town, disagreed; he favored the 1887 local option, which would eliminate the sale of liquor in Beadle County. When asked for his views on the reform, he said, "Local option won't hurt my business one cent. I'm working for it because I believe it will improve trade."[36]

Earlier that year, the territorial legislature gave counties the option of voting on the issue of whether or not there would be sales of liquor in their communities. The legislature authorized counties to submit the issue to voters if one-third of those registered requested that the option be placed on the ballot sixty days before the election.[37] Protestant churches and prohibition clubs immediately began lobbying their county commissioners in an attempt to close down the saloons in their areas.

Huron's Protestant ministers, like many western preachers, hoped that they could redeem their city and its citizens by ridding the community of "demon rum." Two of Huron's reverends led the local option campaign: Reverends Elisha English of the First Baptist Church and D. S. McCaslin of the Presbyterian Church.[38] Both men had moved to Huron in 1886, and they immediately took the offensive by holding prayer meetings and speaking on public morals. English, hoping to save souls, urged Huronites to strike a blow against gambling, the sale of liquor to minors and drunks, and houses of ill repute. "A blow struck now in Huron is worth ten five years hence. Now is our opportunity," he proclaimed.[39]

English's promotion of prohibition from the pulpit and his activities with the local prohibition club led Emma deeper into the cause, and in 1887 her work for temperance expanded. The First Baptist Church choir, which she headed, began providing entertainment for gospel temperance meetings and mass prohibition conventions in Huron, where English frequently spoke. Music was the first outlet by which Emma left her distinct mark upon South Dakota politics.

Music played a particularly important role in nineteenth-century political life. Reformers sang at political rallies, conventions, and meetings, and quartettes often performed tunes to rouse crowds. Fraternal and voluntary associations such as the Grand Army of the Republic (GAR) and the Woman's Relief Corps, to which Henry and Emma belonged, sang patriotic songs, and the WCTU sang hymns and temperance songs.[40] Reformers published songbooks, and the Dakota Territory was no different: the South Dakota statehood, prohibition, and woman suffrage movements all printed and sold such materials.

Emma used her musical talent to reach out to those who attended prohibition lectures, conventions, and rallies. English supported Emma's contributions, and this was part of a larger effort specifically undertaken by Baptist ministers in Dakota Territory in 1887, though it was not unique to the region or time. Protestant ministers had previously encouraged women, who were more pious than men, to form associations and extend their moral superiority beyond the home. Reverends urged Dakota women to increase their interest in "woman's work"—municipal housekeeping and benevolent, charitable, and temperance activism. Baptist ministers emphasized the importance of reform work to their female congregants, urging them to expand their influence outside of the home.[41]

Beadle County passed the local option in 1887, but the law proved ineffective. Police tended to ignore operating saloons, and thus Huronites like English and the DeVoes continued to push for prohibition the following year.

The statehood movement also became increasingly popular in 1887, when many Huronites came to believe that their basic liberties of freedom of speech and of the press were under attack by Democrats, who, for the first time, held the office of the governor and of a number of territorial appointments, including judgeships. The furor began in the summer of 1887, when Territorial Judge J. L. Spencer, a Democrat, filed charges against the Republican *Daily Huronite* for spreading malicious lies about him.[42]

The editors of the *Daily Huronite* had been especially critical of Judge Spencer, calling him "arbitrary and ignorant of the law." Reportedly, the judge was short with attorneys in his courtroom and quipped, "Is that the best you can do?" When council presented evidence to the court, Spencer asked, "What nonsense are you talking now?" The editors concluded that the judge lacked experience and was unaware of how courts operated in Dakota Territory.[43] They also said that the judge was lax in administering laws of the territory. They claimed that he protected hordes of criminals and set horse thieves, gamblers, and prostitutes free.[44]

After he filed charges against the newspaper, the *Daily Huronite* editors announced that they would fight this "vile attack" and "vindicate—if such a thing is possible under this carpetbagger usurpation—the liberty of the press."[45] The idea that the Democrats, who were often referred to as carpetbaggers in the territory, used partisanship to thwart the basic rights of Dakotans was not new. Since 1883 Democrats had opposed the admission of the Dakotas as two separate states because they feared that they would lose control of Congress. Senators Matthew C. Butler of South Carolina and George G. Vest of Missouri, both Democrats from the "Solid South," opposed the admission of two Republican states. In 1886, when the U.S. Senate debated a Dakota statehood bill, Senator Vest, who was then suffering from neuralgia and encouraged to leave Washington, DC, for a more temperate climate, climbed out of his sick bed to oppose statehood for the Dakotas.[46] Naturally, Democrats were unpopular in the territory.

Loyalty to the Grand Old Party ran deep in the territory, where voters frequently elected veterans of the Civil War to office. Supporters were proud of their heritage; their party led the nation during the Civil War, saved the Union, and abolished slavery in the process. Anyone looking to secure the support of voters in Dakota Territory could not overlook the political power the veterans wielded.

Huronites and other Dakotans rallied behind the press. Many of the territory's leading papers sided with the *Daily Huronite*, saying that newspapers had the right to criticize courts and individuals. Even former Territorial Governor Gilbert A. Pierce said, "When it comes to the point when a citizen is to be fined or thrown into jail because he thinks a judge is a nincompoop, and says so, we are rubbing pretty close on judicial tyranny."[47]

The DeVoes probably agreed with Pierce's conclusions. They had been supporters of the statehood movement since 1883, when Henry served as a Faulk County delegate at a Dakota Citizens League Meeting in Huron. There 188 delegates debated "the advisability of calling a [statehood] constitutional convention."[48] Roughly 20 percent of the nonfarming population supported statehood, and the group included many ministers, lawyers, businessmen, and newspaper editors. Those who advocated dividing the territory in half and admitting both into the Union attended Protestant churches and supported the Republican Party. The DeVoes, like many other supporters, lived in town, and for a time Henry worked for a banker before owning his own shoe and boot store. Henry had also served under General Ulysses S. Grant in the "great race after Lee's army," and he favored the Republican Party over the Democrats.[49] Emma's involvement in the statehood movement was unique in that men dominated the effort.[50] She was drawn into the statehood movement through music.

In 1888, the National Republican Party included statehood for South Dakota in its platform. The members proclaimed, "South Dakota should of right be immediately admitted as a State in the Union under the constitution framed and adopted by her people, and we heartily indorse the action of the Republican Senate in twice passing bills for her admission,"[51] and they condemned the Democrats in the House for playing partisan politics and violating the principles of self-government.

Statehood supporters planned to hold a meeting to determine how admission into the Union could be achieved. The convention, which they dubbed "the most grave and important convention to which you have ever been, or probably ever will be summoned," was necessary to draw up plans against those who favored perpetual territorial status for Dakota Territory. Their list of grievances against the federal government, then controlled by the Democrats, was long:

> Your manhood is outraged and humiliated. Rights are invaded, justice is denied, public improvements are held back, rightful political power is withheld, a voice in your own government is insultingly refused. . . . Confederate brigadiers, who have been but lately pardoned for their own unprovoked acts of rebellion against the government, dare to insult the loyal people, and old soldiers of Dakota with charges of revolution, for simply demanding that right of local self government, and that admission into the Union, which belongs to them under the laws and constitution of the country.[52]

After hearing that the meeting would be held in Huron, Henry and Emma began writing songs at their piano with the intention of appealing to the veterans of the state by tying the issues of statehood to the Civil War. They believed that these themes would inspire those who had yet to fight for the formation of two states.[53] Emma also decided to form a special singing group for the occasion, the Statehood Quartette.[54]

One of the songs that received much applause on the evening of the meeting was "Mr. Carpetbagger." The lyrics reflected the frustration of the statehood supporters with their current governor, Louis Church, whom they perceived as a despot hoping to benefit from the misfortune of territorial citizens. Dakotans believed that Church was a Democrat outsider forced upon the Republican citizens of the territory by President Grover Cleveland. The lyrics, reprinted in the *Daily Huronite*, painted Church as an individual who thought he was king "sittin' on de throne" in Bismarck, the territorial capital.

Another song, "Two State Injine," caught the attention of delegates. Using a slave dialect, the DeVoes referred to Church and other Democratic leaders in Dakota as:

> *Broken down politicians, comin' from de east,*
> *Comin' to Dakota for to have a long feast,*
> *Dey send some from York state, and some from Tennessee,*
> *But dem politicians can't boss over me.*

Representative William M. Springer, who favored creating only one state out of Dakota, was not immune from the sting of the DeVoes' pens. Portrayed as a political boss, "De ol boss Springer" supposedly "pull de string, open all de mouths of de carpetbag ring," and fixed the caucuses, which had detrimentally impacted the men and women of the territory.[55]

In "The Dakotas Are Coming," the DeVoes linked Dakota's territorial status to slavery: "Then down with usurper and off with the chain. . . . and three for the twin states noble and brave who dare to be free and refuse to be slave." Freedom and admittance into the Union was far better than a colonialism in which Congress treated Dakotans like slaves, the couple concluded. Former Democratic "slaveholders" in Congress deserved at least one punch for their efforts to keep South Dakota out of the Union, according to the DeVoes: "Now give one to Springer and make it a stinger; And then one to Butler and make it a cutter; And then one to Vest."[56]

According to Henry, when their song "Severance of Church and State, or Lewis [sic] K's Lamentation" was "first sung at a statehood meeting in Huron . . . the sentiment was very strong for making two states out of the territory." After the meeting, delegates suggested that the statehood songs be published for the upcoming state campaign. The couple agreed, and they printed and sold the "Dakota Campaign Song Book" out of their home.[57]

Throughout the fall, Henry attended to business at his store while Emma and her quartette continued to inspire the forces. Drawing large crowds, they performed at meetings across the state. The quartette even drew the attention of the press. An October edition of the *Daily Huronite* repeatedly encouraged readers to attend the grand division and statehood meeting to hear the quartette sing songs of statehood.[58] In November, the campaign came to a close with the election of 1888.

Huronites gathered in the opera house to hear the election results. Men remained on the main floor while women filled the upstairs gallery. Around midnight, when it appeared that the Republicans had won the presidency and taken control of the House of Representatives, the crowd cheered and the ladies waved their fans, gloves, and handkerchiefs. The *Daily Huronite* reported, "Men hurrahed, whistled, threw their hats, canes, coats, etc., into the air and yelled loud enough to be heard in Wessington" (about thirty miles west of Huron). When states tallied their final votes, the Republican Party retained its majority in the Senate, regained the House of Representatives, and won the presidency. According to the

Daily Huronite, "Everybody was happy—especially republicans."[59]

Pleased with Benjamin Harrison's victory, Huronites planned a "jollification meeting." Republicans came from across the state to attend the jubilee, and a street procession kicked off the event. A martial music band marched through the city, and a carriage drawn by cream colored horses that featured dummies representing President-elect Harrison and his vice President, Levi P. Morton, attracted the crowd's attention. Men carried torches and brooms, which symbolized a "Clean Sweep with Harrison." Bands from Huron, Miller, and St. Lawrence played in the parade, and hundreds of men marched with signs, some carrying pans, fiddles, and horns. Two roosters—one dead, a symbol of the Democratic Party, and one alive, who had crowed for Harrison before the election, brought up the rear of the procession.

Organizers invited ladies to hear the addresses at the opera house. Emma's Statehood Quartette sat on stage along with the men who had played a prominent role in the campaign. When the quartette sang "Severance of Church and State, or Lewis K's Lamentation," the tune nearly "brought down the house. It was a peculiarly fitting selection for the occasion and the rounds of applause that followed its singing indicated how keenly the vast audience appreciated the sentiments of the song," reported the *Daily Huronite.*[60]

In February 1889, the lame-duck Congress recognized that its efforts to keep out two Republican states would not succeed. The Republicans would see to it that the territory of Dakota would be divided and admitted as two separate states. Democrats begrudgingly supported a bill that included statehood for Montana, Washington, and both states of Dakota. The bill allowed each state to legally hold constitutional conventions and gave the president authority to admit each.

In 1889, South Dakotans continued to fight for prohibition, and many of those who endorsed this issue also supported woman suffrage. Residents of Pierre and Huron competed to be state capitol. Many other residents hoped for the opening of the Great Sioux Reservation, which lay west of the Missouri River.[61] Emma and Henry focused their attention on constitutional prohibition and woman suffrage.

Temperance workers kicked off a final prohibition campaign in Huron. Prohibitionists from every political party and the WCTU attended the meeting to unite in favor of constitutional prohibition, an issue to be submitted to voters in October 1889. In this crucial election, voters would have the opportunity to approve the state constitution and decide whether or not the state would be admitted into the Union as dry or wet. Not surprisingly, Emma's quartette club provided entertainment for the two-day meeting.

The convention was a particularly important time for Emma, who learned from more seasoned workers about how to organize a campaign, which she would call upon later. She heard numerous addresses and watched as the convention of eight hundred discussed how to secure prohibition. She absorbed every speech and thought offered by ministers, WCTU speakers, and other delegates on how the cause might succeed. Reverend William Fielder submitted a plan that had worked in Beadle County in 1887. "Organize each county thoroughly," he advised. "Employ a paid agent" and "don't forget the literature."[62]

Delegates formed the Non-Partisan Constitutional Prohibition Organization and established an executive committee of seven, which included one woman. That woman was Philena Everett Johnson, a WCTU member and future president of the South Dakota Equal Suffrage Association. The executive committee directed the campaign and drew up the plan of organization, which divided the southern half of the territory into districts to distribute literature, schedule meetings, and canvass voters. They established headquarters in Huron, though only one of the committee members lived there, and pushed for the establishment of prohibition and campaign glee clubs.

Although the WCTU was part of the Non-Partisan Constitutional Prohibition Organization, the union was still a separate organization and worked for prohibition in its own way. The association provided its own speakers for the campaign, distributed the union's temperance literature, and pressed its own organizational plans. The WCTU scheduled schoolhouse meetings and employed several organizers over the course of the campaign to reach "into every nook and corner where meetings could be arranged."[63] The union sent an organizer to every county and formed a chapter in every town and schoolhouse to swell support for the cause.[64]

Although Emma did not play a major role in the campaign battle, she slowly began moving from the background of the prohibition movement to the front stage by helping to canvass Huron's voters on the issue. In June, she demonstrated her speaking skills at the Third District Convention of the WCTU held in St. Lawrence, about forty miles west of Huron, where she presented a paper entitled "Constitutional Prohibition and

How to Secure It."[65] The speech was reported in the press, and Emma recalled that this was the first time she "attracted public notice and began to develop as a public speaker."[66]

Emma's speech in St. Lawrence, which represented a major shift in her involvement with the cause, was brought about through presentation training provided by the WCTU. The organization gave thousands of nineteenth-century women the skills and training to become public speakers at a time when many colleges and universities refused to admit women to take part in rhetoric and elocution classes. National camps and training schools taught temperance women parliamentary procedures and how to influence public opinion.[67]

Emma received some of her training from the Kansas WCTU state organizer, Dora A. Evans, who reportedly had "great skill and experience in the work of instructing women." The Huron WCTU secured her services for five days, during which Evans held meetings and gave speeches about parliamentary usage and how to hold an ideal WCTU business meeting.[68] These brief courses offered Emma the chance to practice her public speaking, master her organizational skills, and learn how to win over hostile audiences, all skills she called upon as an organizer for the woman suffrage movement.

Attending the June convention in St. Lawrence and giving her speech changed the course of Emma's life. Being recognized as a skilled speaker was something she had not experienced heretofore. Had she not attended this district meeting and given the conference paper, it is possible that Emma may have continued to be a local leader, working for numerous reform movements in Huron and directing her glee club. Instead, WCTU convention delegates and president Helen Barker saw promise in her skills.

Just as Emma concluded her speech, a telegram from the Farmers' Alliance, then holding a meeting in Huron, arrived. The alliance asked the WCTU to send a delegation to its convention, and Barker chose Emma along with two other women.[69] Being selected for this task was a great honor for Emma. She had made an instant impression upon Barker, a seasoned organizer and speaker for the Territorial WCTU who believed that Emma had the ability to influence and persuade those opposed to prohibition. The three women left immediately for Huron. Two days later, when WCTU delegates elected officers for the district, they voted Emma superintendent of franchise, and thereafter she became one of the leading women activists in the suffrage battle.

Other constitutional prohibitionists swooped into Huron to attend a prohibition meeting on the same day as the Farmers' Alliance in an attempt to secure the support of the agrarians, like the Non-Partisan Constitutional Prohibition Organization. Although the prohibition alliance was nonpartisan, Flora M. Swift noted that the organization "was in no sense non-political." Prohibitionists hoped to win the support of every organization and political party in the state. As Swift recalled in her summary of the campaign, the Non-Partisan Constitutional Prohibition Organization was "*all*-partisan . . . for they certainly took a great interest in political parties, and they took very great pains too, that the right kind of men were sent to represent the people in the political gatherings." Their strategy paid off when the Farmers' Alliance unanimously passed a platform that supported state and national prohibition.[70] Later, the Republican Party passed a prohibition plank, and all of their candidates stood for prohibition, including John Pickler, the congressional nominee, and Arthur C. Mellette, their choice for state governor.[71] By contrast, the Democrats stood in opposition.

In the midst of the prohibition campaign that summer, the Beadle County Agricultural Association named Emma superintendent of the Woman's Day at the Beadle County Fair, the final day of the event. Emma asked many of South Dakota's leading reformers who favored woman suffrage and had ties with the WCTU to address the crowd on the issue of suffrage. In preparing for the event, she worked closely with Philena Everett Johnson, Helen Barker, and Alice Pickler, wife of John Pickler (who was sometimes called "Susan B." Pickler for his support of woman suffrage and for Susan B. Anthony). Huron seemed to be the best place to hold such an event, as the city was centrally located and nicknamed "convention city" by Dakotans.

Emma had long been a supporter of woman suffrage, but what accounted for her increasing interest in 1889? Why did she suddenly embrace the cause and step forward to serve as one of the leaders of the movement? She had never traveled to Bismarck to help secure voting rights for Dakota's women, as Alice Pickler and Helen Barker had, nor had she attended any of the constitutional conventions, encouraging delegates to include women in the state's electorate. In August 1888, John Flaherty had killed a prostitute in a whorehouse located on Kansas Street, just a few blocks from Emma's home.[72] In April 1889, Flaherty was tried for murder, and the *Daily Huronite* documented the gruesome proceedings. The recollection of the murder and the publicity of the trial may have been the final straw for Emma, who objected to the lawlessness that had invaded her street. Clearly the ordinance to suppress whorehouses failed miserably, and Emma may have come to believe that if South Dakotans gave women the ballot, they would vote for candidates who would actually rid their towns of vice rather than just issuing empty campaign pledges to do so. In other words, her vote would help clean up the city; if women had the right to vote, she concluded, brothels and murders could disappear from Huron.

If this was the case, she was certain she would not fail. At that time, she had almost ten years of successful reform work, including her deep involvement with the WCTU and political campaigns. The temperance movement had given her the opportunity to hone her lecturing, organizational, and administrative skills.

Like Emma, many leaders of the National American Woman Suffrage Association cut their teeth in leadership positions within the temperance movement during the 1880s. Anna Howard Shaw served as the national superintendent of the WCTU's Franchise Department and became its national lecturer. Carrie Chapman Catt was also an active member of the Charles City, Iowa, branch of the WCTU and eventually became its state lecturer and organizer.

South Dakota suffragists hoped that the delegates to the constitutional convention would agree to submit the issue of woman suffrage to voters at the 1890 election (as they had promised in 1885), and Alice Pickler, South Dakota's superintendent of the franchise for the WCTU, emphasized the necessity of beginning suffrage work in 1889. "It is very important, therefore, that we begin now to educate sentiment on the question of equal suffrage, and while we strain every nerve, and work and pray with all our might this summer for prohibition, let us arrange for every county and district convention to have something on this subject of equal rights," she wrote.[73] By scheduling pro-suffrage speakers for the Woman's Day at the Beadle County Fair, Emma followed the advice of a friend and colleague. As superintendent of franchise for the WCTU's Third District, she intended to make certain that the women of her region fully participated.

Emma planned to meet with each superintendent of franchise from the WCTU's Third District at the Woman's Day. At this meeting, she hoped to draw up a plan of work for the upcoming campaign. Upon learning of Emma's idea, Philena Johnson helped by attempting to push the women of the Third District to work harder for women's enfranchisement. "The woman suffrage campaign is not second in importance even to the prohibition campaign, and I do not expect that the women of the Third District will be behind the noble women of other parts of Dakota in seeking to elevate fallen humanity by striving to clothe the womanhood of our land with political power," she concluded.[74]

In the midst of all this activity—the final push for prohibition, planning for the Woman's Day at the county fair, and beginning her work for the woman suffrage movement—Emma's mother passed away at the age of eighty-one. Delia had been living with the couple since 1882. Emma was Delia's youngest daughter and sixth child. She had been ill since the beginning of the year, so her death came as no surprise to the DeVoes or to one of Emma's sisters, who, along with her husband and daughter (also named Emma), had come to visit, perhaps believing it would be their last chance to see Delia before her death.[75] Nonetheless, this certainly complicated matters for Emma, who had a great deal of work to complete within the coming weeks. At the same time, her mother's death encouraged Emma's new career as a suffrage organizer and lecturer. To deal with her grief, Emma later recalled, "I threw myself into suffrage work at that time."[76]

When the first of October—the day of the election for constitutional prohibition—finally rolled around, the women of the WCTU worked at polls across the state. In Huron, Emma and other members of the chapter organized a parade of young children who marched through the streets of the city singing temperance songs and carrying pro-temperance banners bearing slogans such as "Tremble, King Alcohol, We Shall Grow Up." The girls dressed in white, as a symbol of their purity, and the boys wore prohibition badges. The procession appeared to have the effect temperance women had hoped for, as the children "were cheered on every side by the crowds that gazed upon them."[77] The women's presence on the streets and at the polls in Huron resulted in one of the most orderly and civilized elections ever seen. The *Daily Huronite* reported that not one drunk appeared at the polls or on the streets that day and that there were no major disturbances recorded.[78]

Prohibition passed by a slim majority. Suffragists who were active in the campaign for constitutional prohibition immediately turned all of their attention to the upcoming suffrage campaign. With many years of experience behind her, Emma was now ready to step out on her own and help lead the South Dakota woman suffrage movement.

Emma unveiled her plan of work to the superintendents of franchise at the Woman's Day, which fell just three days after South Dakotans had ratified their state constitution. She planned to visit local unions in her district, where she would distribute woman suffrage literature, encourage those in favor of the issue to subscribe to the *Woman's Journal* or to the *Woman's Tribune*, and organize local equal suffrage chapters.

The topic of woman suffrage was popular at the fair, where people crowded around the platform bandstand to hear the suffragists and ministers. The speeches varied by the orator; Reverend Helen G. Putnam presented an engaging address on "Women in the Professions," and Sophia Harden examined "Women of the Farmers' Alliance."[79] The *Daily Huronite* reserved special praise for Helen Barker's speech "Woman's Work," calling it "one of her best."[80]

At the end of the day, twenty people crowded into the DeVoes' home for a meeting on woman suffrage. Barker called the meeting to order, and by the end of the evening attendees had drafted a call for a woman suffrage convention and decided to establish a suffrage club. They sent the announcement, which referenced Thomas Jefferson's Declaration of Independence but omitted the word "men," to the local paper, and requested that all state newspapers publish the notice, which read:

> We, the undersigned citizens of South Dakota, believing in the principles embodied in the Declaration of Independence that "All are born equal, endowed by their Creator with certain inalienable rights that 'to secure these rights' governments exist" and that "they derive all their just powers from the consent of the governed" and recognizing the fact that up to the present time, these "self evident truths" have been overlooked in their application to the women of Dakota in denying them the right to the elective franchise, we rejoice that the convention called to frame a constitution for the government of this new State, recognized the importance of this great question and provided for its submission to the people at the next general election. The issue is before us and *Nolens, Volens*, we must meet it. The time is brief and we must haste. We therefore call upon all friends of equality and justice to meet in the city of Huron, Monday afternoon at 2 p.m. Oct. 21, 1889.
>
> Let us come together and plan wisely for the campaign that is already upon us.
>
> It is important to the future of South Dakota.[81]

Experienced reformers—prohibition workers and speakers, newspaper editors, and statehood workers—signed the call and formed the core of the votes for women campaign in South Dakota. More than half of the people who signed the notice supported prohibition and had been active in the 1889 campaign; many were members of the WCTU or Farmers' Alliance. Women who signed the document included Barker, Libbie A. Wardall, Reverend Putnam, and Emma. Reverend English, Reverend M. Barker, Alonzo Wardall, and Henry represented some of the men who favored granting suffrage to South Dakota women.[82]

Recognizing that time was short and that the issue of prohibition had been secured with the assistance of the WCTU and speakers who came to Dakota Territory from across the country, suffragists looked to national women's rights leaders for help. Anthony was an obvious choice as she had previously stumped for suffrage across the West.

Hoping to draw attention to the cause and inspire home workers, they wrote letters to the famed orator, asking for her assistance, and made plans to attend the national convention in Washington, DC.[83] Henry told Anthony, "My wife looks upon you as a dependent child upon an indulgent parent; your words will inspire her."[84] Anthony agreed to come, but she arrived after the equal suffrage convention met in Huron.

Delegates to the convention established the South Dakota Equal Suffrage Association (SDESA) and elected officers. Samuel A. Ramsey, a prominent attorney from Woonsocket, became president. Ramsey had been a delegate to the 1889 constitutional convention and was a member of the Democratic Party. Vice president Alonzo Wardall lived in Huron and was a member of the Farmers' Alliance. He was also a member of the Republican Party and administered a crop insurance plan for Dakota farmers. Reverend M. Barker became secretary; a strong Baptist, he was president of the Prohibition Alliance in North Dakota. His wife, Helen Barker, served as state organizer. Delegates elected Sarah A. Richards, who managed a six-hundred-acre farm, as treasurer. The executive board consisted of the state officers and Reverend William Fielder, a staunch supporter of prohibition and state president of the South Dakota Enforcement League. Emma rounded out the committee, serving as assistant state organizer.[85]

Two days after the establishment of the SDESA, Emma announced an exciting new opportunity for the working women of her town. The Huron Woman's Christian Temperance Union planned to establish an Industrial School for Working Girls and Women, headed by Emma. The founding of such a school seemed logical to the women of the local WCTU; after all, the local working men had the opportunity to join orders, lodges, and the Young Men's Christian Association for their benefit, while no such opportunities existed for the working women in their community. The industrial school would fill that gap. The school would offer educational courses at no cost to the girls, discuss topics important to working women, provide community support to them, and care for any sick or particularly needy working females.

Perhaps in an attempt to save some of Huron's prostitutes, the school also sought to "throw a sisterly influence for good around each member; [and] to aid each member in securing suitable employment." Emma emphasized that the school would benefit those who attended, as well as those who provided the aid. "It is one of the beautiful compensations of this life that no one can sincerely try to help another without helping herself," she noted. The Baptist church agreed to hold the first school meeting.[86]

The day after that meeting, the *Daily Huronite* reported that a number of young women attended, and there they discussed reading and writing—the most pressing needed skills facing working girls and women. They formed a reading class and convinced Professor R. R. Wardall, a penman, to offer a writing class to the girls. Some of the young women also expressed interest in taking vocal lessons.[87] To raise funds for the school, students began gathering recipes for a cookbook. To ensure that the young women of her school found suitable employment, Emma established a labor bureau where local businesses and families could post job openings, and she located its headquarters at Henry's shoe store.[88]

With the SDESA in place, Emma began working in earnest for women's enfranchisement, frequently calling upon her previous experiences in the statehood and prohibition movements. Emma regularly called upon the skills she had learned in the WCTU while stumping for suffrage. Although the campaigns of the 1880s had prepared Emma to battle for the ballot, she still had much to learn from her mentor, Susan B. Anthony, who came to manage the South Dakota campaign and lived in the DeVoe house for more than six months. Although the idea of working so closely with the seasoned suffragist thrilled Emma, some in South Dakota bristled at the thought of Anthony taking control of the local campaign and publicly proclaimed their outrage.

2

THE SOUTH DAKOTA WOMAN SUFFRAGE CAMPAIGN

ON NOVEMBER 4, 1890, SOUTH DAKOTA VOTERS DEFEATED THE WOMAN suffrage amendment to their state constitution by a wide margin. Alice Stone Blackwell, daughter of suffragists Henry B. Blackwell and Lucy Stone, reported on the loss in the *Boston Woman's Journal*. Mistakes may have been made, she conceded, but she encouraged suffragists not to think of what might have been. Blackwell had long believed that the amendment would not pass because of the state's size, the large population of Russian, German, and Scandinavian immigrants, the distances between communities, high travel costs, a drought, the recent passage of a prohibition amendment, and the opposition or lack of support from political parties.

Although the suffrage amendment was unsuccessful, the 1890 South Dakota campaign was not a total failure, asserted Blackwell. The money spent and the hours of labor dedicated to the passage of the amendment were not wasted. South Dakota's women would eventually become citizens thanks in part to the work of the speakers and organizers in 1890. "The lesson of Dakota will be worth all that it has cost," she concluded.[1]

Suffragists anticipated victory in 1890, but the campaign was the first in a series of failed state elections fought by the National American Woman Suffrage Association.[2] The state-by-state approach remained the association's dominant strategy until 1913, when attempts to secure enfranchisement by a federal amendment gained increased interest. Some of the problems suffragists frequently encountered in South Dakota appeared elsewhere in the 1890s. A statewide depression hampered fundraising efforts, as downtrodden farmers and their neighbors failed to consider woman suffrage as a solution to the economic dilemmas they faced. (By contrast, Colorado voters supported suffrage, and the Panic of 1893 fueled support for the reform.) The state's political parties rejected suffrage planks, fearing that they would lose votes. Finally, funding and the ties between temperance and suffrage workers in South Dakota led to frequent disagreements between NAWSA and SDESA leadership.

As Blackwell acknowledged, suffragists learned a great deal from this campaign. Many of NAWSA's twentieth-century generals—Anna Howard Shaw, Carrie Chapman Catt, and Emma—participated and made a number of discoveries about elections, voters, and organizing, which they applied to future battles. To win a referendum, Catt believed that suffragists needed to secure support of local organizations and political parties, have sufficient funds, and have well-organized and excited campaign workers.[3] Emma compiled her own list of dos and don'ts after the failure, which she employed in the successful 1910 Washington campaign. Aside from serving as a training ground for young leaders, South Dakota also illustrated a major ideological shift occurring within the suffrage movement, as exemplified by Emma's political style.

America's women's rights movement, once considered a radical reform, had grown increasingly conservative over the years. Recognizing that radical tactics had resulted in ineffective results, suffragists distanced themselves from their past and began using more conservative rhetoric to educate the public about the benefits of woman suffrage. Pursuing public respectability, suffragists began to literally recreate their image by using new arguments and paying more attention to dress. Many of these changes can be attributed to the rhetorical training women received from the WCTU and brought with them into the suffrage movement. The women of the WCTU delivered women's rights addresses, which were often controversial, yet they sidestepped the antagonism often encountered by other women's rights supporters by couching nontraditional ideas in language and images that nineteenth-century audiences recognized.[4]

Emma's methods were particularly effective with South Dakota men and women because they seemed familiar. Her arguments, when coupled with her appearance and behavior, also a tactic of the WCTU, resulted in Emma silencing critics and winning new allies. She gained praise from the press for her demeanor, beauty, and singing ability, but she also aroused anger from her colleagues for her controlling methods. Susan B. Anthony, the matriarch of the movement, played an important role in shaping Emma's political style.

Anthony's train pulled into Huron on November 13, 1889. The DeVoes opened their home to the venerated reformer, inviting all those who wished to call on the noted suffrage leader to do so between the afternoon hours of 4 and 5:30 that day.[5] Later that evening, the couple took Anthony to the county courthouse, where she proceeded to speak for two hours. Emma, who had plans to visit neighboring counties to stump for suffrage, listened closely.[6]

Leaving Huron, Anthony continued her tour of South Dakota, which ended in Aberdeen. There she spoke at the annual meeting of the Farmers' Alliance. After hearing her address, the agrarians passed a pro-woman suffrage resolution to "do all in our power" to secure woman suffrage at the 1890 election "by bringing it before the local alliances for agitation and discussion, thereby educating the masses upon the subject."[7] Emma, the other members of the SDESA executive board, and Philena Everett Johnson—a member of the WCTU who would later become president of the SDESA—traveled to Aberdeen to hear her address and meet with the national leader.

Together, they adopted a plan of work for the upcoming campaign. Anthony expected organizers to visit every farmhouse in the state, to converse with the owners about the issue during the winter months, to organize equal suffrage committees in every district and village, to canvass voters, and to leave suffrage literature for opponents to read.[8] Anthony's plan of work was similar—nearly identical—to Emma's. Emma had drawn up these plans earlier that fall and published them in the *Union Signal* nearly a week before Anthony arrived in the state. Emma's agenda suggests that she played a much larger role in shaping the South Dakota campaign than historians and suffragists have given her credit for. Smaller in scope than Anthony's proposal, Emma would visit local unions in the central part of the state, where she would distribute woman suffrage literature, encourage those in favor of the issue to subscribe to the *Woman's Journal* or *Beatrice Woman's Tribune*, and organize local equal suffrage chapters of the SDESA.[9] One major difference separated the two proposals, however: the campaign plan drafted by Emma centered on the work of the South Dakota WCTU.

Anthony had reservations about having the Woman's Christian Temperance Union as an ally. The nationally recognized leader insisted that the campaign fall under the command of the South Dakota Equal Suffrage Association, not the WCTU, the Grand Army of the Republic, the Woman's Relief Corps (an auxiliary to the GAR), or political parties. "Each may do splendid work for suffrage within its own organization, and we shall rejoice in all that do so; but the South Dakota and the National-American Associations must stand on their own ground," she advised.[10] Presumably Anthony worried that these organizations would use the campaign to push their own agendas rather than the issue at hand—women's enfranchisement.

Consequently, Anthony told Emma and the other SDESA officers that the issue of woman suffrage be held "entirely outside and above all other political, religious or reform questions—that is, keep it absolutely apart by itself." For example, she directed suffragists to avoid linking votes for women with the prohibition issue, which the WCTU promoted; instead, she advised them to focus solely on the issue of suffrage and "to wear just the badge of yellow ribbon—that and none other," referring to the white ribbon of the WCTU.[11] Anthony believed that the suffrage and temperance causes were separate and that linking woman suffrage with prohibition in any way would result in failure.

Emma, who had never been employed as an organizer, soaked up every word uttered by her mentor. Even though Anthony's time in South Dakota was short, Emma had time to speak with and listen to the seasoned organizer, who had nearly forty years of experience in the campaigns for women's rights, temperance, and the abolition of slavery. She heard Anthony speak at least twice and enjoyed the personal time with her when she stayed two times as a guest in her home. After Anthony's departure from the state of South Dakota in November, Emma began her first organizing tour in Hyde County.

Emma's initial work fell under the auspices of the WCTU, and these early tours must have been difficult for her, as she tried to follow Anthony's advice to keep woman suffrage and prohibition separate. But, as superintendent of the franchise of the Third District, she could not avoid working with the WCTU until a local or county equal suffrage association could be organized as an auxiliary to the SDESA.[12] Presumably, she combined her work with the SDESA and WCTU until local clubs could stand on their own.

Anthony's instructions about the campaign were clear, but given that the WCTU had trained Emma in public speaking, she continued to use some of its techniques in her public lectures. For instance, Frances Willard, president of the WCTU, believed that music helped deflect criticism from hostile audiences, and she instructed speakers to sing a tune to make their audiences more receptive to the cause of temperance.[13] "A solo from some sweet woman's heart and voice . . . will utterly transform your audience as to its receptivity, its support, its mental elevation," she said.[14] Emma, who undoubtedly admired Willard, applied this WCTU technique to her earliest meetings with great success.

Aside from the influence of the WCTU, the statehood campaign also shaped Emma's style. Singing excited audiences at statehood rallies. Recalling the thrill in the air after singing "Severance of Church and State, or Lewis K's Lamentation," the DeVoes came to believe the same enthusiasm could be experienced in the suffrage campaign through the use of music and song.

Before Emma departed Huron, her husband wrote and arranged a song based on his strong interest in securing voting rights for women. Well before the South Dakota campaign began, Henry favored the enfranchisement of women. Injured during the Civil War, he relied on the aid and care of Union nurses, who tended to his needs while he regained his strength; as his health improved, Henry promised to help women win this battle.

"A Soldier's Tribute to Woman" praised women for standing by their sons, husbands, and brothers during the Civil War. The chorus emphasized the need for the nation to pay its debt to the women who had helped to preserve the Union:

> Yes, they nursed and brought me through, when the fever laid me low.
> In my dreams I now can see them, while they're flitting to and fro.
> Then I swore to help the women, for their hearts were loyal too,
> And my vote shall go to free them, for they nursed and brought me
> through.[15]

Written in the first person (from the male perspective), the lyrics sound as if they should be sung by a man, but Emma was the only one who sang this song. No Civil War veterans joined her on stage, except Henry, who once sang a duet of the song with his wife at the GAR hall.

During her nine-day trip through Hyde County, Emma formed seven local chapters of the South Dakota Equal Suffrage Association and then closed with a county convention in Highmore. She credited Anthony for her success. "Had it not been for the advice and help of Miss Anthony I could not have done it," Emma admitted. "She gave us such instruction, such help, that workers like myself, for instance, feel that we can do something."[16]

That winter, a lack of suffrage literature threatened to undermine the campaign. The SDESA's lack of funds and a statewide depression exacerbated the problem; making matters worse, the WCTU, which recently secured the passage of prohibition in South Dakota, depleted its funds in the preceding year. The SDESA could not afford to purchase any newspapers, leaflets, or suffrage tracts and distribute them statewide, nor could readers part with funds to cover the costs of the literature. Emma lamented, "Oh, if we had some money! I go to organize Hand County next and have not one single leaflet; and I cannot promise them any." If voters only had access to literature, she believed that they would come to support the issue in the November election as they had done the previous year with prohibition.[17]

During the winter months, South Dakotans devoured books, magazines, pamphlets, and newspapers. Publications provided entertainment for those living in isolated areas and broke up the monotony of the day. As Dakotan Mary Dodge Woodward noted in her diary, "Without material to read we could not live here [in the winter]."[18] Freezing temperatures and blizzards forced families indoors, giving them plenty of time to read all sorts of literature, including suffrage newspapers and pamphlets, in front of their blazing fires.

Upon receiving the pleas from South Dakota, editors of the *Woman's Journal* agreed to make their papers available to readers free or at a reduced cost and decided to supply the SDESA with pamphlets for a minimal fee.[19] Clara B. Colby, editor of the *Beatrice Woman's Tribune*, made her paper available to every family in South Dakota with the understanding that readers would submit a payment at a later date, when they had the funds.[20] The WCTU donated ten thousand suffrage pamphlets in foreign languages, which pleased Emma, who believed that the leaflets would greatly benefit the campaign.[21] Anthony mailed fifty thousand copies of a pro-woman suffrage speech to South Dakota residents, half of them to the men of the Farmers' Alliance, by Senator Thomas W. Palmer of Michigan, who favored a Sixteenth Amendment to the United States Constitution to enfranchise women.

Emma braved the winter weather and kept her appointments in Hand County, where she organized eight woman suffrage clubs without literature. Her listeners eagerly joined the movement. The *South Dakota State Journal* reported that Emma "met each and every objection to equal suffrage, and as she with that great sledgehammer in argument—facts and figures—destroyed them, there seemed to be but one verdict by the entire audience—'We are willing to give woman the ballot.'"[22] Even though Emma weathered South Dakota's bitterly cold winter to reach out to Hand County voters, a blizzard forced her to return to Huron before her final engagement at the county convention.

During her two tours of Hyde and Hand counties, Emma learned that the ties between women and veterans ran deep. At the Hyde County convention, she spoke of women's work with the Union soldiers and then sang "A Soldier's Tribute to Woman." When Emma finished singing, a former Civil War soldier immediately called out, "Three cheers for the women!" At a meeting in Highmore, Emma told listeners that the women of the town would serve them lunch, and a veteran said, "Can't you see the hand of woman in that? They used to do that the same way at our reunions after the war, and I shall vote for them next November!"[23]

During the campaign, Emma became a persuasive speaker. She learned to gauge her audience and understood how to appeal to them. She frequently used patriotism and the memory of the Civil War to establish a relationship with her audience—a tactic the statehood leaders and the Republican Party also used to galvanize residents in the territory and a method employed by the WCTU to appeal to listeners. This strategy was quite effective because many of South Dakota's voters were also veterans of the Civil War and members of the GAR.[24]

Appealing to the memory of her audience members, she asked men to help women as the women had helped them during the Civil War. "As I cared for you when you were weak and I was strong as I cared for you in your weakness, I ask you to help me and mine now that you are strong and I am weak."[25] From her position as the wife of a veteran, she appealed to the former soldiers in the audience, who most likely had mothers, sisters, or daughters who had worked in some capacity during the Civil War. Her request challenged popular views of the war, which, by the 1890s, had nearly forgotten women's contributions.[26] By identifying women as politically weak, Emma suggested, but did not insist, that men should help women.[27] It almost appeared as if Emma was asking for a favor, but her appeal was well-suited for her audience. Women had worked hard during the war, and men could thank them by voting in favor of the woman suffrage amendment.

Over the course of the campaign, Emma learned not to force her opinion on listeners. Once, a young man approached her after a speech to say that he would not vote for woman suffrage. Emma recalled the exchange that followed:

> He said: "If I knew how corrupt politics were in his county I would not
> be in favor of women voting, that he could not think of voting for woman
> suffrage on that account." Said I what is the matter with your politics? There
> are only three divisions of society: the home, the church and the state. Let
> us see: perhaps it is the home that is at fault. The young man was offended.
> "No," said he, "our women are as talented and our homes equal to any."
> Then perhaps it may be the church that is at fault. The ministers may be
> corrupt. No, their ministers were as pure and their churches equal to any.
> Then said I there is only one place left, the state, and that is the only place
> you exclude women. Admit them to your politics and they will be all right,
> but he was not satisfied.[28]

With the ballot, Emma suggested, women would be able to uplift men from the cesspool of politics, but she did not insist or demand anything from the man with whom she spoke. "He was prejudiced," she concluded, "and when I meet a man that is prejudiced I think there is no use arguing with him, and I offer a silent prayer for the Lord to have mercy: not only on his soul, but on his everlasting thick skull."[29]

As Emma's last statement indicates, instead of scolding men for their shortcomings, she made them laugh. At the same lecture she said, "I do not say that the men of to day are to blame for these laws. They are not to blame for the laws they find on the statutes, but they are to blame for the laws they leave there."[30]

She also convinced others to give, even when they had little money for the purchase of food or other necessities. When Carrie Chapman Catt asked an older man why Emma excelled in fundraising for the SDESA, he said, "I guess it is because she sings so pretty."[31]

Reverend Olympia Brown, who later traveled to South Dakota, believed that Emma's success stemmed from the fact that she could "always be trusted to please the audience and to offend no one."[32] In other words, she was conciliatory to both men and women. She never challenged the traditionally held ideals of womanhood but instead acknowledged and embraced the differences between the sexes. She believed that women were more moral than men and, when compared to men, tended more to abide by society's laws. Women therefore had an obligation to clean up their city and state governments by serving as municipal housekeepers. Her ideas were in step with other Americans during this time.

Although she had achieved great success in Hyde and Hand counties, the stormy winter weather limited her organizing opportunities, and she took some time off. During her break, Emma turned her attention to the Industrial School for Working Girls and Women. School activities could not take Emma's thoughts away from the campaign, however. Concerned that the suffrage movement might fail, Emma hoped that Anthony would travel to South Dakota for the remainder of the campaign to help the troops win the battle. "If Miss Anthony would only come here, if we could only have her here on the ground, we should be assured of victory. My home should be hers and she should lock us out whenever she wished to be alone," Emma confided to Clara Colby.[33] A week later, Anthony agreed, and she announced she would travel to South Dakota that spring and make Huron her headquarters.

By February the weather had finally improved such that Emma could begin traveling again. She had not organized any equal suffrage clubs since the end of the year, and after more than a month's rest she began her third organizing tour in Beadle County. Her trip through her home county was more extensive than her previous trips, and in total she spent more than a month organizing Equal Suffrage Association (ESA) clubs. In the middle of her lecture circuit, she returned home several times, once to observe Anthony's seventieth birthday.

South Dakota suffragists, however, had little to celebrate in spite of the organizing work of Emma and others. Suffragists had failed to make much of an impact on voters because of lack of funding, inclement weather, and apathy. SDESA officers continually wrote to Anthony requesting financial assistance. Eventually things became so bad that Alonzo Wardall, SDESA vice president, traveled from Huron to the first National American Woman Suffrage Association meeting in Washington, DC, to ask for money.

For the previous twenty-one years, the suffrage movement had consisted of two groups: the National Woman Suffrage Association (NWSA) and the American Woman Suffrage Association (AWSA). NAWSA, formed by the merger of these two associations, adopted the AWSA's more conservative tactics and ideology and dropped the controversial reforms the NWSA had once supported. Anthony, who headed the efforts in South Dakota, directed a campaign which reflected these emerging beliefs. Later in the decade, the formation of one single organization had tremendous consequences for western states, which proved more capable of reaching out to the West Coast and Rocky Mountain West states than the two separate associations had. Organizations across the West would dot the landscape thanks in part to the efforts of NAWSA in the 1890s.

Wardall, along with Congressman John Pickler and his wife, Alice, appeared before the NAWSA to make a personal appeal to delegates. Wardall encouraged state auxiliaries to send at least one worker to South Dakota. The amendment could be carried, he asserted, with financial assistance; otherwise, it would go down to defeat. Delegates sympathized with the leadership of the fledgling organization and appointed a South Dakota Campaign Committee, headed by Anthony and staffed by Clara B. Colby and Alice Stone Blackwell. Colby and Blackwell were second-generation suffragists. Colby, born in 1846, earned her bachelor's degree from the University of Wisconsin. In 1881, she became vice president of the Nebraska Woman Suffrage Association and began publishing the *Beatrice Woman's Tribune* two years later.[34] Blackwell edited the *Woman's Journal* from her home in Boston. A number of states pledged money for the upcoming campaign, and a suffragist from Montana promised $250.[35]

After NAWSA raised $5,500 for the South Dakota fund, the SDESA executive committee determined they could run the campaign. They asked that Anthony turn over the money. Their demand angered Anthony, who believed that the SDESA had outlined no plan of effective work for the campaign. On top of this, many members of the board, like the Reverend M. Barker and his wife, Helen, who served as secretary and state organizer, respectively, considered the woman suffrage and prohibition causes to be inseparable. Helen Barker also served as president of the state WCTU, which proved to be a major conflict of interest.

When Anthony refused to give the South Dakota fund to the state association, she offended many of South Dakota's suffragists, who believed that they knew how best to conduct their campaign. After all, they had just secured two important victories in their state—constitutional prohibition and statehood. If they used the same formula that they employed in those cases, focusing on organization and song in particular, they felt confident that they would win. Anthony, by contrast, believed that she knew best, and she used the power of the purse strings to control South Dakota's campaign. Emma and Henry sided with her.

Although the disagreement centered upon the role temperance would play in the campaign, the matter also reflected more general tensions that occurred between local and national leaders. Frustrated by Anthony's attempt to control things, South Dakota suffragists tried to discredit the leader. Newspapers reported that the South Dakota reformers called Anthony "a mean old thing" and "arbitrary." They claimed that she wanted "to be boss of everything," and the women of South Dakota could not get "along with her."[36] Marietta Bones, former vice president of the NWSA, charged Anthony—who had sacked Bones during the merger of NWSA with AWSA—with embezzling from the South Dakota Fund, and she also claimed that SDESA President Samuel A. Ramsey opposed Anthony's plan of work.[37] The DeVoes disagreed with this assessment. Anthony was Emma's friend and confidante. All winter long Emma wrote to her, shared her organizing experiences with her, and looked to her for advice.[38]

By the end of March, reinforcements made their way to South Dakota to serve as speakers and organizers for the cause. Matilda Hindman of Pennsylvania arrived first. She had worked as an organizer and speaker in numerous campaigns, most recently in Washington Territory. California women raised money to send Hindman, while Minnesota pledged funds to secure the labors of Julia B. Nelson, who followed Hindman into the South Dakota battle. Not quite forty-eight years old, Nelson had dedicated her life to the cause of equality for women and African Americans. She taught at freedmen's schools in Houston and Columbus, Texas, and later accepted a position as the principal of an African American school in Tennessee.[39]

After Nelson, the Reverend Anna Howard Shaw, NAWSA's national lecturer, arrived. Born in 1847, she held a theological degree from Boston University Seminary as well as a medical degree from Boston University Medical School. She began her speaking career as a lecturer for the WCTU and, at the time, was considered one of the best suffrage orators. Anthony followed soon after.

The town of Huron held elections for mayor and city council on April 1, 1890, a few weeks before Anthony's arrival. The *Daily Huronite* described the event as "the most spirited and vigorously contested of any in the history of Huron."[40] During the election, someone printed a number of tickets with Emma's name listed for street commissioner, and she received at least twenty votes, even though the office was an appointed position, not an elected one. Although the act was reportedly an April Fool's Day joke, Emma used the opportunity to promote her causes, writing in an open letter to the mayor and city council that "it is evident there is a desire in the public mind that women shall at last be recognized as suitable persons to hold any office." Emma saw an opportunity to help protect families and clean up local politics by taking this position. In the same letter, she pledged to "use no intoxicating liquors during my term of office." She would also "allow no employee under my charge to spend his time in saloons playing 'sinch' at the public expense." Hoping to avoid the accounting problems that had plagued the city, she also promised to account for all water taxes and other money she collected and to keep the streets in good repair and cleared of snow and mud.[41]

Many of the voters in Huron agreed that the city government needed a change, and they believed Emma was up to the task. A number of citizens planned to submit a petition to the council asking for her appointment to the position of street commissioner. The editor of the *Dakota Ruralist* wrote, "If it be a part of a woman's duty to keep her house clean and orderly, we see no reason why she may not with equal propriety devote herself to the task of keeping the streets in proper condition; and we believe she would do so more thoroughly than a man. We trust the members of the Council will consider this subject seriously."[42] The idea of electing women to municipal offices was not foreign in the West. Western women were increasingly making inroads in city governments. Just three years earlier, voters in Syracuse, Kansas, elected an entirely female city council, and residents of Argonia, Kansas, elected the first female mayor in the United States.[43]

The Huron city council rejected the petition to nominate Emma, unanimously appointing one Alex McIntosh instead.[44] It is unknown precisely why the council rejected Emma, but it seems likely that the mayor and council had their fill of reformers who objected to the licensing of saloons, which provided the bulk of funds for the local schoolhouse. More importantly, the saloons would permanently close at midnight on the last day of April, so her campaign pledges held little interest to those in favor of similar reforms.

Emma must have been excited to see Anthony return to South Dakota that month, and over the course of the 1890 campaign the two became close friends. Anthony, affectionately called "Aunt Susan" by her followers, came to think of Emma and Henry as her niece and nephew and likened their home to that of her brothers.[45] On the road frequently and living in the same house for months, the two women learned a lot about each other. Undoubtedly, Anthony passed along invaluable information to Emma about woman suffrage, lecturing, and organizing. She also helped Emma develop her own speaking style. Their approaches differed, but the two shared some important similarities.

Anthony, once considered a militant suffragist for her defiance of the law to secure the ballot for women, encouraged Emma to avoid confrontational tactics.[46] By 1890 Anthony had worked for woman suffrage for nearly forty years. Over time, she began to realize that opposition to woman suffrage was too strong, so she softened her rhetoric and became less aggressive.[47] When a younger, less experienced suffragist proposed that women turn out to vote on election day, Anthony explained that her plan would not work.

> Hundreds have recommended your plan, so it is nothing new, but it is
> utterly impractical. There can be but one possible way for women to be freed
> from the degradation of disfranchisement, and that is through the slow
> processes of agitation and education. . . . Therefore do not waste a single
> moment trying to devise any sort of insurrectionary movement on the part
> of the women.[48]

Throughout the course of her work for woman suffrage, Emma followed this advice.

Only a few years earlier, Anthony had come to believe it was important to work towards the single goal of woman suffrage. In the past, she had thrown her support behind controversial issues like divorce reform and economic independence for women. Her position changed over time, however. In the 1880s, Anthony became displeased with suffragists who worked for a variety of reforms, not just women's enfranchisement. She preferred that suffragists concentrate on the passage of an equal suffrage amendment first and foremost.[49] In her thirty-one years as a suffrage lecturer and organizer, Emma worked only for woman suffrage, and she carefully avoided associating other controversial issues with votes for women.

In addition to working only for equal suffrage, Emma adhered to a strict policy of nonpartisanship, which Anthony began to support in the 1880s.[50] Unfortunately, politics and economics complicated matters for suffragists that summer.

South Dakotans struggled to make a living growing crops that year. A severe drought reduced crop yields, and many farmers hit hard by this decline moved from South Dakota to greener pastures. Henry and Emma were similarly stressed. They had already mortgaged their two farms to buy Henry's shoe and boot store. They had nowhere to turn, and with so many suffering, few could afford to buy shoes. Henry sought relief from the Huron city council in June, asking for a reduction in his city taxes. They agreed and reduced his bill to $3,500.[51]

With so many feeling the pinch, conditions were ripe for the formation of a party that would push for reform to help the people of South Dakota—agrarians and the working class. In June, the Farmers' Alliance and Knights of Labor held a joint convention in Huron and formed the Independent Party, which demanded "free silver" (unlimited coining of silver to loosen credit), an Australian or secret ballot, railway transport reform, telegraph and telephone service at cost, and other items. The party, however, did not include a plank for woman suffrage. When later asked why the party had not included the measure in their platform, Henry L. Loucks, president of the Farmers' Alliance, admitted they did so to woo voters; woman suffrage was too controversial for the party to adopt, and they could not win if they backed such a reform.[52]

The decision to form a third party angered Anthony, who had come to South Dakota on assurances that Loucks and Alonzo Wardall had the power to force the Republican Party to put a suffrage plank in their platform. They had admitted as much to the reformer when they told her that they were responsible for securing the adoption of a prohibition plank by the Republicans and that their influence led to the passage of the amendment.[53] She concluded that the Independents failed to support woman suffrage and prohibition "for the avowed object of *winning* the *votes* of the *anti-prohibition* and anti-*woman suffrage foreigners* among them."[54] The formation of the Independent Party practically ensured that the amendment would fail.

The decision to form a separate party of farmers and laborers upset the Republicans, who feared they might lose control of the state legislature to the Independents. Party members expected defections to be especially high in counties east of the Missouri River, and Beadle County was not immune to the draw of the movement.[55]

Although Aunt Susan opposed the establishment of a third party, Henry, who was a member of the Knights of Labor, broke party ranks and joined, hoping that the Independents could improve his and Emma's economic situation. In July, he attended the Beadle County Independent Party convention, and delegates nominated him for state senator. He withdrew his name from consideration, however, and instead became one of the nominees for state representative.[56]

Suffragists from across the state, including Emma, signed a call to hold another suffrage convention in Huron on July 8.[57] They demanded the meeting because the current campaign manager and secretary of the SDESA, Reverend M. Barker, was "gravely negligent of his duties." Under his leadership, the association had lost the support of farmers and laborers. Local people constantly cried for speakers, but Barker frequently ignored their calls. Plus, he failed to mail literature to the state workers. Out of twenty engagements, Helen M. Gougar had received literature for only four places.[58]

Barker's appointment had displeased Anthony. Even though the association had no money, the SDESA had agreed to pay him $100 a month. Upon hearing of this arrangement, Shaw told South Dakotans, "Not one of us, myself least of all, will consent to take out of the contributions from friends of suffrage one dollar to pay towards a salary of $100 a month to any man as secretary."[59] Afraid of defeat, President Samuel A. Ramsey agreed to call an executive committee meeting to appoint a new secretary and campaign committee.

The election took place at the Huron suffrage convention the day before the Independent Party meeting opened. Nearly everyone opposed the meeting date for fear that voters would believe that the suffragists had formed a coalition with the third party.[60] Many worried that if they met in the same place and at the same time as the Independents, they would be unable to secure the support of the Republican Party, which had previously endorsed the issues temperance women had lobbied for. Their strongest supporter, John Pickler, remained a Republican. It seemed doubtful that he alone would be able to secure a suffrage plank. The editor of the *Aberdeen Daily* and *Aberdeen Weekly News* reported that the women of Huron, including Emma, had manipulated the women of South Dakota into calling a convention to "hob-nob with the independent" party against the advice of their executive board. Reportedly, the women called the meeting "not to forward the interest of the cause, but to bolster up" the candidacies of some of the women's husbands: Alonzo Wardall, who was a possible candidate for one of South Dakota's United States' Senate seats, J. W. Harden, also a potential candidate for Congress, and Henry.[61]

At the July meeting, the SDESA officially disbanded, and delegates formed a new group under the same name. They discussed forming a new board composed solely of women, because of all the gaffs they encountered with their nearly all male board, but this did not happen.[62] William F. Bailey, described as "the right man in the right place" by Henry B. Blackwell, replaced Reverend Barker as secretary, but he received no salary.[63] Delegates elected Philena Everett Johnson president, Irene G. Adams became vice president, and Sarah A. Richards remained state treasurer.[64] Named to the state executive committee, Emma resigned, preferring the position of state lecturer and organizer. Henry remained active, too. Appointed to the music committee to prepare a campaign songbook, he also designed the association's badge. The insignia consisted of a brass star on which hung scales displaying the words justice and equality. The crossbar included the association's acronym, "ESA," and below the S hung a hook to tie a yellow ribbon.[65]

Members of the executive committee included Anthony, Judge D. C. Thomas, and Helen M. Barker, the former state organizer and wife of Reverend M. Barker, who the SDESA retained as a member of the committee.[66] The reconstituted organization sympathized with Anthony and her campaign plan, welcoming "to our state that able, fearless and true friend of humanity in general, and women in particular, Miss Susan B. Anthony and her talented assistants who have come to spread the gospel of justice and equal rights among us."[67] From that point on, Anthony and Bailey directed the campaign.

That summer was one of the hottest on record, and days for organizers and speakers were long. One of the highlights that season was the admittance of Wyoming into the Union, making it the first state in the Union to have equal suffrage for both men and women. SDESA secretary Will Bailey likened Wyoming's admission to the American Revolution's battle of Trenton. "It is the beginning of the end," he proclaimed.[68] South Dakota shared a large portion of its western border with the Equality State, and suffragists hoped that a commitment to women's rights would spread throughout the land, beginning with their state. In August, the city of Mitchell hosted the second state equal suffrage convention, with the state Republican Party convention opening two days later.

Here Emma had the opportunity to spend time with suffragist Olympia Brown, the president of the Wisconsin Woman's Suffrage Association (wwsa) and a Universalist minister. Anthony invited Brown to participate in the final days of the campaign, beginning with the Mitchell convention. Brown had long been interested in the campaign for women's rights and recalled that after reading an account of a woman's rights convention in 1850, "young as I was, the idea seized upon me. The speeches stirred my soul; the names of the participants loomed up before me as the names of great heroes often inspire young boys." Drawn into the campaign for equal rights, she later circulated petitions in favor of married women's property rights, attended the founding meeting of the American Equal Rights Association, and toured Kansas in the 1867 battle for woman suffrage. Upon arriving in Mitchell, Brown learned that the boarding rooms filled quickly; asked to room with another suffragist, she replied that she would choose "that young lecturer, Mrs. Emma Smith DeVoe." During the short time they were in Mitchell, they forged a lifelong friendship, with Brown frequently calling upon Emma to organize and speak in Wisconsin in later years.[69]

The August meeting focused solely on the enfranchisement of women, and music played a prominent role at the convention. The DeVoes had clearly urged the association to adopt methods that had succeeded in the statehood movement. The campaign songbook sold for ten cents a copy and included Henry's song "A Soldier's Tribute to Woman" as well as many similar tunes with different lyrics from the statehood movement. "What's All the Stir" had been previously known as "Six Hundred Thousand Strong," while "The Dakotas Are Coming" became "South Dakota is Coming." The famous "Severance of Church and State, or Lewis K's Lamentation" became "The County Boodler's Lament." For her part, Emma led the South Dakota Female Quartette, which sang many of Henry's compositions at the meeting.[70]

The three-day convention drew crowds of five hundred in the afternoon and one thousand in the evening. They came to hear the famed orator, Anna Howard Shaw; nawsa's vice president, Anthony; and their home worker, Alice Pickler. New faces included Carrie Chapman Catt, state lecturer of the Iowa Woman Suffrage Association, and Laura M. Johns, president of the Kansas Equal Suffrage Association, who had come to provide further assistance to the campaign. As suffragists expected, Republican delegates attended the meetings, and according to Henry Blackwell, they "showed a deep interest."[71]

The suffragists hoped that the Republican Party would pass a woman suffrage plank, as some leading party men had promised, but the issue failed. Republicans opposed the issue out of political expediency. A Republican from Brown County explained, "Give women the right to vote and seven-eighths of them would knife the republican party on the first opportunity. They would be found in every third party move that might be inaugurated from time to time. . . . Indeed, they belong to the Loucks party now."[72]

As the summer wound down, some farmers chose not to harvest their fields. Instead, they and their families began moving out of South Dakota in hopes of finding a better life elsewhere. This complicated matters for the suffrage movement. Speakers attempted to sway discouraged and impoverished voters to support woman suffrage, but many thought the cause insignificant. "They are so busy thinking about bread and butter they can't give thought to this matter," Laura Johns noted. Other citizens appeared more concerned with the coming winter than with the subject of women's enfranchisement.[73] Emma hoped to stimulate interest by again holding a Woman's Day, this time at the state fair.

The South Dakota Agricultural Board named Emma superintendent of the day, and she began planning the event soon after her appointment. A procession kicked off the celebration and drew a crowd of shopkeepers and fairgoers. The spectacle featured the Knights of Pythias Band of Huron, the Aberdeen Guards (formed in 1890 as an auxiliary to the GAR and composed of daughters of Civil War veterans),[74] the Woman's Relief Corps, the WCTU, the GAR, and five hundred children. Nearly everyone except the band and children traveled to the fair in carriages, and a few women came on horseback. The lead carriage included Anthony, Shaw, Brown, and Emma.

The procession, which stretched for a mile, arrived at the grandstand, where Emma welcomed listeners to the Woman's Day. Visitors, hoping to get a glimpse of Anthony or to hear Reverend Shaw speak, crammed into the gate leading to the platform. Before the speeches began, the South Dakota Female Quartette sang "Glorious Dakota" and the Aberdeen Guards entertained the crowd. Olympia Brown spoke first; her address, called "forcible and earnest" by the *Aberdeen Daily News*, was followed by a "stirring song" sung by the quartette, with Emma playing the organ. Emma Cranmer, vice president of the state WCTU, followed. The final two speakers included Anthony and Shaw. Emma introduced each woman, but before she presented Anthony, the roar of the crowd chanting "The Honorable Susan B. Anthony" was so loud that it drowned out her introduction. Shaw gave the final speech of the day and received great praise from the *Aberdeen Daily News*, which was often unfriendly to the cause of equal suffrage.[75] In all, suffragists deemed the day a success, but the final months of the campaign were less celebratory.

As the election drew nearer, several issues plagued the campaign, but one in particular upset Emma: invited speakers from outside of the state who antagonized South Dakota's political parties. Unlike other workers hired by NAWSA, Emma avoided alienating these groups. Suffragists needed votes from all men, regardless of political affiliation, she believed. She determined that blaming the parties for women's disfranchisement was both ineffective and contrary to the conciliatory approach she preferred. Earlier in the year, when she visited the Black Hills, the editor of the *Deadwood Pioneer* praised Emma for refraining from divisive speech and from the "censure [of] any political party or class of men for being slow in considering the claims of women."[76]

Emma's style as a nonpartisan speaker differed from that of other NAWSA suffragists. Upon arriving in Madison in early October, Emma learned that Catt had denounced the Independent Party, thus offending party members who might have supported suffrage. Rebecca Hager, secretary of the Lake County Suffrage Association and an active member of the South Dakota WCTU, told Emma that an Independent candidate said "no suffrage speaker should get up on their platform and abuse them as Mrs. Chapman [Catt] did." Emma quickly sought to soothe the bruised feelings, arranging to speak to an assembly of Independent delegates with Henry Loucks to "let them see that the suffragists *of the state—the home workers* are not opposed to any party." She immediately asked William Bailey to tell Catt to stop condemning the parties. "She will do more harm than we can possibly do good," Emma wrote.[77]

Even though Emma made amends with Independents in Madison and with their leader, Wentworth Independents remained offended by Catt's comments. Hager had arranged for Emma to speak at their Independent meeting, but they refused to admit her, and she had to send statehood leader General William H. H. Beadle in Emma's place.[78]

Other speakers could similarly offend listeners. Upon arriving in Flandreau, Emma learned that Anna Howard Shaw had offended the president of the Flandreau Equal Suffrage Association, who was also the wife of the local Republican newspaper editor. She called Shaw a bitter woman who argued with Republican Party men. These allegations worried Emma. She instructed William Bailey to pass along the information to Anthony so that their leader might "tone Anna down before she goes to the [Black] Hills."[79] Emma believed that Shaw's sarcastic style could backfire on the suffragists.

In her own speeches, Emma was careful not to insult or challenge the ideas of the political parties upon whom she believed the future of the woman suffrage amendment rested, for which the press applauded her. Women were commonly associated with nonpartisanship in the nineteenth century, and Emma stuck closely to this image, which was part of women's political culture. While in Emory, Emma appeared onstage with a Democratic candidate and the chair of the township's Democratic committee. Irish Catholics, who supported the Democrats, populated the crowd. To appeal to her listeners, she insisted that suffragists were nonpartisan, although many had husbands who were Republican or Independents and their sympathies probably lay with their spouses. Her address, which made the listeners laugh, was so successful that she even managed to convince a saloon keeper to join the club and to wear the yellow ribbon.[80]

Emma differed from NAWSA speakers and even from her fellow South Dakota organizers in another important way: she was beautiful. Emma used this to her advantage, as most of the other organizers were older and less physically attractive than her. A comparison of photographs taken of Helen Barker and Emma indicate significant differences between the two. Barker, the previous state organizer, was in her late fifties. She had thinning grey or silver hair, thin lips, and hollow eyes. By contrast, Emma was young. A photograph taken around the time she spoke for suffrage in South Dakota emphasized her full lips and stylish hair and clothing. Anthony was twenty-eight years older than Emma and "was not beautiful—in the accepted meaning of that word," recalled suffragist Harriet Taylor Upton; one of Anthony's eyes turned inward.[81]

In the past, the press had criticized female speakers for appearing too manly. Even ministers, who often supported equal suffrage, disapproved of physical styles they deemed as extreme. Recalling an exchange with a young reverend who publicly asked Anna Howard Shaw why her locks were so short, Shaw eventually came to realize that "the young minister was right in his disapproval and I was wrong." She grew her hair long and advised women speakers to be aware of their image. "No woman in public life can afford to make herself conspicuous by any eccentricity of dress or appearance," she explained. "If she does so she suffers for it herself, which may not disturb her, and to a greater or less degree she injures the cause she represents, which should disturb her very much."[82]

Femininity—a quality that distinguished women from men—was a tool that Emma used to sway opponents of equal suffrage. Wearing fashionable clothing such as balloon-sleeved shirts and outfits that emphasized her hourglass figure, Emma silenced opponents who tended to believe that suffragists were unfeminine. Following the adage promoted by Frances Willard, "Womanliness first—afterward what you will," Emma recognized the value of appearing feminine and the importance of first impressions.[83] Even though she favored dress reform, Emma wore the fashions of the day, which were often uncomfortable. Her attention to these details and the positive public responses to her speeches illustrate the power of this concept in the late nineteenth century.

Emma's press notices were full of praise, with newspaper editors calling attention to her beauty, pleasing speaking voice, and singing talent. Even though she appealed to listeners with logical reasoning, newspaper writers concentrated more upon her looks and manners. For example, the *Wessington Herald* referred to her as a "fine speaker" but also "an ornament to the cause she advocates," and the *Onida Journal* summarized her lecture as "delicate, ladylike, soft and convincing."[84] Such characterizations of popular female public speakers were common in the years following the Civil War. The lecture circuit and podium, once considered man's realm, became domesticated and a part of women's sphere in the postbellum era. Like so many other popular nineteenth-century speakers, listeners admired Emma because she brought "the best of feminine sensibilities to the podium."[85]

Although Emma presented herself as a polite, respectable, and proper woman to her listeners, the task was not always easy. In October 1890, someone spread a rumor that Emma spoke of "'free love' on the train." Free lovers embraced the idea that love, not marriage, set the stage for sexual relations. This charge worried Emma. "I am—and have been *very* careful about my conduct on the train—only talking [with] those whom

I am well acquainted with," she wrote. Emma had good reason to worry. Suffragists who supported free love were considered disreputable; if this story spread, Emma's pure image would be destroyed. She expressed concern over the fact that her husband had heard the rumor. Although he claimed not to "care a cent about it," he asked another man what he knew. The situation bothered Emma, who wrote to a colleague, "The only thing that looks queer to me is that if he don't [*sic*] care for it why should he ask Mr. Hoke about it?" In the end, no newspaper reported the rumor, and Emma's image remained untarnished.[86] She later joked about free love with Will Bailey, telling him that Father Joshua Himes, who was nearly ninety years old, would be traveling with her from Elk Point to Vermillion. "I suppose there is some more of my 'free love,'" she kidded.[87]

As the campaign came to a close, another rumor circulated about Emma in Wentworth, a "whiskey town," according to Laura Johns. Reportedly, Emma roomed over a saloon in Wentworth and had a beer sent to her room.[88] Johns repeated this rumor, which was circulated by anti-suffragists and fueled by Helen Barker's comments about the women of the SDESA. Earlier that summer Barker had resigned her position on the SDESA executive board, and she began telling lies about the association and its leaders. Dr. Nettie C. Hall, a South Dakota physician who served as superintendent of election work for the SDESA, reported that Barker spread stories "that we were nothing but infidels—liberals and whiskeyites."[89]

Stories circulated by anti-suffragists failed to tarnish Emma's reputation, but later her actions angered some of her colleagues and led them to question her motives for working for suffrage. Emma recognized early on that she was invaluable to the South Dakota suffrage movement, and she had little patience when Secretary William Bailey and Elizabeth Murray Wardall, superintendent of press work for the SDESA, did not give her the attention she believed she deserved. Almost immediately she had problems with those who planned her lectures and meeting dates for the fall, contending that the scheduling committee was careless in booking her speaking arrangements. Arriving at Hurley, for instance, Emma found that the local newspapers had announced three different dates for her appearance, and she was able to speak to only a small audience.[90] This was a common gaff encountered by organizers in the field.

Writing later from Flandreau, Emma lashed out at Bailey because she had not received her list of speaking engagements and could receive mail at only one post office in the area until she reached Wentworth. Elizabeth Wardall promised to send the schedule to Emma after dinner on an unspecified day, but had not done so. "Has she gotten through her dinner?" Emma asked Bailey. "Now if she can stop eating long enough I would like to hear from you."[91] When not in the public eye, South Dakota's state lecturer and organizer could be blunt.

Emma's demands were not uncalled for, given the number of local and county SDESA chapters she had organized. Bailey finally sent her a list of dates, but to her displeasure Emma found that Parkston and Plankinton, which she termed "two of my best points," had been crossed off her agenda.[92] Emma probably insisted she receive better speaking engagements in the final months of the campaign because she knew that Anthony planned to hire additional lecturers after November to speak in the West.[93] Hoping to impress her mentor, Emma insisted on traveling to places where she would be well received and met with praise from the press. Plankinton, Aurora County's seat, was one of those places. Earlier in the campaign, Anthony and Mary Seymour Howell had been greeted at the railroad depot "by carriages and were guests of the people," and Emma may have hoped for the same reception.[94]

Out of economic necessity, Emma may have sought a place in the spotlight for herself, believing that Anthony would reward her with a paid position after the campaign. During early October 1890, Emma wrote entire letters asking Bailey to give her better places in which to raise money and interest in equal suffrage. By the middle of the month, she finally received a revised schedule that met with her approval.[95]

Within a few days, however, Emma determined that her list of speaking engagements would not help her achieve her goal or receive the press she had hoped for. Emma, who had organized hundreds of ESA chapters and given hundreds of speeches, felt underappreciated placed in remote schoolhouses.

Eventually, she refused to do any more schoolhouse work. She kept the larger towns of Elk Point and Vermillion on her calendar and assigned to Julia Nelson the task of speaking at schoolhouses. Nelson, who already felt as if she had bore more than her share of hard work that year, expressed displeasure with this decision. Recognizing Emma's efforts as self-serving, Nelson told Bailey, "If she wants the glory of being met by a brass band let her have it. I'd rather have the *time to speak*."[96]

Many speakers had visited Elk Point, but the schoolhouses where Emma refused to lecture had received little attention during the campaign. Nelson believed that southeast South Dakota was "where the battle is thickest and here's where we shall meet a Waterloo."[97] Emma's decision to cancel her appointments did not reach the listeners who had already planned to attend, and in the case of two communities, large crowds waited for her. Leading suffragist Nettie Hall, who had learned of Emma's decision, criticized her for the blunder. The audiences she would have spoken to were "easily converted," and "now no one can take them," Hall complained.[98]

Emma's actions, which occurred in the final weeks of the campaign, indicated to some that she was ambitious and selfish. Women were expected to be disinterested and unselfish in political matters, and the manner by which Emma had changed her speaking schedule and her reasoning for doing so appeared contrary to these values. By going against those at headquarters, writing her own schedule, and selecting the communities she visited, Emma showed that she lacked the virtues expected then of a lady. Her impatience and lack of modesty proved to many that she was not as womanly as her audiences believed. Women who served as public speakers were, at least according to nineteenth-century literature, reluctantly called to speak in public for the good of women and children. By contrast, Emma appeared to be motivated by ambition. Discussions about her aggressiveness followed her for the rest of her career.[99]

On the other hand, suffragists may have been mistaken in labeling her tactics as unladylike in that Emma may have been putting the movement's need for money ahead of her own economic interests. The South Dakota Fund had proved to be inadequate, and suffragists regularly appealed to readers of suffrage papers to donate money to the movement. Throughout the campaign, Emma had successfully raised funds for the cause, and in October she secured more than $70 in collections. Nelson, by contrast, had difficulty raising funds, and she collected a little more than $36 the same month. She averaged less than $2 per town while Emma pulled in more than $7 per community.[100]

On election day, Emma worked at the Yankton polls. In a telegram to Elizabeth Wardall, Emma wrote, "Women here are working bravely getting good vote."[101] Five to six women worked the city's polling stations, as they had the previous year when voters supported prohibition.[102] They provided coffee and lunch to voters, sang suffrage songs, and urged voters to support the enfranchisement of women.[103] Despite the hard work of Emma and others—1,600 lectures given, 400 clubs organized, and literature mailed to every voter—the woman suffrage amendment failed by a wide margin.

Shortly after the campaign, the DeVoes packed their bags and returned to Illinois. The depression that hit South Dakota in the early 1890s played a major role in their decision to leave. Henry could no longer make a living in Huron, and he sought to reestablish himself in a community where he could. The couple moved to Harvey, a booming community on the outskirts of Chicago and the site of the 1893 World's Fair. Harvey was located just a few minutes from the White City. Once settled, Emma found herself organizing equal suffrage clubs in Illinois, and within a few years she became known as one of the best fundraisers the movement had ever seen.

3

BUILDING A NATIONAL REPUTATION

SPEAKING AT THE 1892 MISSISSIPPI VALLEY CONFERENCE IN DES
Moines, Iowa, on the subject of fundraising, Carrie Chapman Catt introduced Emma to the audience as a "woman who can get people to give
money even when they have none." Emma disagreed, saying that she did
not have any special ability as a fundraiser. She told the audience, "I never
opened a pocket-book." When people become interested in suffrage, a
"pocket-book will *come* open," she said. Emma never told audiences that
the state suffrage associations for which she worked were poor. Instead,
"I tell them that the cause is growing and that we are going to go ahead,
hire the opera houses, engage the best speakers, and make an active campaign." Her secret to fundraising was: "Get the principle into people's
hearts."[1]

As the story above suggests, national suffrage leaders like Catt came
to believe that Emma was an outstanding fundraiser as well as one of the
country's most popular speakers for the equal suffrage movement. From
1891 to 1895, Emma's reputation as a "money getter" grew, stemming in
part from her ability to raise funds as the country struggled with a massive depression. Others sought her assistance because they recognized that
her conservative presentation offended no one, making the issue of suffrage therefore more likely to pass. During these four years, she became
a national lecturer for NAWSA, helped to establish a number of clubs for
the Iowa Woman Suffrage Association (IWSA) and the Illinois Equal Suffrage Association (IESA), gave an address at NAWSA's national meeting,

participated in the 1894 Kansas campaign, and addressed the 1895 North Dakota legislature.[2]

Emma spent much of her time on the road during these years as she needed the funds to supplement Henry's income. A series of bad investments made in South Dakota meant that Emma could no longer remain a housewife; she had to earn a living if they hoped to pay their debt and maintain a middle-class standing.

With Henry by her side, Emma also joined the Federal Suffrage Association (FSA), one of several dissenting organizations formed in the first decade following unification of the movement. Alternatives to NAWSA began to pop up as opponents to the merger formed their own groups. Splits within NAWSA were quite common and afflicted the association from the beginning. Matilda Joslyn Gage, long-time friend of Elizabeth Cady Stanton and Susan B. Anthony, seceded from NAWSA when she learned the association sought the support of conservative WCTU women. She formed the progressive Woman's National Liberal Union.[3] Emma maintained memberships in the FSA and NAWSA until the FSA fizzled, though her dual association led some to question her loyalty to NAWSA.

For a brief time in the early 1890s, Emma dabbled in Farmers' Alliance politics, but she pulled out presumably because she believed much more strongly in working solely for women's voting rights. Throughout her entire suffrage career Emma remained committed to the belief that suffrage lecturers should not touch upon politics or any other subject besides suffrage, at least when stumping for women's enfranchisement. This concept proved to be more complicated for other women active in the movement. Emma's involvement with the 1894 Kansas campaign and her work in North Dakota exemplify how conflicts over partisan loyalties strained relations between national and state leaders and how successfully Emma, a Populist, navigated the troubled waters.

Henry's decision to move to Harvey, Illinois, had a tremendous impact upon Emma's burgeoning career. Being so close to Chicago expanded Emma's network of colleagues and acquaintances, as many of America's leading female reformers resided in the area. Frances Willard lived in nearby Evanston, while Jane Addams and Florence Kelley lived in the city. Home to the WCTU headquarters and Hull House, Chicago had blossomed into a city full of opportunities for women involved in reform, politics, and the labor movement. The Chicago women's network, which had taken root during the Civil War, linked working-class women who were trade unionists, middle-class reformers, and society women.[4]

When Emma learned that her husband had selected the burgeoning community as their new home, she was ecstatic. The town was close to her sisters, and she told Elizabeth Murray Wardall of the South Dakota Equal Suffrage Association, "I *always* wanted to live in Chicago but thought Mr. De would never think of such a thing."[5] He had considered moving farther south, to Tennessee, but perhaps thought better of the idea after considering that he might be labeled a carpetbagger by locals.

Henry probably hoped that the move might have a positive impact on his pocketbook. One year prior to their move, Chicago had been named the site of the 1893 World's Columbian Exposition, and Harvey was flourishing. Advertisements referred to the Chicago suburb as the "MAGIC CITY . . . ALREADY AN ASSURED SUCCESS!!" Moving to Harvey reportedly was a "Great Opportunity to Make a Profitable Investment" as land values in the area were rapidly increasing, thanks to land speculators.[6] If Henry could not immediately open a shoe store, he was bound to find employment, as the covenant between industrialists and the Harvey Land Association included a clause that required companies, when hiring, to give preference to those living in Harvey.[7] Horace Holmes, a resident of Harvey, recalled that the community attracted many families because the factories in town paid living wages and "children could grow up surrounded by the best influences."[8]

Henry and Emma needed to move to a community that they believed was more economically viable.[9] They had to earn enough to pay the mortgages on their two farms in South Dakota (which were due soon), the upkeep on their Huron home (which they had not sold), and their living expenses in Illinois.[10] Given the material he received from the Harvey Land Association, Henry probably concluded that he and Emma could pay off their debts and maintain a middle-class standing.

The founders of Harvey hoped to build a model manufacturing town, and they supported temperance. They believed that abstaining from alcohol benefited employers and employees, and they therefore prohibited the establishment of saloons in town. Harvey must have seemed a suburban utopia for those who subscribed to such morals. Although the restriction prevented "wets" from purchasing property, community leaders hoped it would induce others to become residents. "It is the 'others' who are preferred," they explained. Every property deed issued by the Harvey Land Association did not "allow, suffer or permit any intoxicating drink or drinks to be manufactured, sold or given away upon said premises, nor any gambling to be carried on thereon, nor any house or other place of lewd and immoral practice thereupon."[11]

Moving to a temperance town with "moral surroundings" and "no fear of saloon influences"[12] appealed to Henry, and no doubt the idea of moving to a community without vice—gambling, prostitution, or saloons—also interested Emma. The fact that the town explicitly prohibited houses of ill repute must have pleased the couple, who had witnessed the negative effects of whorehouses on their streets in Huron. They were exactly the type of owners that the Harvey Land Association hoped to attract.

As they had in Huron, the DeVoes quickly became civic and political leaders within their new community. Henry reestablished his shoe store in Harvey. In 1892, voters elected him police magistrate, and he held court in the basement of his business.[13] He became a member of the local Grand Army of the Republic, and Emma helped to form the Harvey Woman's Relief Corps in 1892 and became its first president.[14]

Emma recalled that she "found many congenial spirits" in town, referring to the men and women she met who held similar convictions about women's enfranchisement, politics, and temperance.[15] Temperance advocates, often portrayed as "crabbed, bitter, rural provincials who wanted to limit personal freedom and control the poor and the alien," were in fact often progressive and supported many "radical" ideas, such as woman suffrage.[16] Almost immediately after settling in town, Emma decided to establish an equal suffrage club. Many of the town's like-minded spirits joined the chapter, and they elected her president of the Harvey Equal Suffrage Association.

The women and men who joined explored the topics of the day and opened the meetings to those who endorsed similarly forward-looking ideas. The motto of the club, "Good Will to Men," reflected their president's conciliatory approach to male voters.[17] Discussions about whether to nominate Mary Livermore, who worked with the Chicago Sanitary Commission during the Civil War and was the first president of the Illinois Woman Suffrage Association, for president of the United States kept the meetings lively.[18] By 1892, the club was the largest in the entire state of Illinois and one of the most active.

Even though Henry set up a new shop in Harvey, he and Emma had taken on too much debt in their first few years of marriage and were living on the edge. Trade in Harvey expanded as more families settled in the area, but Henry could not sell enough shoes to cover his loans. Emma was fortunate to find work as an itinerant organizer for the Illinois Equal Suffrage Association. The association had no funds to employ a state organizer, but the group allowed women who organized auxiliaries to collect the dues owed to the association and use them to pay for their expenses. The IESA received no money. "This is the best method we can as yet devise; but as we grow in strength we hope to keep a paid organizer in the field all the time," Mary E. Holmes, president of the association, explained.[19]

Emma, who had successfully organized more than two hundred clubs in South Dakota, had no difficulty finding suffrage supporters in the Chicago area. She established local chapters of the IESA in Lake and Pullman, which numbered thirty-six and twenty-one members, respectively. The Harvey club, which had ninety-two members at the end of 1891, bolstered her numbers.[20] For every member she brought in Emma received $1, totaling at least $149 from these three clubs alone. Unfortunately, these funds were insufficient to cover the mortgages due on the farms in DeVoe and Huron, and the DeVoes defaulted on the loans. In December 1891, the Faulk and Beadle county sheriffs sold the farms at public auctions at the front doors of the Register of Deeds in Faulkton and Huron.[21]

Losing these farms must have been a major blow to the DeVoes. Even with Emma working the couple could not break even. In an effort to improve their financial situation, Henry began studying law to become an attorney, continued to serve as police magistrate, and managed his shoe store. Eventually he found a buyer for their home in Huron, which sold for $1,500 on June 12, 1893. More than half of the amount, $800, went to pay the mortgage they had taken out on the home.[22] Over the next few years, the DeVoes continually struggled to make ends meet, and consequently Henry remained supportive of the Farmers' Alliance and its objectives to break the power of the moneyed elite (railroads, eastern bankers, and large corporations), whose unregulated power, he believed, had left them broke.[23] He later became part of the local People's Party, serving as treasurer.[24]

Although the details are sketchy, Emma also became active in the National Woman's Alliance (NWA) for a few years. The NWA favored key women's issues (woman suffrage and temperance) and also supported the political and economic reforms urged by the Farmers' Alliance. For a short time Emma was a "platform speaker of growing prominence" within the movement, according to Populist reformer Annie Diggs, and she spoke on the "labor reform platform" in Indiana.[25] Emma never included her work as a spokesman for the NWA in any of her autobiographical sketches, but she clearly had some ties to the organization.

Even though the DeVoes had lost their homesteads, they could celebrate a victory in the war to secure voting rights for women. Illinois women were granted school suffrage in 1891. The act allowed women to vote solely for elected school officials, but at that point most positions were appointed, not elected, so the act had a very limited effect. Still, its passage suggested that change was possible. As soon as the governor signed the bill, anti-suffragists challenged the constitutionality of the act. Decisions handed down by the court limited the rights extended to women. They could vote for offices founded by the legislature, the court concluded, but not those set up by the state constitution.[26]

Before they made their home in Illinois, the DeVoes traveled to Washington, DC, for the second meeting of NAWSA. More than one hundred delegates from thirty states, U.S. territories, and foreign nations attended the convention. Many older, well-known suffragists were present, including Anthony, Lucy Stone, Lillie Devereux Blake, and Henry B. Blackwell. Stanton was absent but there in spirit, as Anthony read a speech she had prepared called "The Degradation of Disfranchisement." Emma was one of the youngest women listed on the program.

During the meeting, NAWSA celebrated the admission of Wyoming into the Union—the first state to include women in its electorate. The event marked an important shift in national politics; according to Anthony and Ida Husted Harper, "Hereafter the Chief Executive and both Houses of Congress will owe their election partly to the votes of women."[27] Recognizing the significance of the event, Henry had written a song for the occasion, "Oh, Sing of Wyoming," which he and Emma sang at the meeting and dedicated to Anthony. The DeVoes praised the state for serving as a true republic, where the government represented both men and women:

O! Sing of Wyoming,
Land dear to woman,
O! blest land, Wyoming,
The glory of the mighty Northwest![28]

Just as they had influenced the South Dakota suffrage campaign, the DeVoes continued to encourage reformers to sing their way into the hearts of voters.[29]

Delegates were eager to hear about the South Dakota campaign, and four field workers—Blackwell, Alice Pickler, Reverend Anna Howard Shaw, and Emma—discussed the challenges they faced on the prairies and in the Black Hills. In an especially engaging speech, Shaw addressed the delegates on the topic of "Indians vs. Women." She contended that the idea of enfranchising Native Americans received more consideration from the South Dakota state political parties than did woman suffrage, describing how Republicans welcomed the Indians at their state convention while the women were "barely tolerated." She noted that voters supported Indian suffrage in greater numbers even as the Sioux performed the Ghost Dance to restore their dominance on the Plains.[30] She recalled meeting a Native American man with two long braids and a feather in his hair, to whom she asked:

> My dear sir, I would like to inquire the extent of your knowledge of political economy. I understand that the people of South Dakota are all required to have a thorough instruction in the underlying principles of government; now, my dear sir, can you tell me if you are well posted on all matters that enter into the politico-economic status of this new commonwealth in which you are seeking the right of franchise?

According to Shaw, he responded by blowing "a cloud of smoke" and uttering, "Ugh!"[31]

Emma gave her first national speech at this meeting called "The Moral and Political Emergency." The crisis of which she spoke related to women's judicial rights. Although the text of this speech no longer exists, Emma may have repeated a case she had cited before wherein police arrested a mother who had reportedly killed her baby. Emma explained that an all-male judge and jury tried the woman. She contended that the men had no idea why the woman committed the crime, as they were not mothers, and could not understand the hardships women faced in the home. She argued that women should be tried by a jury of their female peers, not by those who ruled over them.[32]

The following annual convention met again in Washington, DC, and marked a dramatic shift within the movement's leadership. Two of the association's oldest leaders, Stone and Stanton, stepped down from their positions, and younger women began to fill the empty posts. Anthony succeeded Stanton as president, and Shaw accepted the position of vice president. NAWSA abolished the executive committee, formerly headed by Stone, and replaced it with a business committee chaired by Catt. As the leadership evolved, so did its techniques. These young women had "fresh ideas" about how to best secure woman suffrage in contrast to the pioneers, who had grown tired from campaigning.[33] Emma, who had been appointed national lecturer in 1890, was one of these young innovators. Several years passed, however, before she was able to attend another national meeting.

That year, some younger women began to urge NAWSA to hold their annual convention outside of Washington, DC, every other year to draw increased attention to the movement; in particular, they hoped to hold the 1893 meeting in Chicago, site of the World's Fair. The debate that ensued was an example of the different viewpoints held by younger and older suffragists and the strategies they endorsed. The pioneers, who had fought for a federal amendment to the U.S. Constitution, objected to the plan, with Stanton proclaiming, "When Congress moves, we will move; and not till then." Anthony opposed the plan because she believed that doing so "would exert no particular influence." She was adamant that the annual meeting be retained at the nation's capitol because of the financial benefit to the association; the federal government printed testimony given by suffragists at congressional hearings, which could be obtained by NAWSA at a nominal cost and then sent across the country by supporters in Congress.

By contrast, Catt suggested changes had to be instituted to bring women from the West and South into the suffrage fold. She admitted that there were good reasons for keeping the convention in Washington, "but when a Sixteenth Amendment is submitted," Catt argued, "it will have to be ratified by the Legislatures of three-fourths of the States, and the Western Legislatures will vote it down unless some work has been done with them in the meantime." Thus Catt suggested that by holding conventions in the West, the association might sow the seeds of suffrage sentiment in areas that thus far had shown little interest. Recall, one suffragist said, how an entire state went "wild with enthusiasm" when the Republicans decided to hold a meeting there. Another major drawback to holding the convention in the East could be seen in the state delegations. Western states never sent their entire slate of delegates to the meeting, while those in the East always sent all of the delegates they had been accorded. When the motion to hold the annual meeting at Chicago failed, Mrs. Demmon of Illinois complained, "The result of this vote shows the inconsistency of bringing us Western people here and giving us no chance. Illinois is entitled to nine delegates, and where are they?"[34]

This debate continued at the 1893 and 1894 annual meetings, with women from the South questioning NAWSA's claim of representing all American women. The assertion seemed contradictory to Laura Clay of Kentucky, another second-generation suffragist and cousin of Henry Clay, who noted that the women of the East, not the South, dominated the association. "And why?" she asked. "Because our women know nothing about the National-American. Thousands of people have never heard of the National-American. The way to get them to know us is by taking the convention where they will be compelled to hear us." Catt stated unequivocally that the western women would form their own regional organization if NAWSA failed to move the convention to the West. Henry Blackwell sided with the younger women, noting the benefit of holding meetings in different cities as Frances Willard of the WCTU had done.[35]

Schisms within the movement, like the possibility declared by Catt, were common. In 1892, suffragists decided to form a new group dedicated to securing the enfranchisement of women by a federal amendment called the Federal Suffrage Association. Even when the movement had originally united in 1890 under NAWSA, the decision was not unanimous. Opponents included Matilda Joslyn Gage, Hanson Robinson, Clara B. Colby, and the Reverend Olympia Brown, who later claimed that unification would "be a major setback for woman suffrage" and the techniques the National Woman Suffrage Association favored.[36] The push for a Sixteenth Amendment had been relegated to NAWSA's Federal Suffrage Committee, while state action endorsed by AWSA prevailed as NAWSA's method of choice. Some suffragists believed that this decision orphaned the strategy the NWSA had long endorsed.

Brown, one of the founding members of the FSA, contended that suffragists needed to file court cases to win the rights already accorded to their sex in the Constitution. Brown's idea, based on a strategy touted by Anthony and Stanton during Reconstruction, argued that the Constitution and its Fourteenth and Fifteenth amendments established women's citizenship and guaranteed their right to vote. The concept was not widely endorsed, and the U.S. Supreme Court rejected the idea. Nevertheless,

Brown maintained that the issue was not dead and that suffragists should continue to fight in the courts. Emphasizing the importance of federal work, Brown concluded that a separate organization dedicated to its efforts, not a committee, was necessary. NAWSA was "doing good work," but the group could not reach every voter to educate them on the subject.[37]

Isabella Beecher Hooker, who also attended the meeting to form FSA, said that the territory without equal suffrage was vast, and "women cannot get too many Associations before the public to urge their demands for full and equal suffrage."[38] The diminishing focus on federal work discouraged these women. Brown presented her case to a Chicago audience at a March 1892 meeting. Their appeal won over many in the audience, including the DeVoes. Even though Emma earned her salary through the state-by-state approach, she believed neither strategy could be overlooked. She was so supportive of a federal amendment that she became a member of NAWSA's Federal Suffrage Committee in 1893. Emma's commitment to this method may have stemmed from her close association with Anthony, who had been fighting for a federal amendment to the U.S. Constitution for years. She and Henry joined the Federal Suffrage Association, and delegates elected Henry temporary treasurer, with plans to elect permanent officers at a later date.[39] Other NWSA members supporting the association included Abigail Scott Duniway, Louisa Southworth, and Virginia T. Minor, regional vice presidents for the newly established organization.[40]

Clara Colby, chairman of NAWSA's Federal Suffrage Committee, attended the meeting and agreed with the policy, but she refused to become a member. She believed NAWSA alone could do the work.[41] When asked if NAWSA had "neglected to emphasize" federal work in favor of the state referendum route, Colby said any "cause" for concern "was removed at the convention held last January," when NAWSA formed a committee on the issue.[42]

Upon hearing of the FSA, Henry Blackwell of NAWSA questioned the necessity of forming a new organization. "Without calling in question the good intentions of the organizers of this new Association," he began, "some of whom are old and earnest suffragists, there seems to us to be no need of a new society to work for Federal Suffrage." He reminded readers of the *Woman's Journal* that NAWSA worked for suffrage at all levels and had already established a committee to push for the measure in Congress.[43] Hamilton Willcox of New York believed it would be best for the new association to disband because their arguments for suffrage, which had been made "as far back as 1869," had no foundation in the law.[44] The FSA remained active, but the association was short-lived.

By 1893, the Federal Suffrage Association began to fall apart, although it should be noted that the association was never very strong.[45] The year delegates formed the group, the FSA wrote and submitted a memorial to the members of the United States Congress asking that they pass a bill making women citizens of the United States. During the 1892 election, two members attended the Republican Party national convention in Minneapolis, where they presented a memorial asking that woman suffrage be included in the party's platform. At the 1893 World's Columbian Exposition the FSA held a session on the topic of suffrage. That same year, vice president Olympia Brown's mother became ill, and her husband died. Subsequently, the association became "crippled by the death of prominent officers," and Brown's attention to the FSA naturally flagged. "The failure was a great sorrow to many, and an immense loss to the woman's suffrage cause," she noted.[46]

Concurrent with the formation of the FSA, the Iowa Woman Suffrage Association offered Emma the chance to serve as state lecturer for a few months. Catt, who had lived in Iowa and was already known to Emma, recognized her talent as a speaker in the South Dakota campaign and urged the association to employ her. Like Emma, Catt was a rising star within NAWSA. Both came from the Midwest, Catt from Wisconsin and Emma from Illinois. Before working for temperance, they taught, and the 1890 South Dakota campaign was their first suffrage battle. Unlike Emma, however, Catt had married a wealthy engineer. Given her economic situation, Emma could not turn down the chance to earn a few months' guaranteed salary.

Iowa suffragists knew of Emma's work. Their suffrage paper, the *Woman's Standard*, had regularly featured articles about the 1890 campaign and in 1891 printed Emma's letter "To the Lovers of Freedom in South Dakota," which encouraged local clubs to continue pushing for woman suffrage.[47] Editors reminded readers of her ties to South Dakota and of her indefatigable spirit, as shown by her determination to secure the position of street commissioner in the city of Huron.[48] The connection between suffragists in these two states was strong. It seems only natural, as Iowa was one of four Midwest states that helped to populate the southern half of Dakota Territory.[49]

Even before stepping onto Iowa soil, Emma had influenced the tactics employed by IWSA. In 1890 she had spearheaded the Woman's Day and its activities at the South Dakota state fair held in Aberdeen. After the festivities concluded, she advised every state to follow her lead. "I hope every State will do likewise and have a Woman's Day at their State fair. It seemed to place woman in higher respect (in the average mind)."[50] Anthony agreed with Emma, stating, "I consider the securing of a day for the good gospel of equality of rights for women at every great gathering of the people, the very best means of helping forward our cause." Furthermore, suffragists could assure state fair committees that attendance would increase if they scheduled a Woman's Day and that the receipts from that event would be greater than from any other day, as they were in Aberdeen.[51]

Following her example, the IWSA held a Woman's Day at their state fair in 1891. IWSA President Mary J. Coggeshall noted that attendance at the event skyrocketed. The day, while not as elaborate as the earlier event planned by Emma, included addresses from Margaret W. Campbell and Carrie Chapman Catt. The celebration raised $4,000 more than collected on the same day the prior year. Woman's Day was so successful that the superintendent of fair work for the IWSA urged others to organize Woman's Days at county fairs. "The novelty of the thing will draw, and the idea of a woman's speaking will be an attraction, and we will reach many, both men and women, who seldom, if ever, have heard a lecture on the subject of equal suffrage," she explained.[52]

When the IWSA offered Emma two months of work in the spring of 1892, the state legislature, which had just finished its session, had defeated school, municipal, and presidential suffrage bills and had voted to indefinitely postpone full enfranchisement for women.[53] Although no campaign was underway, the IWSA had outlined its plan of work in a supplement to the *Des Moines Woman's Standard*. The organization had four goals: one, to popularize the idea of woman suffrage by holding "suffrage parties"; two, to convert new supporters; three, to increase membership in local clubs; and four, to have the public talking about the issue.[54] Hoping to awaken suffrage sentiment in the state, the society planned to send Emma to the less organized northern and western parts of the state, where she would form auxiliaries to the IWSA and obtain subscriptions to the *Des Moines Woman's Standard*.[55]

Emma's tour of Iowa was important because it helped to establish her national reputation as an effective fundraiser. As she had in South Dakota, Emma appealed to Iowa's farmers for aid, and they often donated a few cents even though they had mortgaged their property, hoping that they could pay the loan with a bumper crop the following year. This rarely happened. Instead, they frequently lost money buying new farming equipment and seed. Rather than sell at a loss, they burned their crops in the field. From 1885 through 1890, Iowa farmers lost money on all of their crops—wheat, corn, oats, cattle, and barley; the only people to make a profit in agriculture in those years were those who raised hogs, but few elected to do so.[56] They were not any better off in 1892.

The Iowa newspapers and suffrage presses suggested that Emma was especially skilled in raising money for the cause in places where the economic situation was dire. In the May, June, and July issues of the *Des Moines Woman's Standard*, the editors listed the funds she had gathered at each place; this was something that the South Dakota newspapers had not mentioned. Interestingly enough, in those locations where inclement weather impacted the size of the donation, the editors listed the cause in parentheses next to the city. As an example of her fundraising skills, the editors printed a letter from Forest City. After hearing Emma speak, the women planned to pledge $25, but the men told them to double the amount. In just three short months, Emma raised more than $900 in collections and pledges for the IWSA.[57]

The economic hardship she suffered may have helped Emma establish a connection with farmers who were in similar situations. Although not one local secretary ever reported that their state lecturer spoke of the frustrations she faced as the wife of a merchant and farmer and the need for real change in the political and economic arenas (they always reported that she spoke solely for suffrage), Emma's understanding of the economic woes of those tied to the land made her an especially effective speaker in these rural communities where discontented farmers worked. It is not hard to imagine Emma arguing for economic justice within the American political system that would benefit the farmer and working man. After all, she was a member of the Farmers' Alliance movement, and the DeVoes had recently lost two farms.

She must have mentioned, in passing at least, the need for relief from a deflationary economy that had spiraled out of control and the need to manage corporate capitalism, which seemed to benefit the wealthy at the expense of the masses. Such talk only increased her popularity with disgruntled farmers, and at the end of her tour, Mary J. Coggeshall, who had been fighting for equal suffrage in Iowa for many years, concluded that

Emma had found "the vulnerable side of Iowa men and women, for your success has been unprecedented."[58]

Her reputation as a "money getter" increased when she attended the Mississippi Valley Suffrage Conference in Des Moines that fall, an innovative conference put together by Catt, who recognized that midwestern women who could not attend national meetings in Washington, DC, might benefit from a regional convention.[59] Suffragists from across the country could exchange ideas on the best methods and tactics to secure suffrage and raise funds. Catt served as chair for the meeting and naturally appointed her best fundraiser to the committee on finance. At this conference, Emma became known as "the most successful money getter the suffragists have ever had."[60] After the convention, her popularity as an organizer and speaker increased.

The Iowa tour was important in fostering a lifelong relationship between Emma and Mrs. C. Holt Flint of Iowa, a leading member of IWSA who provided guidance to the young lecturer. Flint must have reminded Emma of her own mother, who had died only a few years earlier, and the Iowan may have adopted Emma as her own, as Flint regularly began her letters to Emma with "My dear child" and affectionately signed them "Mother Flint" or "Your Iowa Mother." Establishing a deep friendship with Flint was part of a pattern in the early years of Emma's career; Anthony, Brown, and Flint, all first-generation suffragists, became close friends.

Like Anthony, Flint was from New York. As a child she "loved politics" and "read aloud the speeches of Clay, Webster, [and] Calhoun." Flint listened "with awe and then with absorbing interest" to Abby Kelley Foster and Lucretia Mott at abolitionist meetings.[61] She moved to Iowa in 1853 from New York, and she and her husband purchased land for a large stock farm. In 1880, she became a member of IWSA. Flint filled numerous posts within the association; she was a member of the executive committee and served as vice-president and president of the Third District. Described by Brown as "one of the most loyal advocates of our cause," Flint became one of Emma's biggest supporters.[62]

When Emma told her Iowa mother that she had been named to the executive committee of the Federal Suffrage Association and lecturer for the society, Flint told the young worker to *take care*. Sixteen years earlier, Flint had criticized Stanton's remarks on religion and Anthony's comments on social evils. Her words had angered the two. Fearing Emma's decision to join Brown's group might end her suffrage career and create a rift between Anthony and Emma, Flint told her, "Be careful. If there is a new move made, be very sure that there will be no chance to have it said that opposition has crept into the camp."[63] As Flint learned from her work with national leaders, NAWSA did not "tolerate serious political dissent" but instead "forced it outside."[64]

Over the next couple of years, Emma's reputation kept growing; she continued to organize local IESA chapters and lectured for equal suffrage in several states. Many state suffrage associations, including New York and Pennsylvania, asked her to speak on the topic of women's enfranchisement after they had read of her success in Iowa. She later traveled to Wisconsin where she served as keynote speaker and gave the annual address at the 9th Annual Session of the Wisconsin Woman's Suffrage Association in 1892.[65]

By 1893 Emma had taken on many responsibilities. She served as president of the first district for the IESA and established equal suffrage chapters in her region along with the speaking engagements she secured in other states. Emma recalled that she devoted "all her time" to suffrage work and that she was "in demand everywhere" then.[66] She became as popular as Shaw, and Iowans asked her to return to their state that spring.

In February 1893, Emma asked the *Des Moines Woman's Standard* to publish a letter she hoped all Iowa suffragists would take to heart. She encouraged women to continue to work for suffrage and to thank women's rights pioneers like Anthony who had dedicated their lives to securing reforms that had benefited women. She advised them to write letters to newspapers to "teach a new, broader and brighter view of liberty to the reading public," organize suffrage clubs, and "in that way teach that the women's enfranchisement means a higher and more perfect companionship between men and women, that our interests are one and the same. And prove that our cause will aid our brothers in every way and antagonize in nothing."[67] She did her part by working in Iowa, Illinois, and Kansas in 1893.

That year, the Kansas State legislature passed a woman suffrage amendment to be voted upon in 1894. Laura M. Johns, president of the Kansas Equal Suffrage Association (KESA), believed that the prospects were bright: "Success is confidently predicted. Our foes concede it, but," she added, "there is nothing to indicate that we shall win without effort," and she pleaded for help from NAWSA in the form of money or workers.[68]

KESA kicked off its campaign on September 1 in Kansas City at the Bancroft Tabernacle. Suffragists decorated the platform with sunflowers, yellow bunting, and mottos that read "Equal Suffrage," "Equality Before the Law," and "Taxation without Representation Is Tyranny, Women Are Citizens." More than two thousand enthusiastic people attended the meeting, where they passed resolutions in favor of suffrage and heard from numerous speakers on the issue, including Emma, who had traveled from Harvey. She converted at least one person, "a baldheaded man in the front row" upon whom she unleashed "the fire of her caustic wit."[69] Amidst all the excitement, she promised to raise $2,000 in the state. That number was surprisingly high, given the state of the economy in Kansas and the country at that time. Nevertheless, she believed that she would have no trouble securing the funds.[70]

While in Kansas for the month of September Emma revived defunct clubs, organized new KESA chapters, and raised $800 in pledges, significantly more than two Kansas workers, Amanda Way and Johns, who reported less than $200 combined. Johns praised Emma for demonstrating that "money can be raised in Kansas even at this time of financial depression."[71] Her ability to obtain pledges from Kansans in the middle of the worst economic depression the country had ever seen made her work legendary. As a result of her success in Kansas and elsewhere in the early 1890s, the editor of the *Woman's Journal* later declared Emma "an almost unequalled raiser of funds for suffrage work."[72] Praise for Emma's outstanding accomplishments indicates just how popular and powerful a speaker, organizer, and fundraiser she had become in the three short years since the South Dakota campaign.

South Dakota suffragists, who planned to hold their 1893 state convention in Aberdeen, invited their former state lecturer and organizer to the meeting. She wanted to attend, but admitted that it would be "impossible as I am now at work in the woman suffrage campaign in Kansas." More than twenty-five years had passed since Kansas voters had rejected a woman suffrage amendment in 1867, but Emma hoped that voters would support the measure in 1894 because of the economic challenges facing American families and their government. Emma linked the economic problem to the fact that women "have had no voice in governmental affairs. The *governments* of the world are beginning to *rock* and our own nation in particular is being *rocked* and *swayed* hither and thither as never before by internal eruptions." Equal suffrage could remedy the situation, she concluded, and "we as a nation can prosper."[73] After a short tour of the Sunflower State, Emma returned to Illinois.

Writing from her home in Harvey, Emma shared her Kansas experience with readers of the *Woman's Journal*. As always, she was upbeat about the campaign. "After mingling freely with the people, I have high hopes that the suffrage amendment will carry in 1894," she wrote. Emma reasoned that the people of the state overwhelmingly supported the issue. At the twenty meetings she held in September, Emma reported that Kansans contributed nearly $900 (a bit more than the figure given earlier by Johns) to the campaign even though they had little to spare with the financial collapse and winter quickly approaching. "This, to my mind," she wrote, "indicates something of the moral and intellectual grandeur of those people. The women of Kansas are not 'feeble imbeciles' but earnest, thoughtful, intelligent beings, with quick discernment, ready to do and anxious to work for equality."[74]

Emma returned to Kansas in November for a final six-week tour. The campaign committee, pleased with her work, concluded that she achieved much during her time there. May Belleville-Brown, secretary of the Amendment Campaign Committee, praised her work, carefully documenting her achievements:

> Wherever she has spoken, her work has been thorough and effective, and
> she has left none but friends behind her—friends for the cause and for
> herself as well. She has given the State just what it needed in the way of
> agitation, and just at the right time, and it has been along more than one
> line. She has made new friends for us, renewed the old ones, organized
> strong campaign committees, and secured pledges of funds with which to
> carry on the campaign. She has persuaded many and antagonized none,
> and her gift as a special pleader for woman has been acknowledged even
> by those most opposed to the doctrines taught by her. Almost every place
> she has visited has sent a request to headquarters for her return during the
> campaign, which is in itself a recommendation for the character of her work
> among us.[75]

While Emma was in Kansas, Colorado suffragists won an important victory when the Centennial State became the first to enfranchise women by a popular referendum. The success in its neighbor state thrilled Kansas suffragists, who hoped that their voters would follow Colorado's lead the following year. Colorado's success can be linked in part to the political and economic climate of the 1890s and to the growth of the Populist Party.

Without the support of the Populists, the Colorado legislature might not have passed the bill.[76] Catt, who recognized the importance of their endorsement, recommended Emma as a speaker for the campaign because of her appeal to Populists and miners; reportedly Emma could talk like a Populist "when necessity requires" and "keep her politics to herself when among other classes."[77] But Emma never spoke in Colorado, as she was too busy elsewhere.

Chicago and the surrounding areas also suffered the ill effects of the financial collapse. One hundred thousand Chicagoans were unemployed during the first winter of the depression, and when the World's Fair ended, the homeless took shelter in the abandoned White City. Reporter Ray Stannard Baker remembered that the depression of 1893 was "nowhere else so severe as in Chicago. It was marked by unprecedented extremes of poverty, unemployment, and unrest."[78]

Although Henry and Emma had hoped to benefit from Chicago's economic boom, they suffered when the market hit bottom and land values in Harvey depreciated. Horace Holmes recalled that prices fell "in many instances 50 percent and many Harvey people lost their homes. Many more lost faith in Harvey and moved elsewhere."[79] The DeVoes chose to remain, even though those who favored granting liquor licenses tried to gain control of the temperance community in 1894.[80]

As a result of hard times, radicalism surged throughout the Chicago area, and the Populists attempted to form an alliance between farmers and the urban labor movement in Chicago. The midwestern city was "the ideal place" for the marriage of the two groups, given its economic conditions.[81] For example, when the police beat Populist Jacob Sechler Coxey and his army and then threw them into jail for trespassing on the grass of the United States Capitol in 1894, the working class of Harvey rose up. (Coxey and a group of unemployed citizens from across the country—known as Coxey's Army—marched to Washington, DC, to protest the lack of congressional action and encourage members to establish a public works program.) Henry was among those who gathered in town to protest the treatment of the army, and he was listed among the speakers who appealed for a better government.

Those who protested the current state of the economy and lack of inaction on the part of the national government believed that "the only hope for a return of prosperity to this nation lies in the utter routing of the mercenary pack of conscienceless law makers that prostitute their political positions to money getting and to fill their places with men who will not sell their souls to Wall Street for a mess of pottage." At the conclusion of the meeting, they decided to form a local political party to push these lines of reform.[82] One week later, a small convention met in Cook County to elect delegates to the Populist state convention.[83] For the next few years, Henry supported the third party movement, and Emma was probably just as sympathetic, even though she endorsed nonpartisanship as a suffrage speaker.

Partisan politics often complicated suffrage campaigns, as illustrated by the trouble that was brewing in the Sunflower State by 1894. Laura Johns, like several state suffrage leaders, wore two hats in the campaign. She served as president of KESA and the Republican Women's Association, while Annie Diggs, then second in command, was quite active in the Populist Party. When they kicked off the campaign in 1893, they acknowledged that Kansas women, who held municipal and school suffrage, had partisan ties, but they resolved to work solely for the enfranchisement of women. KESA did not expect or ask party women to "cease their activities or their zealous work for their respective parties," but demanded that those working for the amendment "refrain from argument or reference to their party issues." In other words, suffragists were to present themselves as nonpartisans when speaking for the amendment.[84]

This decision stemmed from a policy passed at the 1890 NAWSA convention, where delegates debated the pros and cons of establishing coalitions with political parties. Anthony and Ida Husted Harper recalled, "It was proved beyond doubt that in the past, where members had allied themselves with a political party it had injured the cause of woman suffrage." Delegates therefore endorsed a nonpartisan policy, which encouraged the organization to keep "strictly aloof from all political alliances."[85]

Conflict over the divided loyalties of Kansas women popped up because KESA chose not to demand that political parties adopt pro-suffrage platforms, even though they had passed a resolution urging the parties to endorse the amendment in September 1893. To national leaders, this decision appeared to be motivated by partisan loyalty. Furthermore, NAWSA leaders believed that the parties' endorsement was essential if the amendment were to pass. The failure in South Dakota and the victory in Colorado proved to national leaders that woman suffrage could be carried only with the support of the parties. Anthony made it "perfectly clear" that if the parties did not adopt suffrage planks, she would not work in the state campaign.[86] Catt, Henry Blackwell, and Reverend Shaw stood with their leader, believing that the national leaders knew how best to secure women's enfranchisement.

In a letter to Johns, Anthony questioned her common sense. The Republican Party's "proposal to leave out the plank now, after they have carried the question thus far, is too wicked to be tolerated by any sane woman!" Shaw concurred, telling Johns, "The man or woman who urges surrender now is more a political partisan than a lover of freedom." Without party endorsement, Shaw refused to work for the issue or raise one single penny for the campaign. She begged Johns, "For the love of woman, do not be fooled by those men any longer."[87] Such strain began to take its toll on Johns.

Treasurer of the Suffrage Amendment Campaign Committee Elizabeth F. Hopkins appealed to Emma for her assistance in the matter. She hoped that Emma could "explain the situation of Kansas politics" to the national leaders and serve as their mediator. "It is *unjust* to Mrs. Johns and their cruel letters to her are *abominable*," she wrote. "Her load is heavy enough without her *friends* adding threats. *I know* and we women of Kansas know that *nothing* would *kill* the Amendment quicker than to make a fight on this plank business."[88] Some female reformers rejected plans to secure the support of the political parties, fearing the impact on women and their work. One suffragist wrote, "If we owe our success to any party we are *honor bound* to support that party, no matter how obnoxious its leaders . . . may be to us."[89] Others did not want to antagonize them.

Hopkins believed that Emma understood the challenges facing the leaders of KESA as Emma had not created any hostility between suffragists and party stalwarts in South Dakota. Johns may have told her treasurer about the time she spent there, and how some of the national leaders, Shaw and Catt in particular, had offended party men whereas Emma had not. Emma was careful not to insult or challenge the ideas of the political parties upon whom she believed the future of the woman suffrage amendment rested, and she worked hard to challenge the opinion of those who believed that all suffragists were opposed to the actions of any party. She firmly supported nonpartisanship while speaking for suffrage and understood the wishes of the local women as well as the fears associated with provoking the party leaders of the state. Hopkins may have hoped that Anthony, who had lived with Emma for many months during the South

Dakota campaign, would change her opinion about Johns and about forcing party planks after hearing from her protégé.

The ensuing battle over the question of planks illustrates the tensions that often boiled over between national and state leaders in the West. Interestingly enough, even though she was a national lecturer for the NAWSA, Kansas women did not consider Emma an outsider. Leaders treated her as one of their own: a spokesman for the particular challenges that they faced in the Midwest. KESA leaders contended that the suffragists from other parts of the country could not understand their situation, but Emma could.

Johns begged Emma to return to Kansas to help with the campaign. Emma had chosen to stay away in 1894 because she believed that someone was trying to keep her from returning to the state. Johns denied the rumors. Praising Emma's previous work, she wrote, "You were *eminently* useful here, and . . . we *want* you." She begged Emma to return. "Say *you'll come*."[90] But Emma did not go back to Kansas.

Anthony, on the other hand, continued to discuss the necessity of securing platforms at major state political conventions. She gave a speech in Kansas City about the need to include a suffrage plank in the Republican and Populist party platforms. "Do you mean to repeat the experiment of 1867?" she asked. "If so, do not put a plank in your platform; just have a 'still hunt.'" Those who favored this method avoided publicity as much as possible, held small gatherings, and relied upon personal contacts to win over opponents rather than seeking out public endorsements by the state's political parties. Anthony's insistence upon pushing for a plank upset Johns and other women, who shared the stage with Anthony. They "whispered angrily and said audibly, 'She is losing us thousands of votes by this speech.'"[91] Anthony, offended by Johns's unwillingness to budge, told her she would have to resign from the KESA presidency if Republican women did not pass a resolution demanding the Kansas Republican Party include woman suffrage as a plank at their June meeting.[92]

Eventually, Johns buckled under the pressure of Anthony's demands. At the Kansas Republican Women's Association, a weak proposal in support of woman suffrage was presented to the women delegates. Johns and Anthony demanded and pushed for a stronger proposal. After some negotiation, the women drew up a resolution that they submitted to the Republican Party. It read, "That we, the Republican women of Kansas, having worked for the best interests of the state, using the ballot with judgment in school and municipal elections, demonstrating the benefits to be obtained, ask the Republicans in Kansas state convention assembled to testify and advocate an equal ballot and a fair count to all citizens."[93]

After presenting the resolution, women spoke in favor of the proposal at the State Republican Convention. Johns and Judith Ellen Foster of the Republican Woman's Association had the opportunity to speak with the resolutions committee of the Republican Party, urging them to support the resolution. Anthony threatened the male delegates, saying, "If you leave [the amendment] out you are dead." Republicans unanimously defeated the measure.[94]

Disappointed, suffragists pushed on and tried to secure the support of the Populist Party. Anthony agreed to campaign for the Populists if they supported woman suffrage and if the issue became one of the third party's planks. After they endorsed suffrage, she stood by her pledge and vigorously attacked the principles, ideology, and leaders of the Kansas Republican Party wherever she spoke, even though she was in effect violating NAWSA's pledge that prohibited the organization from forming political alliances. Nonetheless, many suffragists believed that with Populist support, the amendment would succeed as it had in Colorado.

After the convention, Johns wrote to Emma, explaining what had occurred at the Republican meeting. She concluded that the Republicans had defeated the plank because they feared they would lose the support of German voters. Foster, accused by Anthony of being a hired gun for the Kansas State Republican Party, had in fact helped the cause of the women, according to Johns. (When Foster arrived in Kansas she told citizens, "I care more for the dominant principles of the Republican Party than I do for woman suffrage.")[95] She "did *nothing* to hinder us. She was *helpful* to us. Even Aunt Susan and Miss Shaw had to concede that tho' they dislike her so much," Johns wrote to Emma. If only Emma had come, "You would have saved us money and lots of *harm. . . . We need you.*"[96]

Unfortunately, Emma was caught in the middle—between Anthony, her mentor, and Johns, a close friend, and she was smart to stay out of the state. Anthony refused to believe that her efforts to push for a suffrage plank at the Republican convention had caused a rift between herself and the KESA officers. "If you can tell me what is the real *true inwardness* of the Kansas turmoil—do—I pray," she pleaded to Emma. "I cannot believe it all came out of Miss Shaw's and my intense earnestness to get a plank in [the] Republican platform."[97]

Anthony refused to admit that local leaders might have understood their constituency better than the national leaders. Anthony told Emma that Johns's opposition to pushing for planks had hurt the campaign. As an example, she noted that the Republican gubernatorial candidate did not even mention the amendment while at a political rally, and another leading Republican, former U.S. Senator John J. Ingalls, stood opposed to woman suffrage because his wife, daughter, and mother did not want the right to vote. "That is just what I tried to *make* the *women who* wouldn't ask for a plank see would be the result of no plank—*freedom* to our *opponents*—*silence* to our *friends*!!"[98]

On November 6, voters in Kansas went to the polls to cast their ballots. Suffragists were hopeful that they would win. When Johns learned that voters had rejected the amendment, she and other KESA members blamed the failure of the 1894 campaign on Anthony and Shaw. (Some men resented the insults national leaders threw at them.)[99] Johns did not hold Emma responsible for the defeat they had suffered, and the Harvey organizer and lecturer continued to be in demand across the country.

The Kansas defeat, combined with the failure in South Dakota, may have led Emma to believe that the tactics employed by Anthony and Shaw were ineffective and ill-advised in the West. Just three years later, she told South Dakota suffragists that "it has been demonstrated repeatedly" when "outside influence has come into a state with great display of banner and noise, taking control of the campaign, that we have been defeated."[100] Emma's sympathies seemed to lie with the local people, some of whom preferred to use quiet tactics to lull their opponents to sleep.

The outcome of the Kansas campaign convinced Anthony that municipal and school suffrage were "a hindrance rather than a help toward securing full enfranchisement." Partisan women, who illustrated the power of women's votes in school or city-wide elections, only angered male voters who opposed extending women the franchise. Thus, she insisted that women secure full voting rights rather than accept partial enfranchisement.[101]

In February 1895, the women of Grand Forks invited Emma to North Dakota, where a woman suffrage amendment had been introduced in the legislature. Suffragists believed that the prospects for passage were bright. The North Dakota State Republican Party had adopted a suffrage plank, and they had regained control of the legislature the previous year. The women of Grand Forks had read about Emma's work in various suffrage newspapers and had concluded that she was the best candidate to lobby the legislature on their behalf. Emma agreed to come after securing a hefty salary—nearly $300.[102]

On February 8th, the *Grand Forks Daily Plainsdealer* announced Emma's arrival and later described her as a seasoned suffragist and a "stunner in persuasiveness."[103] Several days later she traveled to Bismarck to speak in favor of the bill before the legislature. She met with some of the leading women then at the capitol, including Elizabeth Preston, president of the North Dakota WCTU, and Emma F. Bates, superintendent of public instruction. Bates took Emma under her wing, offered her office space in her department, and introduced her to many members of the legislature.

By the time she spoke on the floor of the House, she had been in the capital city for more than a week. Emma spoke from her heart, hoping to evoke sympathy from the representatives who would vote for the bill. She began by asking whether physiology should determine who should vote. This delineation made no sense to her, as she worked hard to earn a living as an organizer and lecturer. Women invested their pay in their homes, for which they paid property taxes. But women had no voice in how the government spent their tax dollars. As an example, she illustrated how inequities in taxation generally benefited men but also had a negative impact on families with all girls. "[Farmer] A is a man with five sons, [farmer] B is a man with five daughters, and [farmer] C is a widow with five daughters. Each contributed an equal portion in taxes. A is represented by six votes, B by one and C has no voice."

What about the argument that "bad women" would vote if women received the ballot? "Bad men" greatly outnumbered "bad women" in North Dakota. According to her figures, only one woman was behind bars at the state penitentiary at Bismarck, compared to 107 male convicts. What would be the consequences of this one woman voting, she asked?

Women and men were different, she concluded. Men were courageous, hardy, and intelligent, but women were gentle and chaste. With the ballot, women could elevate mankind from the cesspool of politics.[104]

Colonel W. C. Plummer followed Emma's address. He apologized to the female speaker, saying that "the boys" decided he would speak against the issue. "He advanced no arguments," Elizabeth Preston reported. "His speech was made up of cheap ridicule and would not have been out of place in a bar-room."[105] Aside from his suggestion that women did not want the ballot, his comments were not reflective of typical anti-suffrage arguments. For instance, even though women were disfranchised, Plummer ridiculed women for voting against the Pope moving the Vatican to North Dakota for fear he would begin growing wheat in their state. After Plummer finished, the following exchange occurred on the floor.

Mr. Edwards, the sponsor of the bill, asked Plummer, "Do you not know that the Republican convention adopted a platform favoring woman suffrage?"

"I did not know it until today . . . ," he admitted.

"Is it not the duty of the Republican Party to stand by its platform?" Edwards inquired.

Plummer joked, "It would be if they had been in the habit of standing up to their platform pledges."

Then, in an interesting turn of events, the colonel said he would vote in favor of woman suffrage if the legislature passed the bill.[106] But the bill failed by a vote of twenty-five to thirty.

Disappointed, Preston explained, "With a Republican legislature and a woman suffrage plank in the party platform, it would seem to the uninitiated that there was an easy victory before us. We are reminded of an ignorant passenger, who, on being told that he must not stand on the platform, inquired what a platform was for, when from the conductor came the clear-cut reply, 'To get in on.'"[107]

Although the legislature defeated the bill, Dr. Cora Smith Eaton, president of the Grand Forks Equal Suffrage Association, praised Emma and her work. "No one could have done better than you did," she concluded. Emma, whom she referred to as "the General," had impressed both sides. Even though the battle had been lost, the reports received by Dr. Eaton impressed her enough to ask Emma for future assistance.[108]

Emma Bates agreed. North Dakota suffragists needed a "woman who was exceedingly womanly and pleasant in her personal appearance," and Emma fit their requirements. Furthermore, the state needed someone who was tactful, and Emma was not offensive. Perhaps most importantly, Bates wrote, Emma "did not make herself obnoxious to any man under any condition that I have heard of." Unlike past lecturers who visited North Dakota, Emma was more than a platform speaker. She was an excellent organizer whose skills were "quiet, earnest, [and] tactful."[109]

By 1895, North Dakota suffragists could call on a number of lecturers, but none with Emma's range of skills and moderate political approach, at least according to North Dakota women. Catt offered North Dakota a South Dakota organizer who reportedly supported Populism. Bates, a Republican, rejected Catt's plan and told Emma, "They are not going to send any South Dakota 'Pop' woman in here to organize us, if they want to succeed in suffrage work in North Dakota. . . . It is clearly a political deal which will ruin us in North Dakota if permitted to be carried out."[110]

Bates had reason to worry. Just two years previous, her party recalled a woman suffrage bill passed by the Populists and expunged from the record of the *North Dakota House Journal*.[111] Her own party viewed Populist women as "aggressive and threatening 'harpies' and shrews' whose power destabilized politics."[112] She did not want equal suffragists of North Dakota to be linked to the Populist Party, their leaders, or their ideas. Where suffragists were seen as moderate, perhaps even conservative in the 1890s, the press depicted Populists as revolutionaries, a threat to the country's political and economic order. If a Populist came to North Dakota with the support of the National American Woman Suffrage Association, any future suffrage campaigns in North Dakota would be pointless, and the issue would fail. Bates believed that North Dakotans needed a more moderate approach, and the women of North Dakota threatened to refuse to organize for suffrage without Emma. The state would accept no one but her.

They finally did accept another organizer later that year. Laura Johns, a Republican, went in Emma's place, and Bates rated her "*all right* (nearly as good as Mrs. DeVoe)."[113] Emma's ability to navigate the minefields of partisan politics, talking like a Populist when necessary and then avoiding all signs of affiliation other than suffrage, helped her avoid the stinging criticism faced by some partisan women.

Emma's popularity and skills appealed to Catt, who named her to the NAWSA Organization Committee in 1895, even though many questioned her loyalty to the group. During the next few years, the indefatigable Emma traveled relentlessly through the western states of Montana, Idaho, and Nevada, where she preached the gospel of equal suffrage. Enrolling apathetic women into vibrant, active clubs was tiring. Local suffragists frequently opposed NAWSA's interference in their matters and that compounded the drudgery of organizing. Pledges promised to the association went unpaid, and Emma suffered from the movement's poverty.

4

THE ORGANIZATION COMMITTEE

AT THE 1895 NATIONAL CONVENTION IN ATLANTA, GEORGIA, CAR-
rie Chapman Catt presented a new plan to restructure the National American Woman Suffrage Association and utilize new methods to help secure
women's enfranchisement. Criticizing older suffragists for their inability
to attract members, she claimed, "There are illustrious men and women in
every state, and there are men and women by the thousands whose names
are not known to the public, who are openly and avowedly woman suffragists, yet our organization does not possess the benefit of their names
on our membership lists, or the financial help of their dues." The older
methods of education and agitation, she believed, sparked disinterest
among men and women who favored suffrage and resulted in a weak,
ineffective organization.[1] To which Susan B. Anthony sarcastically replied,
"There never was a young woman yet who had just been converted, who
did not know that if she had had the management of the work from the
beginning, the cause would have been carried long ago. I felt just so when
I was young."[2]

Echoing the call of other Progressive reformers, Catt insisted that the
association focus on organization. She proposed a three-pronged plan:
one, to build local, county, and state suffrage associations in the West
and South with the assistance of the new Committee on Organization;
two, to establish a course of study in political science for women; and
three, to create a finance committee to develop model fundraisers that
local clubs could hold. Money raised by local chapters would be pledged

to the national organization and split with the state suffrage associations.[3] Delegates approved Catt's idea, and over the next five years Catt and her organizers carried out her plan of work.

As Anthony had predicted, the road was rocky. Arguments between Emma and Catt were frequent, and the Organization Committee faced significant financial difficulties, which Catt struggled to overcome. Nonetheless, Catt's experiment illustrates the changes under way within the suffrage movement and underscores the importance of organizers, who introduced dramatic changes within NAWSA and played a crucial role in forming clubs in underrepresented regions. Furthermore, Emma's field experience demonstrates the obstacles facing the suffrage movement and one of its most dedicated workers in the late nineteenth century.

Catt's plan centralized fundraising and lobbying work by linking local, county, and state organizations with the NAWSA so that suffragists could work together. Earlier methods had "always operated in a highly personal and haphazard manner" and had been piecemeal. NAWSA provided no clear focus or goals for suffragists until 1895. For the first time, NAWSA gave guidance to local and state associations through preprinted constitutions and the organization's newspaper, the *National Suffrage Bulletin*, as well as through a "consistent membership system (something no one had ever bothered about.)"[4] Catt also hoped to pool money for woman suffrage through the use of the pledge system, rather than through writing letters begging supporters for funds. By combining funds from various states and local communities, money raised by NAWSA could be used to fund state campaigns where an amendment was pending and passage seemed possible.[5] In short, Catt was reallocating money from one part of the country to another and placing the funds where success seemed most likely.

She patterned her committee on the WCTU's successful model, hoping to build an effective army of fighting suffragists. In the 1880s, WCTU organizers had targeted the western and southern regions of the United States, where their numbers were few, and they established numerous temperance unions. As a result of their pioneering work, the WCTU had a powerful network of local unions across the United States, and in only ten years their membership had quadrupled to 150,000. Another popular women's organization, the General Federation of Women's Clubs (GFWC), had around 100,000 members in 1895. NAWSA's small membership, which stood at 13,000 members in 1895, embarrassed Catt, who confided in suffragist Abigail Scott Duniway that she would "never be satisfied until we can boast of one million members."[6]

Catt's organization plan specifically focused on organizing in the West and South, with paid organizers. She selected experienced suffrage lecturers who dressed well, were tactful, had good manners, and were hard workers.[7] Catt believed that her organizers served as educators and advisors to newly formed clubs and their elected officers. Likening new local suffrage officers to young children, she suggested that "women need to go to the Kindergarten to learn the ways of conducting meetings and the business of an Association."[8] Catt therefore preferred to hire professionals rather than offer opportunities to unpaid volunteers.

Emma was one of five women selected to represent the committee as a NAWSA lecturer and organizer (the other organizers were Elizabeth U. Yates, Laura M. Johns, Annie L. Diggs, and Viola Neblett). Recognizing Emma's skills as an effective fundraiser, the committee offered her $125 a month, the highest salary of anyone on the committee. Fearing that Emma might find the terms of employment unsatisfactory, Catt explained that she would not be paid for chairing the committee, that only organizers in the field would receive funding. Those working in the South would receive $100 a month. Catt promised Emma two months of work in Idaho, where she would organize local and county clubs, raise pledges for NAWSA, and close with a state convention, where she would form a state association, and Catt mentioned the possibility of securing an additional month of work in Montana that summer.[9]

Emma must have been excited. Just two years earlier, Rebecca Mitchell, Idaho state president of the WCTU, asked Lewis E. Workman, a Republican, to introduce an equal suffrage amendment to be put to Idaho voters. Believing that the idea enjoyed support from the Republican Party, Emma drafted a plan to win woman suffrage for Idaho women, and she corresponded with Louise Avery Gillette in Ketchum about her strategy.[10] Her plans collapsed when the legislature defeated the bill, and Emma did not travel to Idaho that year. By this time, however, the Idaho legislature had overwhelmingly passed a woman suffrage bill, to be voted on in November 1896.[11]

Emma had also hoped to travel to Florida that year, where she and Henry owned an orange orchard, and she discussed her plan at length with Mrs. C. Holt Flint.[12] It might be possible to arrange a tour of the state for Emma, Catt said, but she believed that the daughter of an abolitionist would not be welcomed with open arms by southerners. "You must be willing to express your entire approval of the doctrine of white supremacy or they will have nothing to do with you," Catt warned. "They do not recognize the people who do not hate the 'Nigger.'"[13]

Emma may have thought the salary was low, but she agreed to work for the committee and earn a few months' salary while traveling through the Rocky Mountain West. She may have accepted the position with the understanding that she did not have to rely entirely upon NAWSA for support. She had recently been made state organizer for the Illinois Equal Suffrage Association and would receive funds from the state as well as from NAWSA. Henry was now practicing law, and he continued to serve as police magistrate for the city of Harvey. The couple was not financially secure, however; Emma, who had been selected as a delegate to NAWSA's Atlanta meeting, remained at home, presumably because of their financial standing. In May, Emma began her westward trek to Montana.

Catt had heard of an effort to enfranchise women in Big Sky Country and had added the state to the organizer's route in March. In February, Populist John Huseby, a member of the Montana House of Representatives, introduced a bill to extend suffrage to women. All Populists and a majority of Republicans then serving in the house supported the issue. Eventually, the lower house passed the measure, but the senate, which contained "staid old benedicts and confirmed bachelors," killed the bill.[14] Nonetheless, Catt began corresponding with state leaders because she believed there was an opportunity to build on the momentum of Huseby's actions, believing that "sentiment there is strong." Montana's labor unions, which recently met in Great Falls, unanimously passed a resolution in favor of woman suffrage. "We do not have that sort of thing outside of the West," Catt admitted to Emma. "I cannot help but pin my faith to the Pacific Coast. Montana is sure to do something for us."[15]

The West was a particularly important region to suffragists who believed in "its freedom from tradition, its liberality of thought, and its willingness to accept new ideas."[16] For Catt, it was important to focus on the West. She and Emma believed that the enfranchisement of Colorado and Wyoming women showed that western men were more liberal in granting women equality than eastern men. Unfortunately, their enthusiasm for spreading the suffrage gospel throughout the West surpassed their understanding of the special circumstances involving the passage of woman suffrage in these western states.[17]

Emma kicked off her tour of Montana in Miles City, about ninety miles west of the North Dakota border on the Northern Pacific Railroad line. Miles City was a cow town with a reputation for attracting rowdy ranch hands. In 1880, Dr. Lorman Hoopes noted that the town of five hundred fifty people had "twenty three-saloons . . . and they all do a good business; we are going to have one church soon." The following year the number of saloons jumped to forty-two, and their customers drank one thousand bottles of beer a day. By the time Emma arrived, the town's reputation had changed, as merchants with families moved west, opened businesses, and built churches and schools.[18] Emma spoke at one of those churches and organized an equal suffrage club with more than thirty members.[19] Emma's Miles City speech moved Reverend Wilder Nutting, a Methodist minister, who agreed to help the organizer as she established suffrage clubs across the vast state.[20]

Although no transcript of her speech exists, Emma's use of expediency arguments, which became increasingly popular in the 1890s, probably persuaded Nutting to the logic of her ideas. The expediency approach focused on the benefits woman suffrage would produce for society. It did not challenge women's roles as mother or wife, but instead highlighted the fact that men and women were different. This tactic tended to focus on women's moral superiority and their abilities to eradicate poverty, create child labor laws, clean up politics, and improve education, if only given access to the ballot box. The use of separate sphere arguments tended to galvanize local residents to organize at the state level. The Nuttings were particularly active in demanding that a state convention be held in Helena.[21]

After leaving Miles City, Emma traveled west to Billings, where she found that no arrangements had been made for her to speak, one of the difficulties frequently faced by organizers in the field. No letters from Reverend Nutting had been sent to Billings, and not one person had heard from Catt about Emma's visit. Consequently, no notices had been posted about her address. Emma came in on the same train as Judge Milburn, whom she had met at Miles City, and she told him of her dilemma. Being interested in the cause as a prohibitionist, he introduced her to some of the community's leading citizens, including the editor of the *Billings Gazette*, and he arranged for a meeting to be held the next evening at the courthouse.

The county treasurer chaired the meeting and "such was the interest that at the close the editor of the *Gazette* arose and moved for a meeting on the following evening, with an urgent request for Mrs. DeVoe to remain and deliver another address." Flattered by their appeals, she agreed. State Senator O. F. Goddard presided over the final meeting, where they appointed Nina Frizzelle chairman of the local committee and elected Alice Free secretary.[22]

Emma was often frustrated by Catt's lack of preparation during the first leg of her trip through Montana. Frequently, she arrived at the railroad depot without anyone knowing a suffrage organizer would be in town, a fact Catt did not dispute. "Without doubt you will find poorly made preparations in some places [but] that is the fate of the forerunner," she admitted.[23] After traveling through parts of Montana and finding no one to welcome her, Emma began to question Catt's plans. She wrote, "I cannot understand why you request that I come to Montana when I did." Suffrage sentiment was not as strong as Catt believed it would be. Emma thought she had misread Catt's orders. "I read your letter over two or three times to see if I had not made a mistake in reading it. But there it is."[24]

In some Montana cities where arrangements had not been made, Emma often had to act as her own advance agent. Catt praised Emma for her dedication to this type of work. "Mrs. DeVoe has a species of grit which I wish were more common with our workers," she wrote. "At several points she has found the arrangements for her meetings unmade. . . . Instead of sitting down with folded hands, she secured a hall, got some bills printed, distributed them, and had her meeting." Emma had some help from local pastors. She was grateful that Reverend Nutting "had written many letters to different places to interest the people in the work" before she arrived and was pleased that another minister told his friends, "Don't coop Mrs. DeVoe up in a church. Hire the best hall, and set the band to play at the door."[25]

Emma departed from Billings on the Northern Pacific bound for Red Lodge, where residents cordially received the organizer. From there she traveled to Big Timber, where some residents "seemed to feel a little shy of the meeting, lest they should get a raking over for having so many saloons," but Emma "stuck to her text" and did not mention the number of barrooms in town. She focused solely on the issue of woman suffrage and as a result converted a few audience members, who before had feared that suffragists were prohibitionists in disguise. As in Miles City, Red Lodge, and Billings, the women of Big Timber established a woman suffrage committee. The women of Livingston, Butte, Great Falls, and Helena also joined local suffrage clubs.[26]

Emma attracted many elite women and men to the cause using a tactic known as the "society plan," made popular by Catt in the 1893 Colorado campaign. The method was used heavily by organizers in the West and South. Emma had organized clubs in several Montana cities with "leading people as officers. In Bozeman, the State President of the W.C.T.U. was made local president of the Equal Suffrage Club. . . . At Helena we have a fine club. Ex-Senator [Wilbur F.] Sanders's sister is president, an able woman, which proves there is still good material for another U.S. Senator in the Sanders family."[27]

This new strategy represented a significant change in the methods used by Catt and her organizers and was designed to bring respectability to the movement. In the past, woman suffragists had been called fanatics, and cartoonists depicted them as old maids, insane individuals, or disreputable women. To change the image of the movement and its leaders, organizers actively courted elite and wealthy society women. Suffragists also hoped to attract middle-class clubwomen by holding parlor meetings. Both groups of women were important to the movement. Wealthy women had disposable incomes and could contribute to the cause, and they had time to donate to worthy issues. Clubwomen, by contrast, had experience working as municipal housekeepers and therefore could help fledgling suffrage associations petition and lobby for woman suffrage.[28]

Using another new tactic employed by suffragists in the 1890s, Emma also reached out to newspaper editors and politicians. In the past, workers had relied on public speeches to convince voters of the importance of woman's enfranchisement. Recognizing the sway of the press, Catt's organizers directly spoke with newspaper editors and politicians who would publicly support woman suffrage.[29] Before she arrived in Big Sky Country, suffragists were uncertain about the support of the Montana press, but many editors became proponents of the cause after listening to Emma.[30] In each city the press welcomed her, and not one Montana editor ridiculed the organizer or the cause of woman suffrage. The editor of the *Bozeman New Issue* regretted that Emma visited Montana so late in 1895. "If she could have given that august body [the state legislature] one of her talks and then made her canvass of the State, we are satisfied the question would have been submitted to the people and carried," he concluded.[31] Governor J. E. Rickards, former U.S. Senator Wilbur F. Sanders, and state Senator O. F. Goddard were just a few of the state leaders whom Emma persuaded to support woman suffrage.

Members of local clubs represented the best men and women in Montana society, and their ties within their communities and state varied. Prominent female reformers who were already active in civic improvement, municipal reform, and temperance dove into the cause. Leading politicians, their wives, and sisters also chose to support the women's rights movement. Working women—including a physician, a county superintendent of schools, and a newspaper editor—led some of the local clubs across the state. Support from community leaders pleased Emma, who told Catt, "I am willing to have the class of people whom I have interested [in Montana] compared with the people of *any* state in this union for their standing in the state."[32]

While Emma recognized that her pioneering work through Montana was important, she needed some reassurance from Catt that her work was—at a minimum—also satisfactory. Feeling insecure about her efforts, and having read no glowing accounts in the *Woman's Journal* or *Washington, DC, Woman's Tribune* about her work, the organizer asked Catt to recognize her efforts. "So you want a little praise do you?" Catt asked her. "I supposed the consciousness of doing splendid work was all sufficient unto you. But if you want more let me say that we *do* think you have done splendidly and well and that your work has been very successful. But then we knew it would be, so perhaps we had been forgetful about speaking the words commendation. I think you will leave Montana in a fine condition."[33] Emma did as best as she could in Montana, but suffrage clubs there tended to fall apart after her short visits. She left Montana in mid-June to organize in Idaho, beginning in Hope, a small panhandle community near the Montana state line. No one was at the railroad depot to meet her, and she discovered that no one expected a suffrage speaker. Catt explained that she might encounter similar occurrences in the northern part of the state, "but we knew we must get a foot hold there and knew you were just the person to do it. Many a speaker would have gotten back on the train and gone on, but you are not that kind of stuff and it is your way of doing that will help us win."[34]

Emma's use of conciliatory tactics was one reason Catt preferred to send her to Idaho. Catt had learned that local suffragist, Abigail Scott Duniway, had offended three groups of importance in the Gem State: the WCTU, the Mormons, and the labor movement, but she did not elaborate on the circumstances in letters to Emma. Catt knew that she could rely on Emma to secure the assistance of at least two groups she sympathized with, the laborers and temperance women. She warned Emma that labor support might be weak because Colorado's women had not supported Populist candidates in their most recent election, leading former Colorado Governor Davis Waite to blame the new female voters for his defeat.[35] He hoped that Populists would oppose women's enfranchisement as a result of the 1894 election, and Catt feared that Idaho Populists might retaliate against women. Several Populist papers "treated the Colorado election as though the women had been enfranchised by the Populists *only* and then proved traitors to the party that had befriended them."[36]

Abigail Scott Duniway was a force to be reckoned with. She opposed Catt's plan to send an organizer into the state and believed campaigns "should also be managed by home workers, who understand the home situation, and know the home sentiment" rather than outsiders.[37] Duniway owned a ranch in Idaho and for years had been one of a handful of suffrage workers in the state. She believed that she understood Idaho's politics better than any other woman, and part of her rejection of NAWSA's plan may have stemmed from her own sense of importance to the movement. Catt's plan, by contrast, challenged the view that western women knew what was best for their states. Both supported the same outcome—women's enfranchisement—but they differed on strategy.

At sixty-one years old, Duniway had been a long-time supporter of suffrage in the Pacific Northwest. Since the 1870s, Duniway had been working for woman suffrage as a lecturer and newspaper publisher. The publication of her woman suffrage newspaper, *New Northwest*, encouraged the development of woman's rights in Oregon and Washington, but many found her sarcasm and bluntness abrasive. In Jacksonville, Oregon, she was burned in effigy and egged for slandering Judge Prim, who, according to her sources, banished his wife from his home and then welcomed her back for his children's sake.[38] In 1883, when the Washington Territorial Legislature had voted on a woman suffrage bill, suffragists encouraged her to stay away from Olympia for fear her presence would kill the bill.[39]

Duniway favored the still-hunt strategy, a small, quiet effort to secure the enfranchisement of women. Fearing parades or rallies would attract too much attention and arouse opponents, she preferred to win over supporters with gentle persuasion, relying on personal contacts and educational efforts rather than hurrah campaigns. Duniway believed that this type of campaign was best suited for Idaho, but Catt disagreed. She wanted to use a unified or national approach when it came to securing women's enfranchisement across the United States, but she also recognized that she needed to tread lightly.

Catt had promised the Atlanta delegates that the Organization Committee would "respect the desires of the State Associations, and will never put an organizer in the field without the co-operation of the State Organization, where such organization exists."[40] Aware of this policy, Duniway organized a suffrage committee and promptly sent a note to Catt, explaining how she had organized an Idaho woman suffrage campaign committee chaired by William Balderston, editor of the *Idaho Statesman*. In the same letter, she directed Catt not to send a national organizer to Idaho. Catt felt slighted and told Emma that Duniway had "'done us up,' and had practically fixed things to suit herself" because she feared Anthony would dominate the campaign and wanted to manage the Idaho movement.[41]

For his part, Balderston expressed concern that the suffrage movement would get "into the wrong hands."[42] In mid-March, he agreed to serve as chairman of the effort, but when a "rather irresponsible young woman" who identified herself as secretary gave him the four names of those on the committee, he concluded that none of them had the "representative character necessary for the organization of this work." He agreed to postpone the committee's work until Catt sent an organizer "to reach the right people and effect a proper organization."[43]

Balderston's allegations worried Catt. The organization Duniway established in Boise was not composed of the type of women Catt wanted to attract. She told Duniway, "We want a State Association . . . made up of the best people, with the right kind of persons as leaders. [Idahoans] write me that the right kind of people are not the leaders there in Boise City."[44] Although Duniway objected, Catt won the battle, and she sent Emma through the state in the summer of 1895.

After holding only three meetings in Idaho, Emma concluded that Idahoans were "like the Montana people, liberal-minded and hospitable. Our cause is having a respectful hearing, and we hope for great things."[45] She spent the remainder of June and July organizing clubs throughout the state; everywhere she went she found sympathetic audiences and people willing to join local woman suffrage clubs. Remembering the success Emma received when she sang "A Soldier's Tribute to Woman," Catt arranged for Emma to be in Coeur d'Alene during the Idaho Grand Army of the Republic convention, thinking she "might do some good with old soldiers."[46]

Before Emma reached Boise, Catt reminded her of the importance of maintaining her respectability, as Duniway had not been "chaperoned by the right people" in the capital city, and as a result had tarnished her reputation. "If you cannot be entertained in families of standing, we would prefer you to go to the hotel and pay your way," she explained. Catt also warned her to stay away from a Dr. Spalding, who "is under question morally. At least they discuss her there and she and her friends must be steered clear of." Finally, she advised Emma to "Be 'a awful good girl' in Boise. Wear your sweetest smiles and good clothes."[47]

Emma understood the importance of wearing fashionable clothing, and she had built her reputation by avoiding controversial subjects. Besides, Catt had previously told Emma that the women of Idaho believed no woman could bring about change in their state unless she were "good looking" and wore fashionable clothing.[48] Catt need not have worried. Emma would not spend time with Dr. Spalding or her friends. Instead, she would court the leading citizens of Boise through tactics she had developed and perfected since the 1890 South Dakota campaign.

Although she had given numerous speeches since 1889, Emma was nervous about her Boise meeting. Originally, Susan Anthony and Anna Howard Shaw were scheduled to come to Boise, with Emma to follow. Balderston liked the idea, but when Anthony's and Shaw's plans changed and they were unable to travel to Idaho, Catt was afraid that she would have to postpone Emma's trip into the southern part of the state. "Without this preliminary the people [in Boise] were not willing to have you come in," she explained.[49] Although Anthony and Shaw would not be able to make it, Balderston finally agreed that Emma could come and form a local organization. Fearing that he might be displeased with her speech and that she might fail for the first time, Emma prayed for success.

She did not overlook any detail for her meeting at the Sonna Opera House. Emma wore her best "white silk crepe, trimmed in lavender, with cream lace and cut flowers." Judge James H. Richards presided, and Emma lectured for an hour on equal suffrage. Emma was so nervous that she believed she gave a "poorer speech than usual" and blamed Catt for her lack of confidence.[50] But the newspaper reported that the audience listened "with the closest attention" and "frequently interrupted with applause."[51] Following her lecture, Emma organized an equal suffrage chapter and dissolved Duniway's committee.

Emma credited God and her Baptist ties for her success. Catt disagreed:

"While I am very sorry to discount your religion at all, there was an element in the success which I think you did not properly count," namely, Judge James and Frances Richards, newcomers from Payette, who helped bring together Boise's society and the suffrage sympathizers. Nonetheless, Catt was ecstatic: "I cannot find words to express my happiness and gratification at your success in Boise."[52] From there, Emma completed her tour of Idaho and finished organizing in Montana, where she visited the state penitentiary in Deer Lodge to count the number of female and male inmates for her speech as proof that women were more law abiding than men.[53] By the end of her tour, Emma had even won over Abigail Scott Duniway, who admitted that Emma's visit "has been quite successful in permanently organizing the suffrage sentiment which has for a long time prevailed in all the inter-mountain States."[54]

Although she had been victorious in every community she visited, Emma had not received her monthly salary from NAWSA. She had received $59 from Iowa suffragists Mrs. C. Holt Flint and Martha Callanan to cover her travel expenses to Montana. Catt told Emma that she had not been paid because the NAWSA Organization Committee had been unable to balance its books. The committee was suffering from the ill effects of the depression, which still gripped the nation. Pledges raised by organizers were rarely paid, and the committee's account was regularly emptied. Consequently, Catt had to beg from "Dan to Beersheba for funds." Emma had to be paid in two installments for her Idaho and Montana work. Her first check for $166.27 drained the committee's treasury. Catt instructed Harriet Taylor Upton's clerk to send another check the following week with "all there might be by that time."[55]

Emma began to feel that neither NAWSA nor Catt valued her work. Catt had mailed her few letters of praise and had published even fewer glowing reports of her accomplishments. She had not even been paid. Emma began to resent the fact that she had not received the attention and compensation she believed she deserved. She shared her concerns with Reverend Nutting, who told Catt of their conversation; he said that "there was nothing but incompetency" in the New York Office (then located in Catt's home), and that Catt and her workers "did not appreciate [Emma] at all."[56]

Catt believed that Emma was the most talented organizer within their association, but Emma tested her patience. Both women were passionate about securing women's rights, and frequently their enthusiasm boiled over into heated arguments. They butted heads over which course was the best path toward victory. Relations between Catt and Emma ran hot and cold because of the organizer's bluntness and the chairman's brashness, and both of them wished to be in control.

Eventually Emma believed that her advice about when and where to hold the Montana State Convention fell on deaf ears. Emma concluded that Catt wanted to travel to Montana, hold a convention which fit Catt's schedule—not that of Montana suffragists—and bask in the glory of having formed the Montana Woman Suffrage Association. Emma was afraid that she would not receive credit for her own work if Catt came to Montana. In addition, she worried that Catt's dictatorial efforts might offend Montanans, who wanted Emma to head the meeting. Reverend Nutting directed Emma "for the good of the cause" to "take right hold of the matter and not allow some little jealousy on the part of some one else to throw you off of the back and spoil it all."[57]

Catt disagreed with Emma's protests to Reverend Nutting and challenged the idea that any lack of praise from New York meant that Emma's work was not valued. "I am not of a sentimental makeup," Catt told Emma. "I am not given to telling people how much I think of them, but actions speak louder than words and you will find that out some day." She told the reverend that she did not ask Emma to return to Montana for the convention because the organizer would have to pay her own way from Harvey to Helena. She knew that Emma did not have the means to purchase a ticket and pay for lodging and food along the way. To soothe Emma's feelings, however, she invited her top organizer to accompany her, conceding that "there would be great advantages in your presence there."[58]

Many of Montana's suffragists felt comfortable with Emma and confided in her. Sarepta Sanders, president of the Helena club, lamented her own lack of leadership skills, saying, "I wish I had your tact and executive ability. We need a strong leader." Regarding the state convention, she confessed, "I feel a little uneasiness as to the success. We lack workers who are able to make it *go*." The suffragists consisted of a small group in Helena, and "those appointed to do work accept . . . and then *stay away*," Sanders explained. She needed advice on how best to proceed, admitting that she was "a little faint-hearted" over the matter.[59]

Emma did not return to Montana until the following year, but Catt arranged to attend the state convention held in Helena that fall. Emma arrived in Harvey in August, and she remained there for two months, where she had a chance to catch up with her husband.

On her second tour for the committee, Emma went west through Iowa and then onward to Utah, where she stayed with suffragist Emmeline B. Wells, who was president of the Utah Territory Woman Suffrage Association and a Mormon. Wells was active in the equal suffrage discussions taking place in Utah as the territory prepared to apply for statehood in the Union. From 1870 to 1887, Utah women had the right to vote. In 1887, Congress stripped them of this right with the passage of the Edmunds-Tucker Act, which punished polygamous Mormons. In 1890, the Church of Latter-Day Saints disavowed the practice of polygamy, and the women of Utah were free to regain voting rights.[60] While Emma was in town, they undoubtedly discussed the re-enfranchisement of Utah's women.

Emma moved on to Nevada and was scheduled to visit the territories of Arizona and New Mexico. In Nevada, the state legislature had considered a woman suffrage bill. According to the state constitution, the issue could not appear on the ballot until the 1897 Nevada legislature voted in favor of the issue. If the bill passed, the question would go to the voters.

Earlier in the spring, Anthony and Shaw had traveled through Nevada on their way to California. Their visit spurred interest in organizing, and local suffragists appointed a campaign committee, but Anthony and Shaw told Nevada women to delay until the following year. Frustrated, Catt confided in Emma that the two "are all the time in the most innocent and unconscious way doing things to put obstacles in our way."[61]

Although both women drew large audiences, Catt believed that the pair did not understand or appreciate what she and her organizers hoped to achieve. For instance, Anthony wondered "what in the world" organizers were doing in Montana. Catt thought that the famed speaker failed to comprehend the importance of organizing women to counter the popular argument that women did not really want the ballot. The organizations established by Emma also served another purpose in that they played a crucial role in launching future suffrage campaigns.

Aside from misunderstandings over organizational efforts, neither Anthony nor Shaw understood the modern pledge system put in place by the Organization Committee; they preferred to raise funds as they had in the past. Catt learned that California suffragists had asked Shaw to help the women raise funds for their campaign, but Catt doubted that would amount to much. "How do you think they are going to do it? Why they will hold meetings and charge admission [to her suffrage addresses] and after paying her a good price they will put the remainder (?) [sic] in their campaign fund," Catt wrote to Emma. "Isn't that an old fashioned scheme," she asked.[62]

Emma began her Nevada tour in Wells, about sixty miles west of the Utah border. Riding the Central Pacific Railroad line, she organized equal suffrage clubs in Elko, Carlin, Palisade, and Battle Mountain. From there she took the Nevada Central Railroad to Austin and then traveled to Winnemucca and Reno. The V&T Railroad transported her to Carson City, Virginia City, and Dayton, while she went by carriage to Genoa. She spent her last few days in Reno at the state convention, where she helped to establish the Nevada Woman Suffrage Association. She then planned to go to California and return home via the territories of Arizona and New Mexico.

This plan resulted in a great deal of animosity between Emma and Catt, as the chairman of the committee expected her organizer to leave Reno immediately for her tour of the Southwest rather than taking some time off. "You have quite broken my heart," Catt cried. "I do not see what ever put it into your head to flunk right in the middle of the work after I had told you that there would not be a minute to spare since it was necessary for you to start so late." (Emma began working in the fall due to the climate of the region.) Catt continued, "If you were so anxious to go off on that visit you should have started out on your visit before the work in Nevada was begun at all. I did think there was one woman who would stick to her work. This sort of thing is mighty discouraging." Catt was so upset that she insinuated that Emma's organizing work in Montana and Idaho was pointless as clubs fell "to pieces inside of a minute."[63]

Emma was angry. She sent Catt's letter to Henry, describing the difficulties she faced in planning this tour of the Southwest with Mary G. Hay, Catt's right hand in the New York office. Henry promptly wrote to Catt, asking her to review Hay's letters and to "see if you can't find it in your heart to apologize to Mrs. DeVoe for the language you unjustly use to her in your letter of the 21st." The confusion over the trip resulted from those in New York, not his wife. Holding in his hand Hay's letter from September 19, 1895, Henry directed Catt to the "red ink underscores" and the map that Hay had mailed to Emma showing her route. Emma had not immediately rushed off to buy a railroad ticket to the Golden State; instead, she waited for a "whole month for dates, before *starting*," he wrote. Catt's criticism of Emma's organizational efforts in Montana and Idaho made no sense to him. "You have doubtless forgotten the very commendatory letter you wrote her of her work there soon after her return."[64]

In the heat of the moment, Emma had also fired off three mean-spirited letters to Catt, accusing her of "neglect" and "bad management." She called Catt a "dictator" and concluded that she was "selfish, unjust, [and] neglectful."[65] In another letter she blasted Catt for the "fuss" made over her plan to rest for ten days before traveling to Arizona and New Mexico, and Emma even threatened to "quit and come home" if she could not follow the plan she and Hay had worked out.[66] Clearly Emma was hotheaded and quick to rush to judgment, as was Catt.

In response to Emma and Henry's letters, Catt tried to determine how and why Hay had come up with a plan that differed from the one she had drawn up in the summer for Laura Johns, who was initially going to visit these territories. After sitting down with Hay, she "exonerated" Emma "from all blame in the matter." But she still believed that Emma held some responsibility for not first checking with Catt about the California trip. Although her railroad ticket was cheaper than the one Catt had planned to purchase, Catt did not believe the scheduled route met the committee's needs. As she explained to Emma, there was only "one way in which the work could be conducted" in the territories and that was the route she had mapped out.[67]

Emma was "too sensitive by far," Catt told her. Catt was equally injured by Emma's assessment of her leadership skills. "No person could do more than I have done," she wrote. She conceded that Emma's work in Montana and Idaho was exemplary, but as they had previously discussed, organizers needed to take more time in each community to create stronger associations. "We tried one night stands in Montana," but that was too little time. Two nights would reap better results. Catt reminded Emma, "You have no better friend than I."[68]

Emma was lucky that Catt had hired her, because not everyone who attended the Atlanta meeting wanted to employ her. Although the press portrayed Emma as sweet and tactful, some suffragists saw a different side of her. They claimed that she was "jealous minded" and always wanted her own way. If she did not get what she wanted, she would not organize or lecture. "If the best of everything" was not offered, Emma would become angry. This clearly contrasted with the public image that she had carefully built in South Dakota and other midwestern states. Her actual character, known to those inside the suffrage camp, was less warm and welcoming and sparked debate among those active in the cause for years to come.

Some had questioned her loyalty to NAWSA because she had worked with the Federal Suffrage Association. Catt eventually countered this objection, believing that Emma was the best organizer and fundraiser NAWSA had, and as such the organization should offer her a position and pay her more than anyone else.[69] Catt had frequently called upon Emma for assistance before forming the Organization Committee, and she would continue to seek her assistance well into the twentieth century as they battled for the passage of the Nineteenth Amendment.

Although Catt had apologized for lashing out at Emma, Emma refused to travel to Arizona or New Mexico, and she returned to Harvey. Emma wrote to Flint telling her of her decision, who agreed with Emma: "I say *emphatically*, you did *just right* to go home." She encouraged Emma to think twice before she "got on the end of the National pitchfork" again.[70]

By the end of the year Catt scrambled to collect funds to pay her organizers, and she tried a variety of schemes, such as selling calendars, holding a Christmas Shopping Exchange, and mailing chain letters, to raise money.[71] None of these methods were effective, and Catt admitted to Emma that she had resorted to begging to pay off the debts she had accrued over the year. The pledge and dues system, which Catt had instituted in an attempt to centralize efforts, was not profitable because clubs did not send the funds that they had promised. For instance, only six out of fourteen Montana clubs mailed their dues, and even fewer had mailed their pledges of $25 to $100.[72]

Emma believed that the Organization Committee's economic problems stemmed from Catt's inability to manage money. She concluded that Catt was wasting funds; a good example was the planned route through the territories of Arizona and New Mexico. By contrast, Emma was frugal when it came to spending money. She shared her feelings with Flint, who told her to "have patience with poor Carrie. Her enthusiasm led her into contracting debt." Flint admitted that Catt was "not always practical" and "does not estimate the force required to overcome the obstacle to reach it," but reminded Emma that she dove into the work and committed herself to the cause.[73]

Much of Emma's anger must have stemmed from the fact that she had to pinch pennies because of the bad investments she and Henry had made during their first decade of marriage. She had to work to keep their household afloat. By contrast, Catt had married a wealthy engineer and did not have to work to help support herself and her husband.

Emma remained at home until January, when she attended the 1896 national convention in Washington, DC. She addressed the convention several times, reading a speech prepared by Flint on the subject of fundraising, and gave her second national speech, "The Liberty of the Mother Means the Liberty of the Race." "Hitch your wagon to a star," she began, quoting transcendentalist Ralph Waldo Emerson. "Your 'wagon' is that which carries you along, down to bondage or up to liberty, and the women who are asking for full enfranchisement have hitched their wagon to the bright, beautiful and most promising star in the firmament—the star of liberty." Give women political rights, she argued, for as "long as the mothers of the race live in an atmosphere of subserviency, in harmony and dependence, so long will they bear children to fill almshouses, asylums and prisons." A mother must be enfranchised, Emma concluded, "because she cannot bequeath to her child that which she does not possess."[74]

In her report as a NAWSA organizer, Emma boasted, "I have traveled 12,180 miles, given 61 evening addresses, held 49 afternoon meetings, collected $511.13 in cash and $1,810 in pledges, organized 12 clubs and two committees in Montana with a total membership of 269; 23 clubs in Idaho, with a membership of 860; and 10 clubs in Nevada, with a membership of 175. My total and other expenses have been $513.32." Emma's achievements as an organizer stood out, especially when compared with the work of others employed by the committee. That year, all of the NAWSA organizers had formed more than one hundred clubs throughout the country, and Emma formed forty-seven of them herself.[75]

This impressive record was made even more so because the work in Idaho, Montana, and Nevada was difficult. Catt explained to the delegates of the national convention the daunting task she and Emma faced in 1895: "We did not have the name of a single person in Idaho who was interested in our cause, and but two names in Montana." Before her trip through these two states, women in these small communities felt as if they were the only supporters of woman suffrage and "dreaded to make a public movement. Now these scattered advocates are gathered together into an active, living force."[76] Although the clubs were not in great shape, Catt recognized that publicly declaring their actual state would only alienate Emma and serve no positive purpose.

After Emma returned to Harvey, she began corresponding with Catt about her assignments that spring. Catt planned for her to spend two months in Wisconsin and hoped that she would accept work in Montana and North Dakota, but Emma's salary became a sticking point. NAWSA's Business Committee offered her seven months of work at $100 a month. If she were on the road for less than seven months, she would receive an extra $25 a month, making her salary $125 a month. Emma apparently considered $700 a paltry sum, to which Catt replied, "I do not consider that $100.00 per month and expenses is a small salary at all." Catt had to beg for every penny of Emma's salary, and besides, Catt wrote, "You will remember that it is the largest one paid." Emma questioned Catt's reminder, writing in the margin of Catt's letter, "Do you believe it is the largest salary paid?"[77] According to the *Des Moines Woman's Standard* and Catt, Emma was the best fundraiser NAWSA had, so why shouldn't she be paid more? Besides, Catt knew that Emma needed the salary.

Catt also addressed Emma's complaint that she did not receive sufficient credit for the contributions she had made to the woman suffrage movement in 1895. Catt pleaded guilty to Emma's allegations and reassured her that her work had made a difference. "I think your work was fully appreciated by all the Business Committee and I am very sure it was appreciated by myself," she admitted. Fearing she might lose her leading organizer as a result of a misunderstanding, Catt asked Emma to "tell me frankly wherein I have erred [and] I will do the very best I can to rectify my error."[78] The women eventually ironed out their differences, and Emma spent two months in Wisconsin and then traveled to Montana in April.

Catt feared that it would be much more difficult to organize in Montana. Hard times had hit ranchers, prices for cattle and sheep had tumbled, and letters from women in the state spoke of hard times. Dejected, Montana suffragists had failed to answer letters. Helen M. Reynolds, then working for Catt, called Montana's women "an inferior race of beings to take so little interest in their own concerns."[79] Both women hoped that Emma would infuse the apathetic Montana suffrage movement with enthusiasm.

Emma's first stop was in Glendive, the Dawson County seat. The committee had done all they could to arrange a meeting for her, but they feared that she would be discouraged by what she found. They sent posters to a Methodist minister and asked him to open his church for a meeting, but he was not encouraging. At least he was not opposed to enfranchising women.[80] Emma found conditions just as Catt had described, but she succeeded and established a local club. From there she traveled to Miles City and then on to Billings and Livingston.

Emma had formed clubs in all three communities the previous year. Unfortunately, the Billings group folded when she left town, and when the president of the Livingston club moved, the club disintegrated. She had to establish new organizations in both areas because Catt believed they were too important to be overlooked, and Catt pledged to send a NAWSA member every six months to see that the Billings club did not fall to pieces.[81] In both places Emma was successful.

As she traveled west to Butte and Helena, Emma had to deal with fractures within the local suffrage community, which complicated her efforts. She was an organizer, not a mediator. Nonetheless, the situation required her to sit down with women of the community and come up with a resolution that worked for everyone involved and also helped the cause. In most cases, she followed the advice of those in New York.

In Butte, members of the sole woman suffrage club in town dissolved the chapter because some of the women wanted to hold secret meetings, perhaps out of fear of being associated as suffragists. Some of these women also belonged to secret societies and were therefore accustomed to closed meetings, while others reportedly preferred open meetings.[82] After spending a week in the mining community, Emma identified the sources of dissension and formed eight different clubs (seven separate clubs and a county organization).[83] Complaints about one member nearly caused others to withdraw from the Helena Equal Suffrage Society.[84] In an attempt to ease the conflict between the women, Emma helped establish the Helena Business Woman's Suffrage Club, as directed by Catt.[85]

As she made her way through Montana, a letter from Henry gave her hope that she might be able to stop working for Catt's Organization Committee. In the letter he promised that if they received his aunt's money in the fall, "There will be no more need" of Emma's working. They might even be able to pay off the mortgage in a few years. In addition, Henry told his wife that their home was "going to be a good investment yet" as the city hall was probably going to be built on the south side of 154th Street, which "will help our property."[86]

Things seemed to be looking up for the DeVoes; Populists were gaining ground in the United States, and the political storm brewing excited Henry, who believed that the issue of free silver would squash the Republicans in the November elections and loosen the circulation of currency.[87] Many people believed that the country needed a change, and the people of Montana, especially the farmers and miners, embraced the

Populist Party, which had firmly established itself in the state.[88]

Emma's Populist sympathies helped her to forge relationships with women who held similar views about the economy and politics. Ella Knowles Haskell, a Populist and Montana's assistant state attorney general, became a close friend of Emma's. She was exactly the type of woman she and Catt hoped to attract to the cause. Haskell worked hard to become Montana's first female attorney and earn a spot within the state government. She was someone that understood how to achieve a goal and also knew how government worked. Emma believed that the apathy in Montana could be due to the fact that the women lacked real leadership at the state level; the current president of the Montana Woman Suffrage Association, Harriet P. Sanders, was not performing her duties.[89]

Sanders was not to blame for her lack of interest, however; she had not wanted the position and accepted it only after coaxing. A lack of motivation and leadership was common in the suffrage movement in the late nineteenth century. Organizers constantly had to battle apathy among local members and state officers. As a result, Emma resolved to encourage women who had earned their standing in the community on their own to become state officers of the Montana Woman Suffrage Association instead of seeking women who were related to leading politicians. She advised Haskell to run for president of the association in 1896, and she did.

Society women were less reliable than Catt had hoped. When organizers left town many elites often lost interest. Once excited about the prospect of winning the support of these women, organizers became dismayed by their apparent lack of sustained interest. Catt complained that many people "announce themselves as suffragists," but not one society woman "has amounted to very much as a working force."[90]

In the summer of 1896, Laura Johns traveled through Idaho for the Organization Committee. She found no suffrage club in Boise and could not interest any society women to work for the cause. Recognizing that Boise needed a club, she established a new one without the assistance of elite women. William Balderston mentioned to Catt that society women had not been included in the newly reorganized club. Angered by his comments, Catt replied that if "the society people will not work somebody must and we must take those who toil."[91]

While Johns and Emma were in Idaho and Montana, Catt continued to wrestle with the issue of money. For the second time in two years, Emma was not paid on time. Catt was "humiliated" to have to tell Emma that her salary would "probably have to come along in driblets as we can get it in." In 1896 pledges were fewer, and she had no money in the treasury to write a check.[92] She had hoped to send Emma on to Texas and Oklahoma Territory in the fall, but hard times prevented her from doing so. Somehow Emma eventually received her pay.

At the 1897 national convention, Catt lavished praise on Emma's Montana work. She had spent nearly three months in Big Sky Country. "To reach her appointments she was forced to travel by rail, stage, wagon and buckboard, and through storms and mountain cold. Yet every discomfort was met with courage, and from hard conditions she wrested victorious results," touted Catt. Emma formed new chapters and revived old ones, establishing eight clubs in the largest city in Montana. The results were spectacular:

> For two years the Committee on Organization has felt a sort of guardianship of the work in Montana, keeping in close correspondence with its clubs and officers, trying in many ways to encourage, inspire, and instruct, but the days of its tutelage are over, and the National Association will find in this new auxiliary an independent, strong association, with a campaign on its hands which it gives evidence of being able to guide to a sure victory.[93]

Emma had established an association that Catt believed would now thrive on its own.

The women of Idaho, recently enfranchised, also thanked Emma for her efforts. Mell Woods, daughter of Emmeline Wells, explained, "Without the aid of the devoted women, Mrs. DeVoe, Mrs. Catt, Mrs. Bradford, and Mrs. Johns, who made the arduous journey across the continent to organize our clubs, plead the cause and teach us how to work and win, we should not be celebrating Idaho's victory tonight." The work of the organizer was dangerous and tiresome, Woods explained. Emma, who had arrived in the summer of 1895, took "wearisome stage rides over dangerous mountain roads to reach towns isolated from the railroad line—organized clubs in almost every town of importance in Idaho, a State whose area is 84,800 square miles, almost double that of New York."[94]

Although Emma successfully revitalized Montana associations and helped the women of Idaho secure citizenship, she did not receive a merit raise the following year. In the winter of 1897, Catt informed Emma that her salary would be cut from $125 to $100 a month because collections and pledges had been shrinking as a result of the poor economy. (Evidently, Catt had not cut Emma's pay in 1896, when she earned $125.) Free silver had not galvanized voters as Henry had predicted; instead, the Republicans won the presidency in the November election. The wages of workers had not kept pace with inflation, and the Business Committee concluded that "our suffrage workers ought to be willing to share the same fate in the interests of our work." Recalling their 1896 disagreement, Catt emphasized, "This is the highest salary any one will receive, and some of those who received $100.00 last year were reduced to $50.00 or $60.00. Kindly let me know if this agreeable."[95] Emma concurred, perhaps recognizing that she would not receive a higher offer. She needed the money. Apparently the funds from Henry's aunt had not come as they had expected.

Catt had hoped Emma would organize in Iowa that year, but Flint advised her to stay away. "Think of it," she explained. "They have not put your name as speaker in the [National Suffrage] Bulletin, for any state."[96] Emma initially agreed with her, and Flint announced that she was "mighty glad" that she "refused to be a puppet" for Catt.[97] Emma's decision confused Catt. "I did not understand that you would not go out," she wrote.[98] Less than a month later, Emma changed her mind and began organizing in Iowa.[99]

In the fall, she donated two weeks of her time to the Kentucky Equal Rights Association. She formed organizations in six towns, revitalized two clubs, and spoke at the convention at Covington in October, the largest woman suffrage convention ever held in Kentucky.[100]

After this tour, Emma did not work for the Organization Committee again. Rumors flew over a supposed feud between Emma and Catt.[101] Before the end of the year, the South Dakota Equal Suffrage Association approached Emma with a plan to bring her back in 1898. In November, South Dakota voters would once again have the opportunity to vote on the issue of woman suffrage, and the officers of the SDESA hoped to mount an effective campaign to secure citizenship for South Dakota's women. But campaigns were costly, and the SDESA's treasury was nearly empty. The economic hardships of the time made it especially difficult to raise funds in the state. SDESA officers recalled that their former state lecturer and organizer, Emma Smith DeVoe, had the ability to raise funds from those who did not have any money to spare.

They unanimously agreed to extend an offer to Emma to serve as their financial field agent and organizer of county and precinct work. Secretary

Clare M. Williams explained their circumstances: "Of course we realize that money is the chief corner stone of our campaign work. Money we must have," she insisted. "Now we must have your help. We know you are a good money getter."[102]

Being at home when the letter arrived, Emma quickly responded. She believed that the task of raising funds in South Dakota was of "Herculean proportions." But she admitted, "I feel a love and duty calling me back to my virgin field of active suffrage work . . . if we can agree upon terms and conditions that shall govern the campaign, I am willing to put my best endeavors into the work." Emma listed one stipulation. She refused to raise funds for the SDESA if she did not have some authority to determine how it would be spent. She cited a previous campaign as an example, where she saw $2,000 that she had raised "fritted away in big salaries that brought few votes."[103]

Recognizing the dire economic situation in South Dakota, Emma hoped to raise $1,000 outside of the state, and she emphasized the importance of keeping outsiders (NAWSA lecturers) from speaking in the state until the SDESA determined it was appropriate. Although she had not lived in the state since 1891, Emma recognized that some might view her as an outsider. To avoid any confusion over the matter, she instructed the SDESA to advertise her as a South Dakota woman. "I have owned a farm in Beadle Co. in my own right for the past 8 years. I was the first person in the state to pay $10 for a life membership in the E.S.A., and I spent 10 years there," she reasoned.[104]

Emma recommended that the state establish a "still-hunt" campaign. She advised the SDESA to tell their lecturers and workers that the campaign would focus solely on woman suffrage and "*under no circumstance touch upon any phase of politics, religion, temperance or any other subject foreign to woman suffrage pure and simple.*"[105]

Her terms were these: she asked that the SDESA pay her $100 a month and all expenses. This salary, according to Emma, was much less than she would charge other states and "much less than I have worked for, even when I had no responsibility," she wrote. (Emma failed to admit that she had received $100 a month from NAWSA's Organization Committee.)[106]

President Anna R. Simmons agreed to all of her terms. "I shall feel so relieved to have you at the head (with all your experience) of our E.S.A. in S.D.," she admitted. In a moment of desperation, Simmons, whose own health was failing, offered Emma the position of acting president of the

SDESA. Simmons did so because she believed that Emma's close ties with Catt would benefit the campaign. NAWSA officers had seemed hesitant to help the SDESA because of Simmons's association with the WCTU. Recalling the 1890 campaign, they probably feared that the ties between temperance and suffrage would result in another failed campaign, and Catt preferred to send funds to states where success seemed more likely.[107]

Emma accepted on the condition that she be made chairman of a campaign committee composed of SDESA officers. She then unveiled her plans to raise funds by forming the South Dakota Advisory and Soliciting Committee, made up of prominent suffrage workers outside of the state. The committee would raise funds for the campaign and select the speakers they believed could aid the cause.[108]

By February, Simmons began to waver over her decision to have Emma serve as chairman of the campaign and acting president. Alice Pickler, who had known Emma for many years, advised the SDESA "to go slow and not give her too much power." Simmons had also just heard a rumor that Emma was "at a cross points with the Nat'l E.S.A," and she feared that appointing her chairman of the campaign and acting president might antagonize the NAWSA, which had "more influence in the states than Mrs. DeVoe." Simmons believed that there was some truth to the rumor because Emma had told her she would not go to the annual NAWSA convention. (She wanted to start working immediately, and she decided to remain in Harvey so that she could quickly travel to South Dakota.) "This *will be the test*," Simmons wrote. "If she signs we will know all is well between her and the National. If she refuses then we can't have her."[109]

Simmons ended up burning the contract they had drawn up because many other South Dakota women who had worked in the 1890 campaign objected to Emma. They believed that she desired too much power. Emma Cranmer advised Simmons, "Drop her at once. She will rule or ruin and create discord."[110] Simmons wrote to Emma, informing her that "for the sake of harmony" she could not chair the campaign or serve as acting president. Instead, they offered her the position of field worker.[111]

Plans changed, however, and by the end of the month Simmons believed that Emma should manage the campaign. She told the SDESA treasurer, Mrs. Bennett, that delegates to the national convention offered "many assurances of Mrs. DeVoe's value as a worker and money getter." Some were jealous of Emma, but most—including Catt—praised her work.[112] Catt hoped that Emma would chair the campaign and raise the necessary funds to mount an effective effort. Catt wrote that Emma could alleviate a great deal of stress Simmons felt regarding the financial standing of the SDESA because she was "fond of money-raising and managing financial undertakings."[113]

When it came to Emma, there were two divergent points of view: those who believed that she was more trouble than she was worth, and those who saw her as one of the best fundraisers and workers in the country. The famed organizer was either a hellion or an angel, and the debates continued well into the twentieth century, when Emma became president of the Washington Equal Suffrage Association.

Simmons promptly sent another contract to Emma, who began mulling over the prospect of going to South Dakota. After discussing the issue with Flint and Haskell, she decided not to accept the position. "You have my full sympathy in this trying time yet I cannot consent to take your place now," she wrote to Simmons. "So do not depend upon me." The complications over whether or not she would chair the South Dakota campaign had upset Emma. The flip-flopping over the decision probably led the organizer to become disheartened with the cause.[114]

From 1898 to 1900, Catt continued her experiment without her best organizer, and after only five years, NAWSA dissolved the Organization Committee. Highly critical of her predecessors, Catt had not understood that sentiment for woman suffrage was not very strong in the late nineteenth century. The association had actually lost members since 1895. In 1900, only 8,900 members belonged to the association.[115] Nonetheless, the Organization Committee was part of a significant shift that occurred in the woman suffrage movement. Catt and her committee essentially modernized the association.

In 1898, Emma dropped out of the suffrage movement altogether. The following year, the *Woman's Journal* reported that "a slender woman from Harvey," presumably Emma, did not gather suffrage petitions for the Illinois legislature because her husband "had been ill all winter."[116] For the next few years Emma remained in Harvey, devoting her time to the Woman's Relief Corps and nursing her husband—who was frequently ill—back to health. It is unclear how the couple made ends meet without Emma working. Perhaps the money from Henry's aunt came through, or they were able to live off Henry's salary for a few years as the economy improved. The woman suffrage movement hobbled along but secured no new victories.

Henry's illness became more severe over the years, and in 1905—seven years after leaving the movement—Emma convinced her husband to move to Washington. She encouraged Henry to move west because she feared that she would become a widow if they remained in Harvey; the "physicians and healers" they hired could not cure her husband, and she hoped that a change in climate might help. She would stop at nothing to see that he was well again. "Money was no consideration," she explained to her family. [117] As soon as he recovered, Emma returned to her life's work, determined to secure suffrage for women in the Pacific Northwest. At fifty-seven, Emma had the energy to secure the first suffrage victory in years.

5

THE NORTHWEST CAMPAIGNS

"WE DIDN'T FIGHT FOR THE BALLOT. WE JUST WORKED OUT THERE in Washington. We were on the best of terms with the politicians, and when either Republicans or Democrats had meetings we were given an opportunity to talk to their audiences," Emma said to her listeners at the Methodist Church of West Allis, Wisconsin, in 1911. She explained how the women of Washington, just eight months earlier, won the right to vote using nonpolitical ways. "All of our meetings were informal. We had suppers and cooked good things to eat. We sold cook books. We had contests and gave prizes for the women who devised the best plans to build comfortable houses and the most useful and labor saving contrivances to aid in household work."

By working for the cause, suffragists proved that Washington women wanted the ballot. But, she emphasized, "We worked for our vote in womanly ways, for we weren't men and we didn't want to be men; therefore we didn't propose to try to get our vote in the way that men would."[1] Washington represented the first suffrage victory in the United States in fourteen years. The Pacific Northwest campaign ended the doldrums that had stretched from 1896 until 1910 and had a very visible domino effect upon other western states. By 1914, nearly all western women, with the notable exception of New Mexico, had become voters.

The fourteen-year dry spell was, however, an important period in suffrage history. During this time the movement went through a "suffrage renaissance" or period of regeneration. When Carrie Chapman Catt became NAWSA president in 1900, she expanded the society plan that she and her organizers used. To publicize their efforts, increase recruitment, and educate the public, suffragists deposited literature at local libraries and offered texts on the subject to schools. They canonized suffrage leader Susan B. Anthony and reached out to younger college-educated women, all in an effort to make the issue of woman suffrage appear more mainstream and less radical.[2]

The Washington Equal Suffrage Association (WESA) went through its own period of rebirth when Emma became president of the association in the fall of 1906. At that point, the movement in Washington was lifeless and had been for nearly eight years. The association had only a few members and a tiny executive board. Emma injected WESA with fresh blood and revitalized a dying movement, providing the executive committee with a new vision of how to secure woman suffrage and the energy with which to rebuild the state organization.

Washington women had been laboring for years to become citizens. From 1883 to 1887, the women of the territory had been enfranchised, but in an interesting turn of events, the territorial Supreme Court overturned the act passed by the legislature, claiming that the title did not adequately describe the bill's intent. Determined to grant citizenship to women, territorial legislators passed a suffrage bill in 1888, called "An Act to Enfranchise Women," which the court again voided. The justices argued that Congress had not given territorial lawmakers the authority to enfranchise women. Delegates to the 1889 constitutional convention opposed including woman suffrage in the state constitution but agreed to give men the opportunity to vote on the issue when they ratified the constitution. The amendment failed. Again, suffragists attempted to secure equal suffrage in 1898, but voters defeated that measure.[3] Following this campaign, Washington women effectively stopped working for equal suffrage. By 1904, only one suffrage club remained in the entire state.[4]

Interest in woman suffrage was alive and well in the neighboring state of Oregon, however. In 1904 Oregon suffragists Dr. Annice F. Jeffreys Myers and Jefferson Myers attended the NAWSA convention and extended an invitation to the association to hold its 1905 annual convention in Portland, the site of the Lewis and Clark Centennial Exposition. NAWSA leaders agreed for a number of reasons: first, they wanted to hold their initial convention on the West Coast; second, they wanted to take control of the upcoming 1906 Oregon campaign; and third, they hoped to increase interest in working for woman suffrage in Washington by drawing women from the Evergreen State to Portland. Delegates from the East would travel north to the Puget Sound region, where they would wake Washington women from their slumber. In short, the Portland convention would galvanize suffragists in the region, including the women of California.[5] The 1906 campaign drew many NAWSA speakers from across the country, including Emma, giving her the opportunity to reacquaint herself with national leaders and spend time in the field honing her skills.

Four years later, Washington State became the first in a series of western states to enfranchise their women in the twentieth century, and Emma celebrated this achievement. The triumph in Washington can be credited in part to the campaign directed by Emma, which consisted of "*partly speech making and partly still hunting.*"[6] Rather than relying solely upon the quiet methods of the past, WESA's president began to slowly endorse and use more modern tactics, such as publicity stunts and parades with a womanly twist, often referred to as more masculine techniques. Younger women who favored new techniques dove in, advertising the movement in new and unique ways. For instance, Dr. Cora Smith Eaton climbed Mount Rainier and drove a "Votes for Women" banner into its peak.[7] Emma used a special train, which she called the "Suffrage Special," to transport NAWSA convention delegates from Spokane to Seattle; along the way, they conducted a whistle-stop campaign. Suffragists held open air rallies at the Alaska-Pacific-Yukon Exposition and even participated in parades with a feminine touch. The following year, California suffragists successfully built on the newer methods used first in Washington State.[8]

Although Washington suffragists were finally victorious in 1910, the triumph came at a cost. In 1909, Emma and NAWSA split when, in her opinion, the organization dealt with what she believed was a state issue. Rather than concede to its demands, she chose to part ways. Emma later formed her own group called the National Council of Women Voters, another organization associated with a series of NAWSA ruptures.

In the winter of 1906, Emma began organizing and lecturing in Oregon. This was Oregon's third campaign for woman suffrage. In 1884, voters defeated a woman suffrage amendment by a vote of more than two to one. Oregon's second attempt to enfranchise their women in 1900 was much less contentious, as suffragist Abigail Scott Duniway employed the techniques of a still-hunt campaign and corresponded with newspapers, brewers, and the liquor industry to tell them that the women of Oregon did not intend to vote for prohibition if enfranchised. Her techniques boosted support for equal suffrage, but they fell short of winning over a majority of voters.[9] Emma played a crucial role in the state's third try directed by NAWSA, not Duniway.

Duniway remained committed to utilizing the still-hunt technique, but NAWSA's leadership disagreed with her out-of-date strategy. The method, Anthony insisted, was a failed policy. Education and agitation was the winning solution, she argued. Concurring with the veteran, several of Oregon's leading suffragists opposed Duniway's tactics and backed those endorsed by Anthony. Clara B. Colby, who had moved to Portland in 1904, supported national control of the campaign, believing that Duniway's "sharp tongue and inept political management" undermined the efforts of reformers.[10] In 1906, NAWSA took control of the Oregon fight for the franchise.

Colby may have encouraged her old friend to come south and establish suffrage clubs, as she recalled Emma's "strength as an organizer" and remembered how her sweetness, in contrast to Duniway's vinegar, attracted listeners.[11] Emma and Colby's ties went back to the 1890 South Dakota campaign. In January 1906, Colby announced Emma's decision to work in Oregon, reminding *Portland Woman's Tribune* readers of her "national fame" and her ability to convert opponents and make "believers enthusiastic to give and to do." The Pacific Northwest was "very fortunate to have her within call," Colby concluded.[12] Ironically, Emma, a supporter of the still hunt and opponent of campaigns controlled by outsiders, agreed to work in Oregon. More than likely Emma's need for funds overrode her principles, and she went south to earn a paycheck.

She began her tour in Douglas County, situated in the Cascade Mountain range. Even though she had not spoken on the subject for many years, Emma quickly fell back into her routine of organizing clubs and speaking for suffrage; she even brought Henry's sheet music with her and sang at meetings. Emma continued to use the same techniques and rhetoric that had worked so well in South Dakota and the western states she had visited in the 1890s. As expected, she drew the attention of Civil War veterans, who promised their votes for suffrage after hearing her speak at the Soldiers' Home near Roseburg. In every community she visited, she secured the support of its leading men and women.

The snowy winter weather and short days made traveling through Douglas County difficult. Fortunately for Emma, she had worked in similar situations, and the inclement weather did not deter her. In some cases the weather made travel to mountain communities impossible, and she had to skip at least one town on her route because the stagecoach driver refused to ferry people up muddy, winding, and poorly maintained roads. Some drivers, however, plowed through ankle deep mud to take Emma to her next stop. Where no drivers could be had, the husbands of suffragists hitched their teams and ferried the organizer to her appointments. Emma appreciated the kindness of these men and told Colby, with whom she corresponded with on a regular basis, "It shows they are in dead earnest in their support of woman suffrage."[13] On the road for hours each day, she made the most of her time by speaking with her drivers and fellow passengers about the upcoming campaign. Traveling to Stephens, she struck up a conversation with her driver about equal suffrage, and he told Emma to tell Oregon women to "jes go an' vote and the Oregon fellers wouldn't say nothin' to 'em."[14] After her tour of Douglas County, she traveled through Lane and Marion counties.

Just as she had in Montana, Emma began to wonder why Laura Gregg, NAWSA's campaign manager, had sent her to Marion County, as she encountered great difficulty in arousing the slumbering suffragists. Few turned out to hear her lectures, and in the case of Gervais, not one person came to her meeting. So instead of speaking in a crowded hall, she addressed a small group that had gathered for a party at a local reverend's home.[15] Discouraged, Emma felt her efforts were futile, but Gregg disagreed. She knew that the county would be difficult to organize, but she believed that the region was important and needed to be organized "by one who could win the people."[16]

Recognizing Emma's strength as an organizer and perhaps recalling events in South Dakota, where she—not Emma—had offended foreigners, NAWSA president Anna Howard Shaw decided to send Emma to Astoria and Seaside, where immigrant voters had supposedly defeated the issue in earlier elections.[17] To galvanize support among middle- and upper-class women in the second largest city in Oregon, Shaw directed Emma to hold parlor meetings. She did not expect much from the women in Astoria and told Emma not to worry. "In the first place the people are largely foreigners and they are not at all an intellectual lot of people, especially at Astoria. . . . I know you will do your very best licks at it and if you cannot work it up nobody can."[18]

As predicted, Emma succeeded. Emma boasted of her achievements in both communities to Shaw, who was pleased with the outcome. Readers of the *Portland Woman's Tribune* learned that she had impressed both immigrants and the middle- and upper-class women of Astoria to come together to work for the cause. "Astoria will always remain as a bright spot in my memory," she wrote.[19] The women of Seaside also responded positively to Emma's style, and she proclaimed that she would "never forget" her visit to the community.[20]

Rainier and Prineville probably also stood out in her memory. When Emma arrived in Rainier she learned that the "saloon element" had hired a hit man to kill two of the city's "best citizens," including the man who had arranged Emma's visit; given the outrage over the incident, everyone agreed it would be better for Emma to return when things calmed down.[21] After a fourteen-hour stagecoach ride to Prineville, Emma learned that its local anti-suffragists declared they would have her arrested if she collected money for the campaign after her meeting. "A peculiar town ordinance made this possible," reported the *Woman's Journal*. After checking ordinances, a local judge declared the action lawful. Even though she might be arrested and jailed, Emma refused to let the anti-suffragists intimidate her. "This trip had consumed so much money and time that I had no idea of leaving the town without some contribution to the cause," she wrote, and she did not leave until she had collected $25. Eventually, Emma won over the entire town, and ministers reportedly cancelled Sunday evening services, encouraging their flocks to attend Emma's lecture in the courthouse.[22]

Pleased with Emma's ability to overcome such odds, Shaw assigned her to The Dalles, where she would work the polls and distribute leaflets to voters. NAWSA's president sent Emma there because she needed workers at the polls who would not offend male voters. Shaw directed all suffragists to act womanly and sweet, in contrast to the bluntness and sarcasm of Duniway. She believed that the city would be a difficult place to sway male voters, but if anyone could do it, Emma could. "We need our best soldiers in the hardest place and I want you there," Shaw confided in her.[23] The measure failed miserably, however.[24]

Emma returned to Washington in June and began working as a suffrage organizer and lecturer; by the fall, she was president of WESA. At the time, Henry worked for the Northern Pacific Railroad as an agent in Melmont, while Emma rented an apartment for $25 a month in Tacoma and saw her husband on the weekends.[25] Because of his railroad connections,

Henry provided his wife with a railroad pass, which she used to travel across the state. As president, she dedicated her first year to forming local and county associations across the western half of the state and establishing a strong organization. She wrote a new state constitution and came up with a system for paying dues and pledges to the association. Emma also convinced many women to accept leadership positions within WESA. She found the task relatively easy because many of her former colleagues or close friends had moved to Washington. Elizabeth Murray Wardall and her husband, Alonzo, who had been active in the 1890 South Dakota woman suffrage movement, had relocated to King County.[26] Elizabeth agreed to serve as chair of parlor meetings, and Dr. Cora Smith Eaton, formerly of North Dakota, headed up the enrollment committee and later served as WESA treasurer.[27]

Thrilled with the changes that she witnessed, Emma encouraged the Washington Equal Suffrage Association to invite NAWSA to hold its convention in Seattle during the 1909 Alaska-Yukon-Pacific Exposition. She explained how the event would help suffragists. "The people in the country and small towns look to the metropolis for their style and manner of thinking, and we would make public sentiment faster."[28] The executive board unanimously agreed with their leader, and Emma traveled to Chicago in February 1907 to extend an invitation to NAWSA.[29] Interestingly, Emma, who had close ties to eastern leaders and to President Shaw, had not considered that such an invitation might prove to be a major blunder, as Duniway found out.[30] The 1909 meeting would permanently scar Emma's reputation.

By the fall of 1907, interest in equal suffrage had blossomed across the western half of the state. Ellen S. Leckenby, encouraged by all the good news, believed that dormant suffragists had finally reawakened. "Six years ago Mrs. Spinning and myself were about the only officers in the state; now look at our splendid executive board," she bragged.[31] Many of these changes could be linked to Emma's leadership, as Dr. Eaton explained to Henry: "Your wife grows upon us and every day we realize more and more what she means to the state of Washington. She has the mind of a statesman, the manners of a gentlewoman and the persistence of an English bulldog, although nothing in her appearance and manners would lead you to suspect this latter."[32] Over the course of the Washington campaign, Dr. Eaton and Emma became close friends, because of the doctor's unwavering loyalty and dedication to Emma's orders. Dr. Eaton also probably recalled Emma's 1895 visit to North Dakota and the overwhelmingly positive reaction she received from both sides of the camp.[33] Unlike some members of WESA's executive board, Dr. Eaton consistently praised Emma's efforts, even if they were out of step with the majority.

Emma devised several plans to secure equal suffrage in the Evergreen State. Perhaps recalling the strength of the immigrant voters in South Dakota, who, suffragists believed, voted against women's enfranchisement, she intended to reach out to this group. WESA's president estimated that one-quarter of voters in Washington were of Scandinavian descent and believed that an alliance with the ethnic group would be crucial if Washington women were to regain the ballot. To "outwit the wily politician," she planned to bring Finnish and Norwegian women to Washington to convince voters of the benefits of suffrage in their nations of origin. Both countries had recently enfranchised their women: Finland in 1906 and Norway in 1907. She also hoped to raise enough money to invite Baroness Aleksandra Gripenberg, the leader of the Women's Rights Society of Finland, to the state. The idea seemed fool-proof, and Emma concluded, "If we can carry out this plan, the politicians will not dare fight us."[34] Shaw agreed with Emma's assessment and concluded that Gripenberg would be "more helpful than a radical socialist" from Finland as she subscribed to more conservative ideas about womanhood supported by WESA's president.[35]

In 1907, Emma accepted the presidency for a second year, although she had considered withdrawing her name because of the high costs that she and Henry had borne over the previous year. She consented to another term because NAWSA promised to provide assistance to the state, but she held off on plans to organize eastern Washington until she had received funds from the group, which had promised to send $250 for organization expenses if WESA could raise an equal amount.[36]

While she waited, Emma began establishing the ties that were essential to the passage of woman suffrage in 1910, in particular the "progressive-farmer-labor coalition."[37] Emma recognized that their support was crucial. As she learned in South Dakota, lack of support from the farmers and union men, who had formed their own party, was one of the reasons the equal suffrage amendment lost. On January 8, she spoke at the state convention of the Washington State Federation of Labor, then meeting in the Independent Order of Odd Fellows Hall in Tacoma. After hearing her address, delegates unanimously supported a resolution on suffrage, which was reportedly the first time they had endorsed the issue.[38] Dr. Luema G. Johnson, chair of the WESA labor unions committee, credited Emma's speech for the victory and expressed her happiness over the vote, writing, "The *resolutions went thru without a dissenting voice. Hallelujah!* Hurrah!"[39]

Emma also tried to establish alliances and networks with other occupational groups and women's associations; coalition building was a popular tactic employed by Progressive reformers.[40] She corresponded with clergy members, teachers, doctors, and nurses of Washington and encouraged those who taught, proselytized, or cured people to form auxiliaries of the WESA. Over the year, she met with numerous women's organizations, including the WCTU, the Washington Federation of Women's Clubs, the Daughters of Norway, the P. E. Club, the Nurses' Reception, and the Woman's Relief Corps, hoping to encourage their support of the measure.[41]

By February, Emma made her way to eastern Washington, where she shared her battle plans with a reporter from the *Spokane Evening Chronicle*. The campaign, she said, "will be carried on in a woman's way. We do not seek in any way to usurp the privileges of men. We are womanly and the more womanly we can be the better for our cause."[42]

While there, Emma established a relationship with the wealthy and flamboyant May Arkwright Hutton, and with her support Emma formed the Spokane Equal Suffrage Association. Born in Ohio, Hutton married twice before the age of twenty-three. She moved to Idaho in 1883, where she met her third husband, Al Hutton. The couple struck it rich when their shares in an Idaho silver mine paid off. Compared to the ladylike Emma, Hutton did not meet Victorian standards of womanliness. Her weight of around 225 pounds, her dress, and her limited education highlighted Hutton's lack of feminine traits.[43] She often called attention to herself by wearing a zebra-striped coat and driving a red automobile. The Spokane press was infatuated with her and published numerous stories about her, prompting Al Hutton to remind his wife not to "make an unholy show of yourself!" as many of the stories "made her appear a buffoon."[44] In addition to her interest in suffrage, she supported the Democratic Party, bringing to Washington a partisan ideology she had forged in Idaho. For a time, the relationship between Hutton and Emma was friendly. They corresponded frequently, and Hutton reminded Emma to "take good care of yourself, because we need you and cannot win without you."[45]

After Emma's visit to eastern Washington in 1908, membership rolls for the association grew to one thousand members. Henry bragged about his wife's achievement, saying that her victory in Spokane was "the biggest thing yet."[46] Leckenby asked her, "Don't you feel as though you had made a triumphal march through the state?" Comparing her to Civil War General William Tecumseh Sherman, she inquired, "Do you whistle [the Civil War song] 'Marching through Georgia?'"[47]

By contrast, others within the organization began to grow restless with their president. Dr. Ida N. McIntire of Everett, chair of WESA's women's club committee and a member of its executive committee, criticized Emma's lack of management and executive skills, which differed from the organizational skills Emma had mastered years earlier. She had been working as an organizer for years, but this was Emma's first opportunity to lead an entire state association. According to McIntire she did not know how to even properly run a meeting of the executive board. Instead, the meetings were "a sort of mutual admiration society" for Emma's accomplishments. Emma had allocated forty-five minutes to reading letters that sang her praises, "the gist of which had already appeared in the Bulletin," but she refused to allow McIntire or Dr. Johnson the opportunity to complete their reports. McIntire gave up an entire day of work and wages to attend these meetings, where she heard nothing but praise for Emma, which left her feeling "disgusted." She admitted that Emma was a "first class" organizer, but "as an Executive I feel that you have not lived up to your opportunity."[48]

Emma either suffered from self-esteem issues, which she had struggled with throughout the 1890s, or she simply had a large ego. Given the dearth of sources, it is impossible to precisely determine the cause of her ailment. Although she had been the most popular organizer and most successful fundraiser for NAWSA in the late nineteenth century, she sometimes had little confidence in her abilities, as indicated by her constant need for reaffirmation of her work as an organizer for Catt. Emma frequently looked to others for reassurance that she met their standards. On the other hand, her ego may have been bruised by the lack of attention from NAWSA leaders. By 1908, Emma's concerns had manifested in her governing style.

In August, when Emma was at home canning, sewing, and resting, she began pondering whether she would continue working as president of WESA. Organizing, not presiding, was her passion. McIntire's words had gotten to her, and money problems continued to plague the DeVoes. She confided all of these problems to her closest ally, Dr. Eaton, who encouraged her to continue in spite of the criticism leveled against her. "I realize it will be no easy task, on the contrary, a great undertaking and difficult one, and subject to criticism from those who are not helping. But my estimate is that you are more than equal to whatever comes and that you are not doing this for praise nor for profit and that if you take the crown, you will also carry the cross," she wrote.[49] Depressed, she offered May Arkwright Hutton the presidency, which Hutton declined, saying, "No woman that I know of can fill that position but Emma Smith DeVoe."[50]

While pondering the decision before her, Emma established a high school girls' suffrage society in Seattle.[51] She hoped that other young women would catch the reform bug. They had different ideas about how to effectively reach voters, and she believed that they could introduce new ideas in the state to electrify the movement.[52]

At the October WESA convention, delegates learned that more than 1,500 people belonged to the association, which represented a gain of more than one thousand members from the previous year. Of all the states in the Union, Washington reported the largest increase in membership.[53] Pleased with her successes, delegates offered Emma another presidential term. Although she and her husband struggled to make ends meet, Emma probably decided to accept the post for another year because she and Henry believed that victory was close, and she had worked so hard to revive interest in the cause. For some time, she had been meeting privately with George F. Cotterill, state senator of Seattle, who drafted an amendment to be introduced at the next session of the state legislature, and Emma deserved and hoped to revel in the glory of having put a fifth star on the suffrage flag.[54]

Members disagreed, however, over which approach they should take. Younger women preferred to use the radical tactics of the suffragettes in England: heckling legislators and holding mass demonstrations.[55] The older women, including Emma, believed in the importance of tried and true tactics like signing petitions and writing letters to their state representatives and senators.[56] Eventually, Emma's ideas won out, and the women of WESA began gathering signatures for a petition. The petitions showed the state legislature that the public—the male voters—supported the issue. To ensure success of the suffrage bill, they sent all of the petitions with 10,000 signatures to each legislator instead of presenting them all at once to the state legislature as they had in the past. State representatives and senators "received letters by the dozen" to vote in favor of the issue.[57]

When the 1909 legislative session opened in January, Emma and long-time Washington suffragist Carrie M. Hill traveled to Olympia to set up WESA headquarters at the Horr residence on Main Street. Suffragists rotated in and out of circulation, but Emma remained until the bill passed.[58] Many of the women who reported to the suffrage headquarters were young, attractive, and inexperienced. Fearing that these younger women might use radical techniques like their English sisters, Emma advised them otherwise. Respectability was the key to winning support for the cause. Recognizing the conservative nature of the Washington State legislature, Emma told them to look and behave as respectable women, for she believed that headlines splashed across the state depicting Washington suffragists as shrieking, hysterical, kicking suffragettes would do immeasurable harm. Instead, she insisted that the lobbyists follow one of her basic principle to win over legislators: "Always be good natured and cheerful."

She also directed the women not to insist that the amendment pass, but simply to ask legislators for their support. "We are not trying to convert the members to women suffrage. We merely ask that the proposition be submitted to the voters of the state," she explained.[59] The tactics employed by Emma and her army surprised legislators who expected argumentative and combative women, like the women who had stormed England's House of Commons, not the sweet, smiling girls who greeted them at least a half dozen times a day. When a reporter asked suffragist Katherine Smith whether it was fair to send "defenseless legislators" new lobbyists every few days, she wryly replied, "Well, it is a little like politics isn't it?"[60]

By January, the house had passed the suffrage bill. When the bill arrived in the senate, cracks began to appear within the suffrage ranks. Emma wanted to hold off on a vote until she was certain that they had a two-thirds majority. May Arkwright Hutton, on the other hand, pushed ahead. Senator George U. Piper later criticized her for being pushy and demanding a vote on the issue. Her unladylike behavior reflected poorly on the suffrage lobby and angered Emma. She later explained that Hutton's "aggressiveness was such that it nearly lost us our success in the state."[61] Eaton implied later, in a gossipy letter to Carrie Chapman Catt, that Hutton talked of buying the votes of five senators at $250 a piece.[62] Nonetheless, Piper secured passage of the bill in late February. Women then seated in the gallery "fluttered their handkerchiefs and silently left." Emma, Jennie Jewett, and Ellen Leckenby walked the bill from the senate to the office of the governor to attend the small ceremony to mark the signing of the woman suffrage bill. There, they met Acting Governor Marion E. Hay. (Governor Samuel G. Cosgrove was ill.) He signed the bill, shook hands with the suffragists, and presented Emma with the pen as a symbol of their victory.[63]

Emma attributed the passage of the bill to the methods employed by her soldiers at Olympia. "Every legislator with whom I have spoken has praised the manner of conducting the campaign and the intelligent, tactful manner of the women who have urged the bill. I believe it is true that we have shown the new type of womanhood at the capitol this winter," she said. More importantly, she added, "There were no hysterics either during the passage of the bill today or during the campaign."[64] Washington women benefited from Emma's insistence on the use of womanly techniques, which were at odds with the methods then being employed by militant suffragists. Police did not arrest one suffragist, and the reformers had not threatened any legislators.

Emma did not mention Hutton and the mistake that nearly cost them the bill, but she intended to punish Hutton by withdrawing an invitation to her to speak at the 1909 NAWSA convention. (Presumably, Hutton had been invited to participate when she and Emma were on speaking terms.) Kate M. Gordon, NAWSA's corresponding secretary, advised Dr. Eaton and Emma to let her speak. "[Your] allowing me to extend an invitation to her for a twenty minute address at an afternoon session will make you appear as though you had not reported the situation and that you were acting magnanimously." Dr. Eaton agreed, saying, "It would mean less publicity to have her speak than not to have her; better let it pass."[65] Emma put her foot down and refused to budge, telling Gordon that Hutton should not be invited.[66] Emma's tyrannical efforts would eventually prove to be her downfall.

Hutton, put off by how Emma had treated her, was soon locked in a struggle for power with the older organizer. The conflict escalated when Hutton received word that she would be eliminated from the suffrage work "if I did not do as Mrs. DeVoe dictated."[67] She and younger suffragists questioned whether they would support Emma for a fourth term. This group of women, called "the insurgents," wished to elect a society woman for state president and amend the state suffrage constitution to forbid the president from receiving a salary. If WESA made such changes, Emma could not continue to serve as president because she was not independently wealthy. The opposition movement made her extremely vulnerable as she depended on women of wealth—many of the insurgent women from Spokane—for funds.[68]

An independent president would be beneficial, the insurgents insisted. A paid worker might not fully support the campaign because her livelihood rested on the battle for woman suffrage continuing, not ending. In short, it was in Emma's best interest to keep voters from supporting suffrage. "If we are to be victorious in this state," Hutton explained, "the best women with the best judgment must be in charge; women who are sincere in their efforts to carry the day for woman suffrage. . . . I do not consider those who make a profession of, and earn a livelihood, in any reform, [to be] the best elements for success."[69]

Two months before the election, members of WESA were asked to sign a pledge supporting Emma's election as president for a subsequent term. Younger suffragists refused to throw their support behind the incumbent and believed that the attempt to thwart the will of some of the WESA delegates smacked of politics. Emma lacked scruples, they concluded. Edith Jarmuth, a potential candidate for the office of president according to the Washington press, stood in opposition to "the preparing of secret slates, and 'discrediting' or 'eliminating' workers in a wholesale manner to the detriment of the suffrage cause" for Emma's economic benefit.[70] Emma was not as sweet-natured, virtuous, or earnest as she had led many to believe. According to her critics, she was a politician.

When the *Seattle Times* ran an interview with Leonia W. Brown, president of the Green Lake Political Equality Club, she said what nearly every suffragist thought about Emma. Was it wise to have "a state president [who is] a professional suffragist," a woman who follows the money from "state to state"?[71] Henry, who was particularly protective of his wife, expressed outrage that "my wife should be bandied about as a professional politician." Brown had insulted his wife, and he feared that the smear campaign would do irreparable damage to his wife's reputation.[72] Those who opposed Emma would stop at nothing to see that she was thrown out of office. He believed that they might offer "fake dues, for fake clubs, with fake members." Fearing the worst, he told Dr. Eaton to "*never* compromise with traitors."[73]

Hutton intended to topple Emma's administration by bringing a large delegation with voting powers to the state convention. She paid dues to the Spokane Equal Suffrage Association for her friends in Seattle and

Oregon and even proposed to pay dues for as many as six people her friends believed could be trusted to serve as delegates. By June, her club had four hundred members, and believing that she had enough votes to oust Emma, Hutton offered Carrie Hill the presidency. Emma would not be left in the cold, however. Hutton intended to offer her the position of organizer with a salary, "but under the control of an executive board who would be absolutely just and fair-minded, and whose interest for ultimate success would be unquestioned," she explained.[74]

Fearing that she would not only lose her executive position to another but also the glory of having secured a suffrage victory, Emma thought of asking NAWSA president Shaw to come and speak on her behalf. Hill thought that would be "bad form" and advised Emma to leave things as they were. Dr. Eaton offered two options that might work in Emma's favor. They could pack the convention with supporters by "splitting up our clubs into clubs of 4 and sending every member to the state convention!!!!" Emma could also use heavy handed tactics at the meeting, forcing the insurgents to "walk out," and form a new suffrage organization.[75]

Dr. Eaton, at Emma's urging, tried to handle the matter with as little confrontation as possible by refusing the dues mailed in by Hutton. She returned the funds, and then committed blackmail, perhaps hoping that Hutton would back down if threatened by something that might tarnish her reputation. Dr. Eaton told her, "I believe you are ineligible to membership in the Washington Equal Suffrage Association because of your habitual use of profane and obscene language and of your record in Idaho as shown by pictures and other evidence placed in my hands by persons who are familiar with your former life and reputation." Eaton was referring to Hutton's swearing at the capitol. The photos and other documents she held allegedly proved that she ran a house of prostitution and that Idahoans knew her by the name "Bootleg Mary." Emma told this story to members of the board in a futile attempt to undermine Hutton's support by younger suffragists. If Hutton demanded that her dues be accepted by WESA, Dr. Eaton threatened to make the evidence public.[76] Hutton refused to be blackmailed by lies and intended to be seated.[77] A man identified as Mr. Savage was sent to Idaho to investigate Eaton's charges and found nothing to support the allegations.[78]

Without any resolution to the conflict, Emma greeted delegates for the NAWSA convention as they reached Spokane and welcomed them onboard the "Suffrage Special" train. Emma had secured the train to transport

NAWSA delegates across the Evergreen State to Seattle. This was the first time a train had been used by NAWSA for such a purpose. At each of the stops, well-known woman suffragists such as Florence Kelley, Charlotte Perkins Gilman, NAWSA president Anna Howard Shaw, and Emma spoke from the train's rear platform, which was decorated with flags and yellow banners calling for "Votes for Women." Along the way, hundreds of people surrounded the train to hear these speakers. Emma would give a short speech and then present the national leaders. Listeners responded positively by offering the delegates fresh flowers and fruit.[79] Emma's plan to win the hearts and minds of Washingtonians through womanly, not militant, tactics seemed to be working.

Washington suffragists benefited from the growing militancy then appearing in the English movement and splashed across newspapers in the United States. When, on June 29th—just days before the NAWSA convention—British suffrage leader Emmeline G. Pankhurst slapped a police officer and was then arrested, newspapers across the globe carried the story. The editor of the *Seattle Post-Intelligencer*, a supporter of woman suffrage, printed the article next to a story about the American suffragists then meeting in Washington. The headline read, "Suffragists in Session; Suffragettes Go to Jail," suggesting that American suffragists sought the ballot in lawful ways by legal action; English women, however, acted in unlawful ways, and the police imprisoned them for their violent methods. Readers of the *Seattle Post-Intelligencer* could not help but view the Washington and English suffragists as different.[80]

The image of the sweet-natured suffragist was shattered soon after, as readers learned what had unfolded at the WESA convention. When Hutton and her camp arrived at the Plymouth Congregational Church, Dr. Eaton refused to seat Hutton's delegates, as she had promised. Pandemonium broke out, with delegates from both sides calling each other names. Some shouted "thieves," while others yelled "liars." Newspapers across the country reported that "there was hysterical weeping and screaming."[81] Some of the insurgents were locked in a chamber and escaped through a window. Finally someone called the police. Between all the hissing and cat calls, Emma threw up her hands and sat down. Eventually, the insurgents walked out, and delegates reelected Emma as their president.[82]

The insurgents appealed their case to NAWSA officers, hoping that they would be recognized by the state association and that a new election could be held. The fact that NAWSA agreed to investigate the matter angered

Emma, who believed that she alone had the authority to make decisions for the state and that NAWSA would never snub her as they slighted Duniway in Portland. Her friends from the East, however, put her on the spot. Asked to testify, she told the board that "we could not agree, and I consider the action of the state convention a closed incident." A solution, she suggested, would be the formation of a new organization by the insurgents. Members of NAWSA's board found her testimony lacking. One woman said, "We have learned some facts from the gentleman from Spokane [David C. Coates, one of Hutton's supporters], but from the dear lady who has tried to pour oil upon the troubled waters we have learned nothing." When Dr. Eaton took the stand, the board found that she would also not provide much detail.[83] They concluded that Emma would have to either patch things up with the insurgents or lose her salary from NAWSA. Emma believed that she had treated the insurgents fairly and had nothing to apologize for. So she refused, and NAWSA fired her.[84]

This event permanently scarred Emma's reputation. Suffragists had previously whispered behind closed doors that she was jealous and wanted things her way, but these statements had never been printed in newspapers, nor had suffragists from across the country seen Emma in this light. Her actions in Seattle proved that she was ambitious and would go to any lengths to remain president; NAWSA treasurer Harriet Taylor Upton, who heard testimony from both sides, declared that Hutton "was not the only prostitute who was in Seattle during the summer nor was she the only one who had her reputation soiled who was attached to the association."[85] Shaw told stories about Emma to Maud C. Stockwell, president of the Minnesota Woman Suffrage Association, leading her to conclude that Emma was "an ambitious, dishonest woman" who "hypnotized our dear Doctor [Eaton]," who had lived in Minnesota and worked with Stockwell.[86]

Emma was particularly upset by NAWSA's action. NAWSA president Shaw and other members of the board had been her close friends for years, and they humiliated her in her home state. Emma believed her guests treated their hosts as "spoiled children" and improperly chastised them for what occurred at the state convention. She told the *Seattle Times*, I "have never before been forced to submit to the ridicule and dictation of any executive board, who had no business to take a hand in affairs that did not concern them."[87] Nevertheless, Emma quickly recovered and found herself in control of WESA at the same time that Hutton formed a competing organization, the Washington Political Equality League. Emma intended to carry out the ladylike campaign that she had envisioned.

Whenever she spoke to the press, Emma emphasized the methods that she advocated and pursued. Emma told *Collier's* that she expected the electorate to vote in favor of the woman suffrage bill in 1910, and "when we do [win]—it will be a triumph for strictly feminine methods." This strategy included never challenging those with opposing views. Instead, she directed suffragists to ignore those with different perspectives. "If we can't, we meet it with sincere and tolerant consideration, or—in the case of irrationally prejudiced persons whom it is impossible to answer—with good-humored raillery," she said.[88]

One component of Emma's plan was the publication of the *Washington Women's Cook Book*. "We had two ideas in view in this. One was, of course, the money and the other was the vindication of the slur put upon suffragists that they have no domestic traits," Emma explained.[89] Speaking against those who said that the publication of the cookbook was a political trick, Emma said that the motives of the association were misunderstood. "'Not that I say'—and Mrs. DeVoe's eyes twinkled, though her smile was demure—'that the book hasn't made us friends among the men.'"[90]

In the same article, *Collier's* reported on the publicity stunts of the Washington suffragists, which they called "a new style of approach in the fight for the equal ballot." Washington suffragists easily adopted a popular male style of politics, consisting of tours, slogans, human interest stories, and billboard advertisements.[91] During the campaign, Dr. Eaton, a mountain climber, erected a "Votes for Women" banner on the top of Mount Rainier. That same summer, the Kangley sisters (Helen, Gertrude, Louise, and Lucy) tried to repeat Dr. Eaton's success, but a blizzard kept them from doing so.[92] Suffragist Adella Parker, head of wesa's publicity bureau, participated in a suffrage play, "How He Lied to Her Husband," and billboards in thirty-five towns read, "Give our women a Square Deal," recalling the progressive agenda of former President Teddy Roosevelt.[93] "Despite the masculine use of publicity," Eaton wrote, "it was essentially a womanly campaign."[94]

Throughout the 1910 campaign, Emma emphasized the importance of personal contacts, a component of her reliance on still-hunt tactics; she told wesa members to ask for the vote, but not to demand the ballot. "Begin my girls with the men you love and who love you. Tell them you want to vote and why. Pledge them to vote Amendment No. 6, and pledge them each to convert one other man who in turn shall convert his man," said Emma.[95] Women sought the support of "her neighbor, her doctor, her grocer, her laundrywagon driver, the postman, and even the man who collected the garbage," recalled Dr. Eaton.[96]

Emma encouraged suffragists to hold Woman's Days at county and state fairs, as she had in South Dakota, and she agreed to serve as president of the Woman's Day at the Puyallup Valley Fair in September 1909. State Senator William H. Paulhamus, a founder of the fair, moved to Washington from Aberdeen, South Dakota, in 1890. Recalling the crowds at the South Dakota Woman's Day and perhaps hoping to draw record-breaking attendance, he encouraged the board of directors to establish a similar day and appointed Emma president of the day's events.[97]

On October 14th, six thousand people, including Governor Hay and his wife, Lizzie—vice president of Woman's Day—attended the fair. Attendees crowded into the amphitheater to hear Emma, Clara Colby, Governor Hay, and Senator Paulhamus speak. In the afternoon, bands, a drum corps, and schoolchildren marched from downtown Puyallup to the fairgrounds, just as they had in Aberdeen. Floats peppered the procession. Marching in parades had provoked tremendous opposition within the American woman suffrage movement in the twentieth century; former NAWSA president Catt, for example, opposed their use, saying, "We do not have to win sympathy by parading ourselves like the street cleaning department."[98] The Puyallup fair parade did not spark debate among Washington suffragists, however, as they agreed in advance that they would not march. Militants, not respectable women, marched.[99] Fearing that she would be linked to the suffragettes of England, Emma rode in an automobile back to the fairgrounds.[100]

As Emma had hoped, the parade and its float demonstrated the femininity of the participants and countered the idea that granting women the ballot would desex them. The suffrage float included six women wearing white gowns, which implied that women were moral and more virtuous than men, and yellow sashes, which represented woman suffrage.[101] Four of the women represented the "free" states of Wyoming, Utah, Colorado, and Idaho. One woman with bound hands acted as Washington, while the Goddess of Liberty stood nearby to free Lady Washington from the shackles of slavery.[102]

Although Emma experimented with some of the suffragette's publicity-generating methods, she publicly rejected the more militant methods that

Washington voters and the press objected to.[103] When Emmeline Pan-khurst toured the United States in 1909, Emma carefully differentiated the suffragists of Washington from the militant English suffragettes who smashed windows, attacked guards, and destroyed government property. "We will not fight. We do not have to fight. We've obtained everything we want. The last legislature treated us very courteously. We are working now, not fighting," she proclaimed.[104] Violent techniques ran counter to the claim presented by Emma that women were naturally pacifists and would not vote for war.

In the midst of the campaign, Governor Hay appointed Emma to the Conference on Uniform Laws called by President William H. Taft, which was meeting in Washington, DC, in January 1910. This trip to the U.S. capital helped to reestablish Emma's reputation as a leader who could get results through conciliatory tactics. As an example, the Washington State press bragged that Emma beat NAWSA at its own game through the use of feminine techniques. At the Capitol for only a short time, she managed to convince Idaho Senator William E. Borah to introduce a woman suffrage resolution on the floor of the United States Senate; Idaho Governor James H. Brady, who was also in town, probably also played a part in Borah's decision to bring the issue to the Senate. NAWSA, which had its own capi-tol lobbyists and had spent "thousands of dollars" on a national campaign, had not been able to do so, but the press reported Emma, who "quietly sought" the support of Senator Borah, succeeded.[105] Borah, a notorious womanizer, was most likely flattered by Emma, who used her womanli-ness to sway the junior senator.[106]

Emma was a celebrity in the capital; she was one of only several women delegates at the conference. After arriving in Washington, "messages began pouring in" for Emma at her hotel. Maryland and DC suffragists asked her to attend receptions and give how-to addresses on securing passage of woman suffrage bills in the legislature. Many were eager to learn how Emma had persuaded the Washington State legislature to pass a woman suffrage bill at a time when the issue seemed to be so unpopular.[107]

Aside from meeting with suffragists, Emma cultivated new friendships with Idaho Governor Brady and Senator Weldon B. Heyburn, both of whom belonged to the Republican Party. Both admitted that the Wash-ington campaign held their interest and, like Borah, offered Emma their support in the final months leading up to the election.[108] On her way home Emma stopped in Boise for one week. She stayed with Governor Brady and told him of her plans to create an advisory committee for the WESA, just as she had hoped to institute in South Dakota in 1898. The advisors would help her solicit funds from outside the state, stump for suffrage, and identify speakers who might sway voters. While in Idaho, Emma met with many of the friends she had made in 1895, including William Balderston, who promised her that they would raise the funds to send a woman to Washington.[109]

Over the course of the week, Emma convinced Brady to chair the committee.[110] Later, she asked the governors of the other suffrage states to join. These executives were important spokesmen for votes for women because they could attest to the benefits of woman suffrage in their states, where women had voted from fourteen to forty-one years. Governors James Brady of Idaho, John F. Shafroth of Colorado, Bryant B. Brooks of Wyoming, and William Spry of Utah, as well as Judge Ben Lindsey of Colorado, and Carrie Chapman Catt, the only woman on the council, joined Emma's committee.[111]

Although she had secured the support from these four governors and the senators from Idaho, Borah and Heyburn, the men from Idaho continually disappointed her. Brady was one of the strongest proponents of the enfranchisement of Washington women, but he never set foot in the Evergreen State, even though he promised to stump for suffrage in the final months of the campaign. Busy running for reelection in 1910, he explained, "Now, Mrs. DeVoe, I want you to feel that I would come over and help you if I possibly could, but, never in the history of this state has any man had the fight made on him that I have had."[112] Even though he did not make a personal appearance, he declared his support in a letter published by the *Seattle Post-Intelligencer* and paid for twenty thousand copies of a pamphlet, "Greetings from the Enfranchised Women of Idaho to the Women of Washington Seeking Enfranchisement."[113] She also asked Borah to speak at the state fair in 1910, but he declined, complicating Emma's plans.[114]

Although they let her down, Emma used select quotes from Brady and the other governors in her speeches to bolster the cause. She told listeners that, according to Governor Brady, Washington voters would "not hesitate for a moment to grant" woman suffrage if they knew of the "real benefits of equal suffrage." If voters rejected the amendment, Governor Spry encouraged Washington women to move to Utah: "With the experience Utah has had, we should not think for a moment of returning to the male suffrage system." Similar experiences could be found in the neighboring states of Colorado and Wyoming.[115]

Emma spent the remainder of the campaign speaking in favor of woman suffrage across the state while her foot soldiers canvassed their voting precincts.[116] She presided over three Woman's Days at the Walla Walla County Fair, the Puyallup Valley Fair, and the Washington State Fair in Yakima, and gave hundreds of addresses at Grange meetings, union gatherings, and numerous meetings of women's associations, all of which threw support behind the amendment.

Farm and labor support never faltered, thanks to Emma's efforts. Fifteen thousand Grangers supported the cause and raised funds to secure its adoption. To promote the amendment, C.B. Kegley, Master of the Washington State Grange, spoke in favor of women's enfranchisement and his wife, Augusta, allowed her name to be "used in any honorable way to advance the interests and promote the welfare of women."[117] C.B. Kegley believed their causes were intertwined and called every local Grange "an Equal Suffrage Association" and promised that they would "remain so until after the amendment is voted upon."[118] The Washington State Federation of Labor unanimously approved a woman suffrage resolution at their convention in 1910 and pledged to work for women's enfranchisement.[119] Emma appealed directly to labor in her speeches and in published articles, linking the ties between equal suffrage and class issues. (See appendix for an example of these effective arguments.)

Aside from securing the support of farmers, laborers, and women's associations, Emma had met personally with owners of the various state newspapers, asking for their assistance. Sidney A. Perkins, the owner of seven Washington newspapers including the *Tacoma Ledger* and *Tacoma Daily News*, promised his assistance, as did the owner of the *Seattle Post-Intelligencer*.[120] At Emma's urging, the *Tacoma Daily News* held a "Kitchen Contest" in the fall of 1910 designed to engage housewives in the campaign and counter the popular misconception that homes and families would suffer if voters enfranchised women.[121] In September 1910, the *Tacoma Daily News* published a women's edition, with Emma serving as editor-in-chief.[122]

In November 1910, the Washington residents voted in favor of woman suffrage by a margin of nearly two to one, just as Emma had predicted. The womanly methods supported by Emma stood out in the minds of politicians and the press. Governor Hay congratulated WESA's president.

"I desire to compliment you upon your management of the campaign just closed. Few people realize the amount of work being done, but it is very evident that the ladylike, quiet campaign you conducted, with appeals to reason and not to prejudice or passion, is the kind that wins," he wrote. The *Tacoma Ledger* reported that Emma's approach "invited careful thought on the part of the electorate." Her conciliatory tactics did not denounce men "as brutes and oppressors" but "as reasonable beings possessed of a desire to do justice and promote the general welfare." [123] No doubt the increasing militancy in England and the distinctions made between English and Washington suffragists also helped the cause.

The suffrage doldrums that had lasted for fourteen years finally came to an end. Washington women had regained the ballot that they had lost twice, thanks to the campaign Emma had run. Success came at a high price, however. The costs of campaigning emptied her purse, and she was worn out from all of her traveling and speeches.

The *Tacoma News* cited the tremendous odds which Emma and her association had overcome. WESA had little money except for the $500 Catt had donated. The rest of the money dribbled in as women held "cake sales and apron showers." With no funds in the treasury, Emma and the other officers were frugal. Rather than eat in restaurants, they cooked their own meals at their Seattle headquarters. If no one offered Emma a room when traveling, she spent the night at WESA headquarters sleeping on a sofa. "The Washington victory represents sacrifices scarcely believable, not only in money but in time and tense devotion," the *Tacoma News* concluded.[124]

After the passage of woman suffrage in Washington, newspaper reporters asked Emma what she and other women planned to do with the ballot. "We are going to rest and think," she said. "We realize that we are under the scrutiny not only of this state, but of all other states, and our procedure is going to be as deliberate as we can make it." Women voters, she argued, would not seek to "overthrow the laws that have been made by men. We contemplate no sweeping reforms. . . . Most of us have the belief that in many matters pertaining to business affairs and legislation, men are superior." She maintained, however, that Washington women could assist in the "making and enforcement of pure food laws, in sanitation, in legislation pertaining particularly to women and children, in civic beautification, and to a certain extent, in the management of the schools."[125] In short, Emma defined a role for women voters that was nonthreatening to political parties and male voters and consistent with the accepted role of women as municipal housekeepers.

She also planned to dissolve the WESA and create a National Council of Women Voters (NCWV) composed of women from the five equal suffrage states of Wyoming, Colorado, Idaho, Utah, and Washington. Emma's plans to form such an association can be linked to 1908, when she began discussing the idea of creating an "organization of the women of the free states."[126] Unlike NAWSA, this organization would be the first suffrage organization made up entirely of women with full voting privileges—school, municipal, primary, and presidential suffrage. Emma thought that women from the equal suffrage states would have much more leverage over state and national politicians than NAWSA, whose members, she believed, had no political clout because they were not voters.

Emma spent the next few weeks relaxing and then traveled east to Boise, where she arranged a meeting with Brady at the governor's mansion. There, "before the blazing logs in his wide fireplace, around the great table in his stately dining room, and on the wide sunny piazza," she strategized with the governor.[127] Fearing the insurgents would once again attempt to wrest victory from her, they agreed that he would issue the call for the formation of the National Council of Women Voters. Emma probably hoped that doing so would silence critics who believed that she was ambitious and dishonest.

Brady announced his support of Emma's council, stating that "the time has arrived when the enfranchised women of the West should extend a helping hand to their sisters in the eastern and other states in securing the ballot." He urged the governors of Colorado, Utah, Washington, and Wyoming to appoint one delegate to the convention to be held in Tacoma. Brady appointed Margaret S. Roberts to the NCWV. Wyoming's Governor Brooks selected Zell Hart Deming. The governor of Colorado named Mary C. C. Bradford; Susa Young Gates was the Utah delegate; and Virginia Wilson Mason represented Washington.[128]

The plan backfired. Rumors about Emma's politicking rose to the surface soon after Brady made the announcement. Clubwoman Katherine Smith, a member of the insurgents, reported that Emma had been meeting with John Lockwood Wilson, a former U.S. senator and publisher of the *Seattle Post-Intelligencer*. In 1910 he decided that he wanted to run for office again. He reportedly asked Ellen S. Fish, who was president of the Seattle Federation of Women's Clubs, if she could promise the clubwomen's vote; when she said she could not, he met with Emma. Smith inferred that Emma "promised to deliver the whole woman's vote." Smith feared that unless they exposed Emma before the formation of the NCWV, she would in fact do so. According to Smith, Emma had "already got in with the politicians here" and "several of the most prominent think she is a wonder. Of course the fact that she is unscrupulous is no detriment in their eyes."[129]

Smith had several ideas about how to expose Emma. *Seattle Votes for Women,* the *Seattle Times,* and the *Seattle Star* could publish a story about how the WESA leadership lost $1,000 and lied about having their books audited every month. Hutton could also sue Emma for slander for the story that she ran a "bawdy-house" and smuggled "whiskey to imprisoned miners in [her] stockings." Smith urged Hutton to act quickly. "After she is elected to a 'National' presidency she will be a sort of goddess and every-thing that would be said about her after that would be looked upon as spite and jealousy."[130]

Publicly, both questioned Emma's attempts to form the National Council of Women Voters by any means necessary. Hutton told the press that the plan to form NCWV was "a huge joke," and Smith tried to dis-credit Emma by politicizing the council and Emma's plans. The NCWV was, according to Smith, a political party for women that would work against, not with, men.[131]

On January 14th, delegates appointed by the western governors met at the Tacoma home of Virginia Mason, the vice president of the Washing-ton Equal Suffrage Association and the Washington representative, where they created the NCWV and drafted a constitution. Heavy snow prevented Gates and Deming from attending.[132] They also outlined the association's goals: one, to provide encouragement and assistance to other states bat-tling for the ballot; two, to improve conditions in the suffrage states for men, women, children, and the home; and three, to help women obtain justice in political, social, and economic spheres. They elected officers, making Emma their leader.

Her selection raised suspicion. Hutton and Smith concluded that she had rigged the election, even though she was not at Mason's house. Instead, she had chaired the last meeting of WESA at the Tacoma Music Hall. Smith declared that Emma's election was "a framed up affair." Emma denied the allegations: "I did not know that I was to be elected president of the national council. I did not know that I had been elected until the report was read in the meeting." Unable to sway women voters against Emma, Smith told reporters that the new organization was merely a pawn in the "hands of a coterie of politicians."[133]

Later, Mason denied that the delegates participated in a political scheme when selecting the council's president, and she challenged those who questioned Emma's ambitions. "Mrs. DeVoe's [moral] standards are of the highest," she declared. "I wish people could be made to understand the object of the council. It is not political. I would not have gone into it if it were." Mason had not affiliated herself with any political party. She belonged to numerous women's organizations, including the Daughters of the American Revolution and the P.E.O. Sisterhood, and had organized the Nesika Club at her home in 1892.[134] Joining the NCWV was merely an extension of her interests. Women who belonged to the NCWV wanted "cleaner streets, pure food and pure water," she argued, as well as "better conditions for our children."[135] In spite of Mason's protests, Emma's reputation as a politician continued to follow her for many years, to the detriment of the council.

After NCWV had been formed, Brady addressed the council. In his speech, he emphasized two themes: the uniqueness of the West and the importance of the NCWV. He described a plan of work for the council: "The free political atmosphere of the West is good soil for a wider and purer suffrage. You can operate in your sister states—in California, Nevada, Montana—until the swing of a powerful western movement will encircle every commonwealth in the Union." The fact that western women like Emma had experience leading successful campaigns was critical to securing woman suffrage across the United States. Unlike NAWSA, the NCWV could "safeguard others against mistakes, indicate the lines of least resistance, and suggest methods of education and organization which are most potent."[136] Over the next nine years, Emma and her National Council of Women Voters, based out of Tacoma, did just that. They provided assistance in various states through organization and education.

The NCWV and Emma also played an important role in helping to secure a national constitutional amendment to enfranchise women, a movement which was nearly dead until 1913, when the council joined forces with younger suffragists who used militant tactics to draw attention to the suffrage movement. Although Emma opposed such methods, she intended to do all she could to see that she and her council, not the NAWSA, received credit for securing woman suffrage for all American women.

6

THE NINETEENTH AMENDMENT

ON MARCH 22, 1920, FIVE MONTHS BEFORE THE TENNESSEE STATE legislature ratified the Nineteenth Amendment, Washington legislators endorsed the constitutional change. Their action, Emma proclaimed, "all but marks the finish of the work which our forefathers began to make this a perfect representative government, recognizing, at last, that women are people."[1] The support of the Nineteenth Amendment by the Evergreen State was important—it was the last western state and the thirty-fifth state, out of thirty-six, to ratify the amendment. "At last," stated the president of the National Council of Women Voters and head of Washington's ratification effort, the "woman's hour has struck."[2]

Emma and her National Council of Women Voters, a relatively unknown and overlooked association in the suffrage literature, were quite influential in the passage of this constitutional amendment. NCWV leadership, along with countless other suffragists, helped to revive interest in a constitutional amendment. They threw their support behind militant suffragist Alice Paul, head of NAWSA's Congressional Committee and the Congressional Union (CU).[3] NCWV participated in a host of activities in conjunction with the CU, which Paul and Lucy Burns formed in April 1913 solely for working toward the passage of a federal suffrage amendment. NCWV leaders spoke to President Woodrow Wilson, testified in front of the House Rules Committee, organized suffrage demonstrations, and met with congressmen, urging them to support a national amendment enfranchising women. The NCWV's alliance with the CU was an important yet ignored coalition of women increasingly at odds with NAWSA's lack of leadership and plans for action in the nineteen-teens.

From 1904 to 1915, Anna Howard Shaw served as NAWSA president. During her tenure, NAWSA was a relatively quiet force that had not adopted a national strategy to achieve votes for women. Conflict reigned under her administration, and NAWSA suffered from factionalism that festered during her final five years in office. The CU and NCWV emerged out of this tension. "Easily prejudiced" and often "aroused to hostility," Shaw greeted "any and all signs of awakening initiative in the ranks," like the CU, "as potential insurgency." Her behavior alienated many longtime supporters of the cause, including Emma.[4]

The CU and the NCWV made an interesting pair. The women of the enfranchised states and its leader did not necessarily support the militant methods employed by Paul and her supporters nor her meddling in state affairs, but they agreed that it was important for all American women to be enfranchised. Both recognized the importance of the western women voters in the push for a federal amendment. The NCWV and their president in particular relied on tactics successfully used in the West and adopted from their western experiences and the biases of western male voters. Regionalism, therefore, played a role in the shaping of battle plans to win passage of a suffrage amendment. Their alliance was short-lived, however. Once Catt took over the reins of NAWSA's leadership in 1915, NCWV threw its support behind her Winning Plan. In 1911, however, NCWV endorsed the state-by-state approach and remained at odds with NAWSA and Shaw.

After the formation of the National Council of Women Voters, Emma intended to relax and travel. She planned to gather her strength for future suffrage battles she knew she would fight until all American women had the right to vote. Some doubted that Emma, who had devoted a great deal of her life to the cause, would actually stop pushing for suffrage even for a few weeks or months. One of her friends, Bernice A. Sapp, joked, "I know exactly how *you* will rest if you go back to Washington, D.C. You will be buttonholing all the senators & representatives on a national suffrage bill."[5] Letters poured in from suffragists across the country asking Emma and the council for help, forcing her to cut short her break.[6] Emma first turned her attention to the states of California and Wisconsin, where suffrage campaigns were pending.

In February, the California State legislature agreed to put woman suffrage on the ballot, which would be voted upon in the fall of 1911. Upon hearing of this decision, Emma traveled to the Golden State, where she spent some time with one of her brothers. Following her visit, she traveled to some of the larger cities in California: Stockton, Los Angeles, and San Diego, where she spoke on the issue of votes for women and organized equal suffrage chapters.[7]

In April, Emma met with John H. Braly of Los Angeles, president emeritus of the Political Equality League (PEL). Braly had been a long-time supporter of equal suffrage and convinced the California Republican Party to include woman suffrage in its 1910 party platform. It is not surprising that the president of the NCWV met with him. The PEL, previously an all-male group supportive of women's enfranchisement, was "the most influential suffrage group in Los Angeles," and Emma knew the value of securing the support of powerful male voters and progressive women, who formed the core of the club's membership.[8] From Los Angeles, she traveled north, where she formed the Butte County Association and gave instructions on how to form a suffrage society in a nearby community.

Upon returning home, Emma learned that Mary Simpson Sperry, a board member of the California Equal Suffrage Association, believed it "would be a great mistake to have Mrs. DeVoe come into the state." Emma admitted that she "was shocked" to hear of this. She had visited Sperry in San Francisco and told her about her California work. Sperry claimed to be pleased with her efforts, Emma maintained, but must have later changed her mind after hearing about what transpired in Seattle at the national convention and at the formation of the NCWV. Other California suffragists disagreed with Sperry and wanted Emma to return.[9] Fearing another visit might create dissension between board members, she decided not to revisit California, even though former Idaho Governor James H. Brady urged her to do so. He believed that she was the only "person in the United States" who could "bring order out of chaos, and start [them] on their road to victory."[10] In spite of Brady's concerns, California women became voters in 1911.

Earlier that spring, Reverend Olympia Brown, then president of the Wisconsin Woman's Suffrage Association (WWSA), sent a telegram to Emma informing her that the state legislature had passed a suffrage bill, giving voters the opportunity to enfranchise Wisconsin women in the 1912 election. Although Brown had many more years of experience stumping for suffrage, she had not secured a victory as her friend had, and Brown admitted that she was "waiting for . . . everything" from Emma.[11] She was uncertain about how to proceed, and Emma advised the Wisconsin leader to canvass voters on the issue of woman suffrage, just as Washington women had done. Wisconsin's legislators, including U.S. Senator Robert M. La Follette, concurred, and Brown asked Emma to come to Wisconsin to lay the groundwork for the 1912 campaign. She agreed.[12]

Emma had been appointed state organizer for the WWSA, and she arrived in the Badger State in the summer of 1911. Rumors about what happened at the Seattle convention continued to plague Emma and consequently the Wisconsin movement. Her opponents shared their disapproval of Emma and her tactics with Ada L. James, president of the Political Equality League, a newly formed suffrage association composed mainly of young Wisconsin suffragists who opposed Brown. Catherine Waugh McCulloch, vice president of NAWSA, feared Emma's involvement would result in further division between Wisconsin women.[13] Later, Washington insurgent Catherine M. Smith alerted James to Emma's ladylike but ineffective tactics "so that your forces will not waste any valuable time and strength by pursuing the wrong methods as advised by Mrs. DeVoe and other enemies of suffrage."[14] Brown finally had to concede that Emma's reputation had become a problem and asked her friend to draw up a "brief concise clear statement of the facts" as they had occurred in Seattle so that she could put a stop to the gossip.[15]

Emma returned home to settle some household affairs and to help Henry with renovations on their Parkland property, called Villa DeVoe, where he had been planting fruit trees and installing an irrigation system.[16] After working in California and Wisconsin, Emma remained at home and began devoting more of her time to administrative work at NCWV office headquarters in Tacoma. Spending time in the field had convinced her of the importance of emphasizing the benefits of woman suffrage, not just explaining how women had secured a victory in Washington. So she decided to have a pamphlet printed that listed the acts of "especial interest to women" passed by the five suffrage states in 1911. The NCWV believed that these examples would illustrate "the kind of laws women voters" sought and counter the belief that "equal suffrage states do not keep pace with the rest of the Union in such progressive legislation."[17] Emma told Lucy B. Johnston of Kansas that the leaflet, printed before California women had suffrage, "*proves* that W.S. benefits humanity."[18]

By focusing on women's achievements since they had been granted full citizenship, Emma and her NCWV reshaped the battle for woman suffrage. Women, who had been voting in their states for more than forty-two years to less than one year, altered the type of arguments presented in favor of woman suffrage. Prior to this time, suffragists had emphasized the potential power of women's votes and their ability to clean up politics. By contrast, the western women voters who had banded together to form the NCWV emphasized the benefits of women having already cast ballots, using legislation to prove women's moral nature and progressive spirit.

Wisconsin voters rejected the constitutional amendment, but three western states were victorious in 1912. After five unsuccessful campaigns, Oregon women became voters. Kansas and Arizona also adopted equal suffrage amendments. By contrast, the issue went down to defeat in Michigan and Ohio, despite the hard work of organizers in both states. Emma extended NCWV offices to the newly enfranchised voters of Arizona, Kansas, and Oregon.

Concurrent with these events, interest in securing woman suffrage through a national amendment began to grow. Support for such a measure had dwindled dramatically since Emma had joined the Federal Suffrage Association in 1892. In 1912, NAWSA's Congressional Committee was nearly defunct, and the federal campaign was in shambles. The budget for the national effort stood at $10 a year in 1912, but the funds were never spent. Twenty-five years had passed since woman suffrage had been debated on the floor of the Senate, and not one House or Senate committee had issued a favorable report on the issue since 1893.[19] Alice Paul changed all of that when she headed up the Congressional Committee in 1912. She immediately drew attention to the cause by planning to hold a suffrage parade in Washington, DC, on the day before President Woodrow Wilson's inauguration on March 3, 1913.

The NCWV agreed to participate in the spring parade, although it is not entirely clear who made the arrangements or exactly how the relationship between Paul—a militant suffragette who had worked in England before returning to America—and the council began. Most likely Dr. Cora Smith King (formerly Dr. Eaton, who had recently moved to Washington, DC) looked favorably upon Paul's plan. During the 1910 campaign, the doctor had shown an interest in utilizing publicity stunts to draw attention to the cause, and Paul's plan of work probably impressed King. Also, Dr. King became Paul's personal physician. She may have written to Emma about Paul's efforts in the nation's capital that spring. Dr. King led the western women in the 1913 parade on horseback, carrying a NCWV flag, followed by a float depicting the nine states of light.

With the assistance of the NCWV, the Congressional Committee revitalized efforts to pass a national amendment to the Constitution in the first part of 1913. After participating in the parade, nine members of the NCWV District Chapter, composed mainly of the wives of western representatives and senators, met with President Wilson, urging him to include woman suffrage on the agenda for the special session he had just called for April 7th. Dr. King, who headed the delegation, and the nine representatives used the same tactics the women of Washington had employed at the state capitol in 1909. They did not demand that the president submit an equal suffrage amendment to Congress. Instead, hoping to convince Wilson of the benefits of woman suffrage, they told him of the progressive reforms they, as voters, helped to enact: mother's pensions, minimum wage laws, and teacher's pensions. They did not threaten him with removal from office if he did not support the amendment—that was not their style.[20] Their achievements did not persuade the commander-in-chief, and he told the women voters that the special session he called did not permit the time to discuss the issue of woman suffrage.[21]

Daunted but not dismayed, NAWSA's Congressional Committee and the NCWV were ecstatic when they learned that a suffrage amendment would be introduced by two western congressmen on the first day of the special session. The women hoped to build upon the momentum of the past few weeks by holding a second demonstration in the capital city on Congress' first day. Women from each of the congressional districts in the United States met at the Capitol, bringing signed petitions to show the popularity of enfranchising women through an amendment to the Constitution. Dr. King, then NCWV treasurer and head of its Congressional Committee, served as a member on the reception committee for the Senate. Senator Henry F. Ashurst of Arizona along with senators from four other suffrage states greeted the women, many of whom were from equal suffrage states and members of the NCWV, as they brought their petitions to the legislature. From there, the women took places in the galleries of the Senate and House, where their petitions were presented.[22]

Following the ceremony, Senator George E. Chamberlain of Oregon and Representative Frank W. Mondell of Wyoming (husband of one of the women who had met with Wilson), introduced Senate Joint Resolution 1, which called for the passage of a federal woman suffrage amendment. The Senate Woman Suffrage Committee unanimously supported the resolution, issuing a favorable report on June 13th, and the Senate planned to discuss the issue on the floor at the end of July. The women of the Congressional Committee and the NCWV had succeeded in awakening congressional interest on the issue of woman suffrage. Although it would be several years before Congress passed the Anthony Amendment, the fact that Congress was discussing the issue on the floor of the Senate was a major victory for both groups.[23]

Although Emma had not been at these events, Paul asked her to schedule a conference of women with voting rights at the nation's capital in August. She hoped that the meeting would keep attention upon the suffrage amendment, increase public awareness of the issue, and convince Congress that the four million western women voters were extremely interested in the issue. Paul promised the president of the NCWV that the meeting of western women voters would receive a great deal of publicity from the press, as there were hardly any women working for suffrage during the hot DC summers. Most of all, the conference might help women secure the passage of a federal woman suffrage amendment. "You can hardly realize the tremendous psychological effect which a conference of women voters meeting here would have just at the time when our bill has reached this critical stage in Congress," Paul wrote.[24]

Paul's personal appeal probably flattered Emma. Since 1911, national leaders had dismissed the significance of her organization and her ladylike skills, which they claimed had never helped win woman suffrage in any state. Pleased with Paul's request, Emma was more than happy to help counter such accusations and to illustrate the political power wielded by western women voters. If she worked in conjunction with Paul, and Congress passed a federal amendment, she may have believed that rumors about her and her methods would finally disappear, and she would be credited with one of the greatest reform campaigns in United States' history. "It may be possible to come to Washington in August," she replied, "but I fear our women will beg for more time." Emma promised Paul her assistance and signed her letter, "I am your friend."[25]

Emma's support of Paul may have also stemmed from her belief that the movement needed new tactics and leadership to secure suffrage. The success of the western campaigns and the failure of elections elsewhere probably led Emma to question the state-by-state strategy. Many western women were citizens by 1913, but women in other regions of the country remained disfranchised. Their campaigns continually failed. Armed with this knowledge, Emma probably came to believe that the federal woman suffrage amendment would be the only way to obtain enfranchisement for all American women.

Emma drafted a letter to her NCWV state presidents, and she reported on the status of the federal suffrage amendment as explained to her by Paul. At the end of July, the Senate planned to discuss Joint Resolution 1, and suffragists were hopeful that the issue would pass. They feared, however, that the resolution would die in the House of Representatives because no committee on woman suffrage existed in the lower house. Instead, the House Judiciary Committee, called the "graveyard" by suffragists because so many bills died there, introduced amendments to Congress.[26] Paul concluded that the House needed to create its own woman suffrage committee if eastern and southern women were to become U.S. citizens.

Based on her understanding of the matter, Emma issued an emergency call for a NCWV conference. "A critical situation has arisen in the National Suffrage movement [and] your help, as women voters, is urgently needed," she exclaimed. "One-fifth of the Senate, one-seventh of the House, and one-sixth of the electoral vote come from equal suffrage states. At this stage of the progress of the Federal Amendment, women voters are the decisive factor. The women yet unenfranchised turn to us for help; we must not fail them."[27] Conference delegates would testify before the House Rules Committee, where a resolution to create a Woman Suffrage Committee would take place. Emma urged those who could not attend to write letters to the members of the House Rules Committee, asking them to create a standing Committee on Woman Suffrage, and to their two senators, urging them to pass Joint Resolution 1.[28]

With the assistance of Emma's contacts in the Senate and House, Dr. King secured a meeting with the House Rules Committee. Suffragists had asked for a hearing before with the committee, but its chairman, Robert Lee Henry of Texas, a Democrat, had refused. When approached by NCWV leaders, he granted a meeting. Emma hoped to capitalize on the fact that her council—not NAWSA's Congressional Committee or the Congressional Union—had secured the hearing.

Dr. King quickly responded to her president's request by telegram. "Absolutely imperative for papers not to advertise situation as victory of Council over Suffragists or attempt to humiliate Henry and Democratic Party," she advised Emma. "Politic thing; now phone Hunt that Henry graciously grants informal hearing because conference is held in August attended by its president, Tacoma women, and other women from west."[29]

Meanwhile, eastern women and several western congressmen hoped that Emma would, following the NCWV's meeting in DC, travel to New York for several suffrage conferences. Knowing of her conciliatory methods, they championed her tactics and questioned more militant methods then being employed in New York, such as parades and street-corner speeches. They hoped Emma could usher in the "gentler and more successful methods used by western women in procuring equal suffrage."[30]

People in the Pacific Northwest rejected militancy, a fact that Emma successfully exploited in the Washington suffrage campaign, and they remained supportive of conservative tactics even after the campaign had ended. As an example, the *Tacoma Ledger* published a political cartoon illustrating the difference between Alaska women, who became voters in 1913, and the militant suffragettes in London. The artist, James North, depicted Alaska women as sweet homemakers, dedicated to their families; their legislators responded to their kindness and womanliness by granting them the right to vote in future elections. By contrast, the militant was manly and offensive to all men, and even man's best friend, the dog, fought her in response to her methods.[31]

The use of nonconfrontational techniques was important in securing suffrage in many of the early suffrage states. Representatives from these states were accustomed to such tactics and bristled at the thought of giving militant suffragists the right to vote. In a speech given on the floor of the U.S. Senate in July 1913, Senator Reed Smoot of Utah told suffragists that he believed in rewarding the ladylike, home-grown tactics used by America's leading suffragists. "Suffrage should be given not to the Pankhursts and the militant radicals among our women, but to those who follow in the womanly footsteps of the American pioneers for suffrage," he stated emphatically.[32]

In addition to calling a national conference of women voters and scheduling a public hearing with the House Rules Committee, the NCWV helped Paul in other ways. Dr. King organized a suffrage demonstration in Hyattsville, Maryland, eight miles from the District of Columbia on July 31. On that day, suffragists from across the country including the enfranchised women of the West brought signed woman suffrage petitions to Hyattsville, where King lived. The CU and the members of the Senate Woman Suffrage Committee met the women, and from there they drove in a caravan to the nation's Capitol where they handed the petitions to the senators.[33]

Years later Paul recalled, "It was very effective because these congress-men that they were going to see were their own congressmen and they were, themselves, voters."[34] The press recognized the significance of the moment, "Heretofore the women of the country when seeking for politi-cal consideration have merely been human units disfranchised. They had to come as beggars and seek the crumbs that fell from the politicians' bounty." This changed when women with voting rights petitioned the United States Senate, and twenty-one senators gave speeches favoring the passage of a woman suffrage federal amendment to the Constitution.[35] Interest in woman suffrage remained high following the submission of petitions to the senators.

The NCWV's August conference kept the press, Congress, and the pub-lic focused on the issue of women's voting rights, as Paul had hoped. The highlight of the convention occurred when members of the NCWV spoke to the House Committee on Rules to urge members to establish a per-manent Committee on Woman Suffrage in the House. The *Washington Times* reported that nearly four hundred suffragists wearing yellow rib-bon badges from the ten suffrage states stood to hear what Emma and other speakers had to say.[36] Emma recalled that people stood in the cor-ridors, and many were turned away, "for all were anxious to get sight of the new women voters."[37] The Democrats, who composed the majority of members, were "gracious, polite and chivalrous." They promised Emma a response by December, but she did not expect a "favorable answer."[38] Just as she expected, the House Committee on Rules did not immediately cre-ate a Woman Suffrage Committee. The event was nevertheless important, as Congressman Henry had regularly denied women the right to address his committee on the issue. The hearing was probably the most important victory achieved by the NCWV and Emma that year.

A second victory was the election of Jane Addams, the most celebrated woman in America at that time, as vice president of the NCWV. At the time, Addams was also vice president of NAWSA, and her acceptance of the position probably created quite a stir within both organizations.[39] Shaw must have been angry with the NCWV for incorporating the celebrity into its leadership ranks and with herself for not being able to keep the two associations entirely separate.[40] By contrast, her adversary, Emma, must have been pleased with the benefits the NCWV might gain from its associa-tion with the famous Addams.

The alliance between NCWV and NAWSA's Congressional Committee upset Shaw, who had grown to despise Emma. Shaw shared her disapproval with Alice Paul following NCWV's convention in DC, and Paul admitted that she was "greatly distressed" to hear that she had offended NAWSA's president. She claimed not to know of the split and suggested that the suffrage movement had benefited from the convention, because, as she later remembered, the congressmen from the West "who had never visualized" the numbers of female voters "could see right in their own capital these voting women."[41] Addams agreed with Paul, who encouraged Shaw not to worry "over evil results from the conference."[42]

Emma remained in the district for the remainder of August, hoping to drum up support for a federal amendment. Believing that eastern women looked to her for assistance in securing national suffrage, she remained determined to achieve that goal.[43] Her calendar filled quickly with meetings at the Capitol. About a week after the NCWV convention, she met with Senators Thomas J. Walsh of Montana and Porter James McCumber of North Dakota. Disappointed to learn that both men were lukewarm on the issue of a national amendment, she told Alice Paul that she feared it would be nearly impossible to obtain a positive vote from both.[44] Emma was no doubt dismayed to learn that she could not use her weight as a voter and president of the NCWV to change their minds about the matter.

Aside from meeting with members of Congress, she also challenged anti-suffrage arguments presented on the floor of Congress. When Senator Benjamin R. Tillman ("Pitchfork Ben") of South Carolina linked woman suffrage to higher rates of divorce, the press asked Emma for a response. The western women's experience provided the answer, she believed:

> Those who oppose woman suffrage often do so in a wholly theoretical way and lose sight of the fact that the experience of the West through many years show them to be in error. The attempt was made in the Senate today to link the increase of divorce in this country with woman suffrage. Of course, there is no relation between the two. If so, we could point to the fact that until last year the State of Wyoming, which has had equal suffrage since 1869, had the lowest percentage of divorces of any State in the Union.[45]

Emma began working her way west in September. She stopped along the way in Chicago, where she helped organize the Illinois NCWV, and in Denver. When Emma finally arrived in Tacoma, she found several invitations waiting for her. Tacoma women were filled with pride when they read about her work at the capital, and at least four clubs wanted to hold receptions for her, hoping to hear of her successes in DC.[46] She bragged of the NCWV's achievements to Margaret S. Roberts of Idaho: "You see my dear Miss Margaret nothing succeeds like success and we surely had success in Wash D.C."[47]

Upon returning home, the president of the NCWV wrote to Paul, encouraging her efforts. "It is a great work, but if you fail to get the favorable vote of Congress this time, do not feel in any way cast down or discouraged. I will be with you in this work, to share your sorrows and rejoice in your victories." Emma understood just how difficult the task was; after all, she had not secured suffrage in any state other than Washington, and that campaign had required many years to come to fruition. Assuming that women would vote as a bloc to aid their disfranchised sisters, she believed that a federal suffrage amendment was within the grasp of women if the suffrage campaigns of 1913 succeeded.[48] For her part, Paul kept working with Emma because of her connections with Northwest politicians—current and former state governors, representatives, and senators working in Washington, DC—which she tried to exploit on several occasions.

Even though Emma wholeheartedly supported Paul and her efforts, the alliance between the two women was doomed from the beginning because their tactics so widely differed. Emma continued to support a nonpartisan approach to securing suffrage and told the women of the council to avoid partisan politics until all American women had won the ballot. Recognizing that an amendment needed support from both parties if it were to pass, she avoided alienating party leaders when working for woman suffrage. Although she valued new methods and even experimented with some of them in Washington, her ladylike strategies differed from those endorsed by younger women of the CU. She advised women to "avoid big meetings; they arouse your enemies" and encouraged suffragists to "always be good natured and cheerful."

By contrast, Alice Paul had lived in England, where she had joined the Women's Social and Political Union (WSPU), headed by Emmeline Pankhurst. The WSPU was a militant suffrage organization, and police routinely imprisoned its members for attacking property and people. Paul participated in suffrage demonstrations and was arrested several times in England. The CU imitated many of the Pankhurst's publicity stunts in the US. Unlike Emma, she demanded that Congress enfranchise women, blamed the party in power for women's disfranchisement, held mass demonstrations, and her group later heckled President Woodrow Wilson.

December came, and the House Rules Committee provided no indication of how they might vote on the formation of a Woman Suffrage Committee. Lucy Burns, vice-chairman of the NAWSA's Congressional Committee, asked Emma for help. Under her leadership, western women bombarded Henry with letters and telegrams, asking that his committee establish a Woman Suffrage Committee, but he refused. Burns told Emma that the Democratic Party was responsible for this defeat and blamed them for being "so short-sighted as to refuse a request merely for a committee who would consider our arguments. It is not as if we were asking them to endorse Woman Suffrage."[49] Eventually Paul and her group concluded that the Democrats must be held accountable for their inaction.

In 1914, NAWSA severed its relationship with Paul and Burns, citing opposition to the techniques used by the younger suffragists. President Shaw favored the split and even likened the CU to Judas Iscariot, in other words, a traitor to the cause.[50] Although Emma did not entirely agree with Paul's strategy and remained supportive of nonpartisanship, she criticized NAWSA's condemnation of the Congressional Union, calling it "stupid. . . . It simply exemplifies the contrast between the new methods and the old. . . . I fail to see why so much controversy has been indulged in because Miss Paul said 'the democrats will be responsible for the defeat of the amendment.'"[51]

The basic problem was the CU's very controversial decision to blame the party in power for the failure to pass a suffrage amendment. The Pankhursts used this policy, and so American suffragists labeled the tactic militant. Conservative workers opposed the political plan because the policy failed to consider or distinguish between the Democrats who favored woman suffrage. For years Emma supported methods which were conciliatory and designed to win over the votes of all men. She avoided antagonizing parties and firmly believed that all parties had to support the issue; she had friends in both parties. For a time she appreciated the efforts of Paul, but eventually Emma came to see this as a foolish tactic and distanced herself from their militancy.

The split between the CU and NAWSA was also a clash between younger militant women and older conservative suffragists. Older suffragists tended to be horrified by the attention-grabbing methods of the younger generation, finding them too extreme. Although the CU attracted several older women, such as Alva Belmont, who was born in 1853, in general the organization was known as the "younger suffragists." Its endorsement of radical techniques led it to be seen "by both outsiders and insiders as the party of youth." These suffragettes wanted to reshape the boundaries of femininity, and they rejected the conservative ladylike behavior promoted by Emma and NAWSA. They supported sensational methods to fight, rather than plead or beg, for the ballot.[52] Although Emma did not support their publicity stunts, she sympathized with Paul and Burns over NAWSA, at least initially.[53]

Neither Paul nor Burns wanted to leave NAWSA, but Emma hoped that this would occur. Her experience at the 1909 Seattle convention convinced her that NAWSA preferred to keep its auxiliaries and their leaders under national control, especially if they refused to accept orders and obey the dictates of the board, which Emma believed benefited no one. Besides, Paul had proven herself where NAWSA had failed.

Emma encouraged Burns and Paul, whom she was "very fond of," to break away from the association.[54] "I have great confidence in your Congressional Union and believe you will grow faster by standing alone than by leaning on any organization. I speak from the fullness of experience," she confided to Burns.[55] Emma used the formation of the NCWV as a guide for other groups dissatisfied with NAWSA's leadership, such as the CU and, later, the National Woman's Party.[56]

As a symbol of her support, Emma agreed to convince Washington, Idaho, and Utah women voters to participate in nationwide processions, open-air rallies, and meetings on May 2, 1914, in support of the Susan B. Anthony Amendment. She had already planned to travel through these states to organize additional chapters of the NCWV, and she was happy to help the CU.

She began in Boise, where she tied her activities to the memory of Anthony. On February 16, one day after Anthony's birth date, the Idaho Council of Women Voters held a banquet in honor of the pioneer suffragist, and Emma established the Boise NCWV chapter. Those in attendance passed a unanimous resolution for "their sisters in the east struggling for voice and representation" and pledged "their moral and political support in their efforts to obtain the submission of a constitutional amendment."[57] They also began laying plans for their demonstrations. Utah and Montana women sketched out similar plans.

The CU contacted Emma while she was in Idaho, hoping to use her connections with Senator William E. Borah to its advantage. The union had been unable to convince the senator to include suffrage in the Republican Party platform, and they looked to Emma, who supposedly had a "close hold on Borah," to secure his support. (The CU must have heard how Emma encouraged Borah to introduce a suffrage resolution in 1909, and they presumed she could sway him again.) She was encouraged to speak with the senator, "to bring all pressure possible to bear for a suffrage plank."[58] Borah promised much and delivered little, however. When the CU asked Idaho women to wire Borah in support of a federal amendment, Emma told Paul that her attempts to secure the support of Idaho women were all for naught. Many Idaho women "argue it should be secured *in the states*, and the Idaho women have passed resolutions commending Borah's stand for his states rights speech, not to my 'amazement,' but to my chagrin and sorrow."[59]

Emma returned home and attended meetings of the NCWV in Olympia, Tacoma, Seattle, and Parkland. Eventually all chapters agreed to participate in the May 2nd demonstration, but Emma had to twist a few arms, including those of fellow Tacomans who were "amused and somewhat displeased over the plan of the eastern suffrage workers for parades and demonstrations in their fight for the ballot."[60] In describing the incident to Paul, she told her, somewhat erroneously, "It is impossible for the western women to understand what you are really doing, for in all suffrage states a 'demonstration' or a 'march' has never been resorted to to get votes." By differentiating between eastern tactics and western methods, Emma emphasized the uniqueness of the West and their efforts to secure suffrage. When she told members of a local council about the May demonstration, "a shout went up at the idea from all of our members, for they never took part in anything of the kind and it struck them as being decidedly funny. They are perfectly willing and anxious to help, but they have thought such methods were only to be read about as occurring *someplace* [else]!! Come west and you will understand their view point."[61]

On May 2, 1914, women across the country visibly showed their support of a federal amendment by participating in the national suffrage demonstration, called the "Greatest Suffrage Day" by the *Suffragist*. Emma attended the rally in Tacoma, where the local NCWV chapter voted in favor of the Bristow-Mondell Resolution (known more popularly as the Anthony Amendment), and she gave an address on the issues facing disfranchised women. She also spoke at an earlier gathering in Portland on May 1.[62] The national demonstration had the desired effect. On May 5, the House Judiciary Committee reported the resolution out of committee without recommendation.[63] The CU's tactics and the pressure of western women voters via the NCWV seemed to be working.

In spite of their combined successes, the relationship between the CU and the NCWV began to erode in the fall of 1914, when the CU sent women to the suffrage states to work against the election of Democratic congressional candidates. In general, most western women living in the Pacific Northwest opposed this action, which ran counter to the NCWV's policy of staying out of political campaigns unless invited.[64] Once again eastern suffragists irritated their western colleagues. Abigail Scott Duniway of Oregon's NCWV believed that sending easterners into western states would make more enemies, not supporters of suffrage. She explained, "The worst trouble I have encountered in all my 44 years of work to get the ballot for women has come from the invasion of Eastern agitators who have tried to take advantage here of what they cannot do at home." She feared that Democratic Senator Chamberlain, a friend to suffragists who had introduced Joint Resolution 1, would become disgruntled by the CU's efforts.[65] The president of the Washington Council of Women Voters, Virginia Mason, agreed. Washington's women were so upset with Paul that even Republican women opposed eastern women working against Democrats in western states.

Emma admitted to Dr. King that "everybody's mad about them coming but myself," but Paul had offended her by sending women into Washington without notifying her first. "I wonder why Miss Paul did not ask me something about the girls coming and tell me they were coming," she asked King. Emma received a letter from Paul only the same day CU worker Margaret Fay Whittemore arrived in Seattle and thus did not have time to prepare for her arrival. Nonetheless, she planned to soothe local opposition by speaking at club meetings. She hoped to capitalize on the publicity that the young women would undoubtedly receive and then invite the women and men of Tacoma to hear CU organizers at a "monster meeting."[66]

Whittemore attended the meeting Emma had arranged for her at the end of September in the Perkins Building, the headquarters of the NCWV. Serving as chair of the hearing, Emma told women from the parties and organizations present that "Miss Whittemore has come to present her case—not our case. We already have the ballot." Whittemore explained that she sought the assistance of western women voters only to gain the ballot. "I do not wish in any way to interfere in local politics. It is only in the national issue that I am interested."[67] In spite of this protest, her desire to defeat Washington Democratic congressmen tied the hands of the NCWV, and Emma told the young woman standing before her that the council's commitment to nonpartisanship prevented the organization from helping the CU.[68]

Dr. King expressed approval of Emma's decision, telling Paul, "I am well pleased with the way she is handling it. She can help more by appearing disinterested and fair and kindly than by espousing the 'policy'— which as a council we cannot do."[69] Emma understood that joining with the CU to defeat the Democrats would only anger western representatives and senators and would dissolve the working relationship that she currently maintained with Washington Governor Ernest Lister, who was a Democrat. Besides, Emma had lived in Washington since 1905, and since that time voters had regularly supported Republican candidates for Congress.

Ironically, however, the NCWV had been drawn into Democratic politics earlier that spring when Emma learned that Judge George Turner was running against her friend George F. Cotterill in the Democratic primary for a seat in the U.S. Senate. Other candidates included Hugh C. Todd and Judge W. W. Black. She vowed to oppose Turner's campaign, but not because of his political affiliation. Cotterill had been a "tireless worker" for woman suffrage, and Turner had served on the Washington Territorial Supreme Court that had declared woman suffrage unconstitutional in 1887. She told Paul, "We are determined that Judge Turner shall not go to the senate to do us more harm in fighting your bill" and promised to fight Turner's candidacy.[70] Turner lost the primary. Black won the nomination and ran against incumbent Senator Wesley L. Jones. Black opposed the work of the CU in Washington, who, he contended, "were carrying out a Republican policy of attack upon the Democratic national administration," and he urged the women to return home.[71]

The Republican candidate remained in DC. Congressional business kept Jones at the Capitol, and he feared he would be unable to return to the state to canvass voters. Jones asked Emma to send him "a list of ladies to whom you think it might be well for me to write [and] I shall be glad to do so." Recognizing her campaign abilities, he also encouraged her to pass along "any suggestions" that he might follow.[72] Likewise, Idaho's junior Senator James H. Brady, also a Republican, asked for her assistance in the 1914 senatorial election—the first elections in which voters, not state legislatures, selected their U.S. senators.[73] Both states reelected their incumbent senators that year. For their part, the CU declared victory in the defeat of five Democratic candidates.[74]

Emma devoted time in the fall of 1914 to working for suffrage in New York, where a bill was pending in Albany. Emma told Senator Jones that the campaign, under the charge of her old friend Catt, appealed to her because "Mrs. Catt as well as myself is strongly non-militant."[75] During her time in the Empire State, she spoke for woman suffrage, raised funds for the cause, and the following year she and Congressman Frank Mondell of Wyoming spent one week stumping for suffrage, emphasizing its benefits in the equal suffrage states of Wyoming and Washington.[76] In the midst of this activity, two western states passed woman suffrage in 1914—the only campaigns the NCWV had helped to fund—Nevada and Montana.

Catt's decision to call upon Emma may have surprised NAWSA President Shaw, who saw the NCWV president as an opponent, not an ally. Catt probably did not want to antagonize Shaw, but she recognized the benefits associated with Emma's participation. For instance, the New York Grange refused to hear from a "regular suffrage speaker," so she invited Emma to speak, believing that "they would be willing to hear a lady [and a Granger] from a suffrage state."[77] Shaw, much to Catt's chagrin, had let one of NAWSA's best speakers and organizers break away from the organization. Being a pragmatist, Catt objected to Shaw's pettiness and enjoyed working with Emma, who had asked her to chair an auxiliary to the NCWV called the Prospective Voter. Asking Catt to head the committee was probably an attempt to bring some sort of legitimacy to the NCWV, which Shaw repeatedly snubbed.[78]

Emma's partnerships with younger and older suffragists expanded in number as the battle for a federal amendment heated up. Younger suffragists rejected Shaw's views on Emma, as someone disloyal to the cause. They recognized her political power and established ties with the veteran reformer. Anne Martin of Nevada, for instance, invited Emma to serve on the Executive Committee of the Women Voter's Campaign Alliance, and she agreed.[79]

At the same time that Emma and Catt became close allies again, relations between the CU and NCWV became less friendly. Perhaps hoping to emphasize the importance of her own organization and downplay the role of Emma and the NCWV, Paul told others that the council's role in the suffrage battle was "nominal." When Paul heard that the NCWV planned to hold a conference of women voters in 1915 at the Panama-Pacific Exposition in San Francisco, she told Whittemore that the event would be of "very little importance" and would "not have any political significance."[80] Paul may have, in fact, been de-emphasizing the NCWV's convention in favor of her own, scheduled to meet in September at the Expo—just a few months after the meeting of the NCWV.

Aside from her work with Carrie Chapman Catt and Paul, Emma also sought the assistance of Washington's first lady, Mary Alma Lister. Ernest Lister, who became governor in 1913, had helped Emma in numerous ways, and she hoped that establishing a relationship with the first lady would be just as beneficial. One afternoon at the governor's mansion, Emma unveiled a plan to publish a NCWV pamphlet about how equal suffrage operated in the suffrage states. Mary Lister agreed to ask the governors from these states to submit short statements about women voters and the benefits of their participation.[81]

Just a few months after meeting with the first lady, the *Boston Post* reported that, according to Judge W. H. Snell of Tacoma, woman suffrage was a failure in Washington State. "Many of us were led to support woman suffrage in Washington by the familiar argument that it would tend to purify politics and make for better government. But, after four years of experience, we are forced to conclude that it has done neither," Snell explained. "On the contrary, it has simply added to the numbers of those who can be used in the interest of corrupt politics, and has resulted in a hodge-podge of ill-digested, sentimental, socialistic legislation which is a menace to the welfare of the state."[82] Snell's comments challenged the image that the western women voters had presented to the rest of the country.

When the story broke, Emma answered his criticisms and denied his accusations, which had been plastered across newspaper headlines in the East.[83] She also turned to Governor Lister for assistance in countering Snell's statements to the press. He quieted her concerns and reassured her, "I beg to say that I know of no one who favored giving the women of the State the right to vote who today opposes it and large numbers of those who were opposed to the constitutional amendment when it was before the people are today in favor of it."[84]

The testimony of the other governors emphasized the importance of women voters and their positive impact upon their states. The governor of Idaho, Moses Alexander, challenged Snell's conclusion that women were no more moral than men and that they sought political influence to the same degree as men. "The women of Idaho are not politicians or place hunters, but they are independent, intelligent and honest and are the most potent force for good government and civic righteousness." Other governors echoed Alexander's comments. Women's votes had a positive impact on the polls, quality of candidates, and moral legislation.[85]

Although Paul was beginning to separate from NCWV leadership, Emma remained committed to the idea of a federal amendment and to Paul's efforts well into 1915. In a letter to Duniway, she criticized eastern women who "were death on the Congressional Union." Even though Emma disagreed with Paul's partisan strategies, she told Duniway that "that girl's heart is true."[86] Perhaps Paul reminded Emma of her time in South Dakota, when she worked day and night for women's enfranchisement. Although she was fond of Paul, Emma and her state presidents could tolerate only so much militancy, and by 1915, they wanted no more of eastern women's meddling in suffrage states.

Their pushiness and mass demonstrations had alienated the more demure women of the West. When Paul and Mabel Vernon visited Idaho in 1915, Margaret Roberts, a Republican party woman and president of the Idaho NCWV, privately told Carrie Chapman Catt, "A large number of our Citizens resent the advent of [eastern] women in our state organizing and telling us how to help other women secure the ballot. We feel that the western women are better fitted to come into the East and help and tell eastern women how to organize." Carefully distinguishing between the eastern and western methods of securing suffrage, Idaho's women, she explained, "came into our citizenship sanely and quietly," without spectacles or parades. Like Emma, she supported Catt's non-militant methods and refused to provoke the men of Idaho or any party.[87]

Frances Munds of Arizona, a Democrat and president of the Arizona NCWV, told Anne Martin of Nevada that she refused to work with the CU because of their work in her state in 1914. "They have such bad judgment and 'butt in' where they are not wanted," she complained. Munds had to constantly make the rounds, apologizing for their efforts. "I was never so ashamed of suffrage women in my life."[88]

In July, the NCWV held its second conference in San Francisco, which, when compared with its first convention in Washington, DC, was a flop. Only fifty-one women attended the meeting, and the men who were invited—Senator James Brady, President Wilson, and Wyoming Governor John Kendrick—only sent remarks. Emma, who worked "night and day" on the convention for six months, must have been disappointed with the turn out.[89]

Paul's convention, held in September, was strikingly similar in title and tone to the council's efforts, and several of NCWV's officers (King and Roberts) signed the call to conference. In fact, the CU made every attempt to reach out to the western women in their push for the passage of a constitutional amendment. Advertised as a National Convention of Women Voters, organizers noted that the convention would be strictly nonpartisan and would urge the voting women of the West to band together to help secure the ballot for eastern women.[90] Forgetting the conferences held by the NCWV in DC and in San Francisco, perhaps in an attempt to take the limelight away from Emma's efforts, the chairman of the convention proclaimed it was the "first political convention of woman voters that has ever been called." Echoing the sentiments of Emma, who believed that the work of the women of the West was invaluable, the call noted that the Susan B. Anthony Amendment could be passed if the four million western women voters united behind the effort.[91]

Even though Emma and some of the NCWV objected to the CU interfering with local and state politics—some of the most outspoken leaders became members of the CU's advisory council, a decision which Emma approved—Paul continued to send representatives to the West, where they appealed to the women for freedom and worked to boycott the Democrats. In 1916, Paul formed the National Woman's Party (NWP), composed entirely of women voters, but not all western women eagerly joined. Women in Los Angeles, Salt Lake City, and Boise passed resolutions opposing the party and its militant methods. Roberts, who lived in Boise, supported conservative tactics and told Catt that she hoped the enfranchised women of the West "will have nothing whatever to do with the forming of a woman's party. This will only be another barrier, to my mind, in the enfranchisement of women."[92]

Copying a tactic employed by Emma in 1909, Paul sent organizers on a tour of the western states on the "Suffrage Special" train and mailed Borah a signed petition from the "qualified" voters of the woman suffrage states.[93] The party sought Emma's assistance in the Evergreen State, but she refused to participate in its events, believing that the "Woman's Party would cause no end of trouble in the home and in public . . . and do more to defeat W.S. than anything." Emma believed that its policy of holding the party in power accountable angered Democratic state legislators, complicating her work in the Northeast and Midwest. She remained, however, supportive of the federal woman suffrage amendment but opposed "*their methods* of getting it."[94]

When Shaw stepped down as NAWSA president in 1915, Catt replaced her. Emma's attitudes toward NAWSA softened because of the change in leadership. Being pragmatic politicians, Catt and Emma resolved to reestablish ties between NAWSA and NCWV to present a united front on the campaign trail. The reconciliation was made permanent at the NCWV 1916 convention. The *Cheyenne State Leader* reported that the alliance challenged Paul's approach. Emma explained, "We believe that the women of the United States will succeed more quickly and certainly with much better dignity by appealing to the sentiments of reason and justice rather than attempting to adopt militant methods."[95]

Emma began working closely with Catt as a member of the NAWSA executive board, and for the first time since 1909, she attended a NAWSA conference. There she played an important role in outlining the plan by which NAWSA would achieve women's enfranchisement. Referred to as the Winning Plan, executive board members decided that national and state associations would simultaneously focus on the passage of a federal amendment and continue working for suffrage at the state level, although the major thrust of the association centered upon securing a constitutional amendment. Emma promised Catt that the NCWV "will stand by that amendment and do our work in the suffrage states for this amendment as it stands here today. They are absolutely pledged to it now."[96] She also planned to continue working in the states as she had since the passage of suffrage in Washington.

In August 1916, Emma returned to the prairies of South Dakota, where she assisted women working for suffrage, and eventually arrived in her old home town of Huron, the cradle of liberty for South Dakota. The centrally located city had hosted the state fair since 1905, and when she arrived, Emma took the opportunity to speak with many attendees. Two Democrats told her they had been in favor of woman suffrage until they learned that the western women voters aligned themselves with the CU to defeat President Wilson, who was running for a second term that year.

Emma explained that this was not the case, and she asked Democratic Governor Lister to provide proof. "Explain the matter that the women voters are still sane, and have not organized to fight the Democratic or any other party," she directed.[97]

Lister explained to R. W. Clarke that the Congressional Union had come to Washington to organize western women voters to oppose President Wilson and the Democratic congressional candidates, but the state's women voters refused to ally themselves with the cu. "Any opposition on the part of women voters in this State to the President and support for him, by women voters of this State, has been given by such voters along political lines and not along suffragist lines," he wrote.[98] In spite of this complication, Emma was confident that South Dakota's women would become citizens.[99] The Associated Press reported that the issue had passed in November, but voters actually defeated woman suffrage for a sixth time.[100] Upon learning the true outcome, Emma told her South Dakota sisters that she felt "ill to know our rejoicing was all in vain."[101]

The South Dakota incident provided Emma with proof that the cu and nwp had damaged the reputation of western women voters, and she concluded that nawsa had to take action. After a board meeting, she advised Catt on this issue of paramount importance. Based on her own experience, she believed that Paul and her supporters would return to the suffrage states and "make a strenuous effort" to organize women voters to work against the Democrats. If that occurred, Democratic voters in the East and South would come to oppose the enfranchisement of women as their counterparts in South Dakota had. Responding to Emma's concerns, Catt promised to visit the suffrage states of Washington and Oregon to counter the plans of the nwp and would try to stop in Idaho, Wyoming, and Montana.[102]

Although Emma was nearly seventy, she refused to sit idly by and let the younger women take control of the movement. In addition to her work with nawsa's board, she agreed to serve as a congressional aide for its Congressional Committee, headed by Maud Wood Park and Helen Gardener.[103] She was much more interested in organization, but she was willing to do whatever it took to secure the federal suffrage amendment, and so she urged newspaper editors to print favorable woman suffrage articles and editorials, lobbied the associates of congressmen, and encouraged powerful constituents to urge their senators and representatives to vote for the amendment.[104] Emma continued to maintain relationships with the state's leading decision-makers and undoubtedly met with each of them, urging them to support the movement in its final hour.

In 1917, the Great War raged in Europe, and in February the United States severed diplomatic relations with Germany. After hearing the news, Catt called an emergency meeting of her Executive Council, and women from across the country met in the national capital for a two-day meeting to discuss what action the organization would take if Congress declared war against Germany. Some women advocated peace, including Emma and Catt, while others favored preparedness. The board members decided that they opposed going to war, but the association would remain behind President Wilson if he declared war against Germany.[105] NAWSA leaders agreed to support the government by offering the assistance of their members. They refused, however, to give up working for woman suffrage.[106] Catt was fiercely criticized for her decision, and undoubtedly so was Emma. Although the issue was ferociously debated, it is impossible to know the extent of Emma's pacifist beliefs, as the only indication of her interest stems from a membership card glued to a page in one of her scrapbooks.

On April 12, six days after the United States formally declared war on Germany and ten days after Jeannette Rankin of Montana was sworn in as the first female U.S. congresswoman, Emma registered with the National League for Woman's Service, which coordinated the activities of female relief workers.[107] Although Emma was a member of the World's Peace Army, she was hopeful, just as Elizabeth Cady Stanton had been after the Civil War, that women would be rewarded for their service to their country. Her decision to work for the war effort was pragmatic. She knew how voters responded to her husband's song, "A Soldier's Tribute to Woman," and hoped that her support of war work would help all American women. She and Henry dove into Red Cross work in Parkland, with Henry serving as secretary and treasurer of the drive and Emma appointed a lieutenant.[108]

While Emma helped with war work, Alice Paul and members of the NWP used even bolder methods to put pressure on President Wilson to support a woman suffrage amendment. In 1917, the party began picketing the White House. Eventually the DC police arrested the picketers, and later a judge sentenced them to Occoquan Workhouse.[109]

As the NWP drama unfolded, Catt began laying plans to establish a new organization of women voters, the League of Women Voters. Some have suggested that she saw the NCWV as a rival to her league, but Catt had strategic reasons for creating her association.[110] As she explained to Congresswoman Rankin, "The Council of Women Voters was a start in the right direction and had a good name, but it did not travel far." Reportedly, the leadership of the NCWV was "anxious" that NAWSA "should take it up and extend its organization and influence," but Catt believed there was "some prejudice attaching to it which will practically make that impossible." She preferred to "organize an entire new group."[111] Clearly the manner in which the NCWV had elected Emma as its president in 1911 continued to offend many women. Plus, Emma's association with Paul may have also led more moderate members of NAWSA to question the respectability of the association and its leaders. Catt respected Emma, but she preferred to establish a new organization, one which more women would want to join. In November 1918, fighting ended on the battlefields of Europe, and Catt began implementing her plans.

She hoped that success was around the corner and scheduled a Jubilee Convention in St. Louis. Before the meeting, Emma approved a plan to merge the NCWV with Catt's League of Women Voters, NAWSA's successor, but not all members of the NCWV agreed with this decision. Margaret Roberts told Catt that she opposed NAWSA taking the name of the NCWV "or in other words stealing it without permission." She informed Emma, "I want right here and now to vote emphatically against the proposition of merging with the National Suffrage Association and allowing them to take our name and as I believe I have written you before leaving our glorious West without a habitation and a name."[112] Roberts' reaction exemplifies the frustration western suffragists continually voiced about the interference by their eastern sisters and their treatment as second-class citizens.

Although not all members were in agreement, their president proceeded to merge the two organizations at the March 1919 convention. Catt appointed Emma chairwoman of the preliminary meeting of the women voters' convention (held at the same time as the jubilee meeting) and a member of a subcommittee at the conference of the League of Women Voters. Emma, Mrs. Raymond Brown, Mrs. Charles H. Brooks, Grace Wilbur Trout (also a member of the NCWV), and Blanche Haines wrote the organization plan for the League of Women Voters, thereby ending the NCWV. The subcommittee decided that the Council of the League of Women Voters would be a national association composed of one representative from each state with full, presidential, or primary suffrage.[113] Emma returned home after the jubilee and continued to finalize the unification process.

After the merger with the league was completed on January 6th, Emma turned her attention to the final suffrage battle: the ratification of the Nineteenth Amendment.[114] The U.S. House had approved the measure in May 1919, and the Senate followed in June, thanks in part to the work of the NCWV and its president. The battle was not over, however; the amendment had to be ratified by the states.

Ratification was the most difficult task faced by suffragists. The "egalitarian" states of the West were slow to approve the amendment, and Washington was no exception. Many of the western state suffrage associations had disbanded, and NAWSA knew very few women leaders in the western states, with the exception of Emma. Governors, such as Washington's Louis F. Hart, who became the state's executive upon the death of Governor Lister in 1919, were generally unwilling to call special sessions of their legislatures to consider the Nineteenth Amendment. A fiscal conservative who hoped to reduce state expenditures, Hart cited the expense of calling a special session, which could not be limited by the governor. In other words, the legislature could consider additional legislation unrelated to the woman suffrage amendment. Emma agreed with Hart's responsibility to the Washington taxpayers, demonstrating her interest in issues of importance to the Republican Party, noting that "a special session has never been held in this state for less than $20,000 and the cost has run up to $75,000 or more." At the same time, she recognized that the amendment was "the next big work to get across" and promised that the NCWV would meet regularly until the amendment was ratified.[115]

Governor Hart eventually came around to the idea, telling suffragists that he would call a special session when enough state legislatures had taken action to ensure that the amendment would not be defeated. Finally convinced that the amendment would be ratified by three-quarters of the states, he promised that he would call for a special session, but set no actual date.[116] With no date in sight, suffragists continued to lobby the governor, asking that he immediately call a special session.[117]

While Emma recognized the high costs of a calling a session, she was sympathetic to the eastern women. She had supported women's rights since she was a child, and Emma was finally in a position to aid all of America's women. For so many years she wanted suffragists to recognize her work and her contributions. Here was the perfect opportunity for

Emma to secure national recognition for her efforts. After Oregon ratified the amendment on January 13, 1920, Emma began to doubt that Washington would ever consider the measure. As chairwoman of the Ratification Committee for Washington State, she told Bernice Sapp that she worried the new governor would not call a special session.[118]

In response, Sapp told her friend that it was best if the governor of Washington did not call a special session in 1920. "As one man said, the eastern women have waited fifty years for Suffrage, another year more or less shouldn't make much difference to them," she kidded. "Let them wait one little year until the western legislatures meet in regular session in 1921."[119] Sapp's comment reflects the animosity that had brewed between eastern and western suffragists for years and continued up to the passage of the amendment.

After the state of New Mexico—the only western state not to enfranchise its women—ratified the amendment in February 1920, the Washington League of Women Voters expressed its humiliation in a telegram sent to Catt. "We were a pioneer State, the fifth to be enfranchised. Therefore we resent the disgraceful humiliation put upon us by the stubborn refusal of our Governor to listen to our united demand for a special session to ratify the Suffrage Amendment."[120] Hart finally yielded to the pressure of the Republican Party and leading women in the state and called for a special session to be held in the winter of 1920.[121] His decision pleased Emma, who wrote, "I rejoice that at last the extra session has been called and hope soon the women of the U.S. and the world will be politically free."[122]

On March 22nd, women from across Washington State crowded into the capitol in Olympia to mark the historic event. The balconies in the house and senate, the hallways, and the corridors were packed. Frances M. Haskell introduced the amendment in the house, which received unanimous support from the legislators. Amidst the cheering, a special committee escorted Emma to the seat of honor, between the state speaker of the house and the governor. Addressing the house, Emma thanked every member from the bottom of her heart. "God bless you everyone!" she cried. Washington senators approved the resolution only twelve minutes after receiving the measure.[123] Only one more state would be needed. Tennessee was the final state to approve the amendment in August 1920.

With the issue of suffrage behind her, Emma found a new crusade. Then in her seventies, she became a party woman and quickly rose up the ranks to become the highest ranking Republican woman in the state.

Although she had emphasized the importance of nonpartisanship during her suffrage career, she had always identified with the Republicans, and within a few short years held a national post, where she pushed for women to be given equal representation in the party.

7

PARTY WOMAN

IN 1922, THE *TACOMA NEWS TRIBUNE* RELEASED THE NAME OF THE recently appointed vice chair of the Washington State Republican Committee, local resident Emma Smith DeVoe. Reminding readers of her long political career, the author recounted Emma's ties to Susan B. Anthony and her untiring devotion to securing woman suffrage in South Dakota, Idaho, and Washington. Called "Washington's leading woman in politics," the writer credited Emma's success to one of her main principles: "Always be good natured and cheerful." Emma, the *Tribune* predicted, would continue to influence state politics for many years to come.[1]

In the years following ratification of the Nineteenth Amendment, Emma became active in the Republican Party. Her time as a party woman, although short, provides a glimpse of the role women played in partisan politics in the early 1920s. The ratification of the Anthony Amendment—a significant accomplishment for women—could be considered the "Great Divide," marking a distinct change in women's political participation, but Emma's party work suggests that women's political styles and behaviors did not change overnight. There were continuities.[2]

Within the party, Emma organized women's clubs for the Republican Party, just as she had for NAWSA, and she scheduled Republican Days at the state fair. Being a partisan was not easy, however, and many women struggled for equality in the party of Abraham Lincoln and Teddy Roosevelt. For example, as vice-chairperson, Emma appeared to be tasked solely with handling women's issues and Republican women's clubs rather than with matters facing the entire party. As an associate member of the Republican Party's executive committee, she and the other female associates continued to face obstacles within the party machine as they had no voting rights as members of the committee. Emma became drawn into party politics through her interest in the League of Nations, an issue of importance to leading Pacific Northwest Republican congressional leaders.

In December 1918, as suffragists lobbied to secure the passage of the Nineteenth Amendment, President Woodrow Wilson crossed the Atlantic, hoping to broker a "liberal peace plan" for Europe.[3] Emma, who had been working for the Red Cross in Tacoma, initially supported the president's efforts. Very quickly, however, she came to believe that his trip changed the man and his outlook. Europeans enthusiastically received the president and his peace plan, called the Fourteen Points. Upon arriving in Brest, the French greeted the American leader with shouts of "Vive l'Amérique! Vive Wilson!" Others on the continent praised Wilson by renaming squares or railroad stations after the American president or by hanging posters that demanded a "Wilson Peace."[4] A year and a half later, when Emma became a vocal proponent of the Republican Party, she told readers that "the wining and dining and prolonged flattery showered upon him by the nations of the East" had resulted in the president's "inordinate vanity" usurping "control of his better judgment."[5]

One critical component of Wilson's peace plan included the establishment of a League of Nations to help resolve future disputes, prevent aggression against people, and to keep the peace. The League, which became part of the Versailles Treaty, was particularly controversial in the United States, and Emma, like many of her Northwest political allies, came to oppose the idea.

In March, while Wilson was still in Europe, Senator Miles Poindexter, Washington's junior U.S. senator and a Republican, gave an anti-League speech in St. Louis, which Emma praised.[6] Questioning the need for such an organization and equating the League with German plans to control the world, he told Missourians, "The Kaiser sought to set up a world government and there is not a doubt but that he believed it was for the best interests of mankind." There were other problems with Wilson's plan to keep the peace; one of the points, known as Article X, gave the League authority to use American troops without a congressional declaration of war if a member nation was attacked. Poindexter, who planned to run for president in 1920, argued that this provision would "put the world in a straight jacket," thereby undermining the sovereignty of the United States and its ability to negotiate with other nations and to handle its own foreign affairs.[7]

President Wilson returned to the United States in June and tried to convince opponents of the importance of the peace plan. For the next year and a half, until the 1920 presidential election, Americans debated the issue, one that has been called "no less important than the great debate of 1787–1789 over ratification of the Constitution."[8] Emma believed that the passage of Wilson's plan would undermine Congress' ability to declare war, an action granted to that legislative body by the Constitution. She thanked Poindexter for "keeping the heritage vouchsafed to us by the blood and suffering of our forefathers unsullied by the personal ambitions of a president."[9] Even though the Constitution gives the president the authority to make treaties, Emma believed that the president "had neither the authority nor power" to reach a deal with international leaders, which ran counter to the document drafted by America's forefathers.[10]

In 1920, when Emma broke with her nonpartisan past and threw herself into the world of party politics, she followed a pattern established by the men in her life. Many of her closest political allies had been Republican—James H. Brady, who died in 1918, William E. Borah, and Wesley L. Jones, to name a few.[11] Henry was a Republican, and she was a second-generation Republican. Her father joined the newly formed party and supported presidential candidate John C. Fremont in 1856.[12] It was thus not surprising that she became affiliated with the Grand Old Party.

Although women had been voting for nine years in Washington, men were still apprehensive about women's inclusion in party politics. The *Tacoma Daily Ledger* reported that the welcoming of women into the party ranks would bring about significant change, not just equal representation. National conventions would become more civilized with "less smoke, less profanity, less free speech in general, less scrapping, less conspiring, less insanity on the floor of the convention hall."[13] Party men had hoped that the women would be content to focus solely on women's issues, but their demands surprised party leaders, Democrats and Republicans alike, who assumed that they could preoccupy party women with "a rag doll and a tea set." Professional politicians, "who believed that they were dealing with a lot of unsophisticated females only interested in the social side of an intensely practical game . . . have revised their judgment." Women who had previously dedicated themselves to municipal housekeeping now wanted to understand the inner workings of the parties.[14]

Emma entered the Republican Party during a particularly contentious period. Since December 1919, Republican women had demanded equal representation on the Republican National Committee (RNC) and had asked that each state be accorded a representative from both sexes. They argued that the states and local committees should adopt a similar structure. In January, women from fourteen midwestern states gathered to urge the party to double the size of the RNC by allowing each state a female and a male representative.[15]

Within the Evergreen State, the issue over who should lead the woman's Republican committee, Sarah Flannigan of Spokane or the incumbent Estella G. Mendenhall, previously appointed by the state chairman, split the women into two factions. Flannigan reportedly wanted to unseat Mendenhall, who "was palmed off on" the women of the state. Flannigan and her supporters believed Mendenhall's work was good but contended that women should be given a voice in picking their leader.[16] The tensions boiled over at the first day of the Grand Old Party's 1920 state convention in Bellingham and angered the male delegates. "Work together, stand together, think together and cooperate with the men," advised one male delegate. "Women are not going to get anywhere in politics if they start bickering and having petty quarrels among themselves," he said.[17] The women's political interest surprised journalists in attendance, who reported that they handled politics "as glibly as if they were speaking of the latest crochet pattern, the next tea they are planning to give or the flower they expect to plant in their window boxes."[18]

The inclusion of women at the Washington Republican convention was especially newsworthy. Frances M. Haskell, the only woman elected to the state legislature in November 1918, was in attendance, as were other prominent Washington women: Emma; Mrs. R. C. McCredie, former president of the Washington State Federation of Women's Clubs; and Mrs. W. E. Burleigh.[19] The female delegates were generally dissatisfied with the state GOP and argued that women voters had not received enough recognition from the party. The women in attendance who were leaders within their county and the state organizations demanded change. They opposed separate women's clubs and wanted at least one female delegate selected for the national Republican convention.[20] They were also hopeful that Emma would be selected as a presidential elector. The men patronized the women. "Be good children," they said, "and you may receive a reward." If they cooperated, they promised the women that they would receive the honor of one female voting delegate, "but if they continue any of the petty bickering that was started here yesterday they will be turned down coldly."[21]

The party women reportedly united in an effort to secure the name of one female delegate to the national convention.[22] By the end of the meeting the press reported that the Republican women left Bellingham "with political laurels tucked under their arms." Women received several honors at the meeting. Republicans partly responded to their demands, selecting Emma as an elector for the 1920 presidential election in recognition of her dedicated efforts to secure woman suffrage. A number of women were elected as alternate delegates to the national convention.[23]

When the Republicans met in Chicago for their national meeting, the lack of female delegates was disappointing. Only 27 women served as delegates (about 3 percent of the convention's attendees), with 129 named as alternates. None were appointed to the RNC. As a concession to women, the party agreed to enlarge the Republican National Executive Committee from ten to fifteen, offering positions to seven women.[24] Harriet Taylor Upton, vice chair of the Republican National Executive Committee, told Ruth Hanna McCormick that the committee was "simply a servant of the National" and that until the RNC included women, women's efforts to effect change would be unsuccessful.[25] Although women had difficulty achieving their goals within the RNC, they nevertheless remained Republicans. Margaret Hill McCarter of Kansas, who spoke at the Chicago convention, pledged that "the womanhood of America will not be found wanting in upholding the great Republican ideals."[26] Emma never wavered in her commitment to the party, and she gave numerous addresses on the importance of registering to vote and casting a straight Republican ticket that year.

In the summer of 1920, Charles B. Welch, editor and general manager of the *Tacoma News Tribune*, asked the former suffragist to write a political column for his newspaper. Flattered, Emma agreed. Called "The Viewpoint of a Republican Woman," Emma's articles were partisan in scope and played a role in the party's efforts to regain control of the White House in 1920 (seven years had passed since Republican William H. Taft occupied the office of the president.) Her column emphasized the benefits of a Republican presidency and the potential problems Americans might face with another four years of a Democratic administration.[27]

Republicans opposed large government and hated to waste public money, and Emma dedicated many of her articles to pointing out just how much the Wilson administration had squandered during the Great War. The examples seemed endless. The War Department had contracted with the Steinburn Camp & Field Equipment Company to build fireless cookers, bread boxes, and other utensils. They delivered only a few items at a cost of more than $170,000. Then, the government turned around and sold the company its own gadgets as "junk," even though it was worth much more. The administration also sold goods to the French at a discount, and it hoarded foodstuffs, which eventually spoiled and had to be thrown out. "I could continue the detailing of these outrageous swindles almost indefinitely," Emma told readers, "but I think the foregoing is enough to convince an unbiased mind that we have had a great plethora of Democratic administration."[28]

When the Democrats finally selected a nominee, Ohio Governor James M. Cox, Emma consistently linked President Wilson's record to the new presidential candidate. Initially, Cox supported the League. As chairman of the Ohio League to Enforce Peace, he believed that the League of Nations would promote tranquility. As a presidential candidate, however, he initially tempered his endorsement and tried to distance himself from the League.[29] Emma, however, continued to hammer away at Cox. "The governor professes to believe the league covenant, as secretly made by Mr. Wilson and foreign diplomats, is a guarantee of eternal future peace, while wiser heads certainly realize it is a war breeder," she proclaimed.[30]

Emma saw the election as a referendum on the League and Wilson's war policies. She encouraged Tacoma readers to think about their first president, General George Washington, who discouraged his countrymen from entering into entangling alliances with foreign nations, and she asked her readers why the country should become aligned in Europe's liabilities when his advice had served the nation so well.[31]

Aside from attacking the Democratic nominee and Wilson's record, Emma also pointed out what Republicans, who had swept the congressional elections in 1918, had achieved in Congress. Naturally, the party woman boasted of the money Republicans conserved. According to her records, they saved Americans nearly $1.5 billion, which totaled about $30 to $150 for a family of five. "Had the Democrats been in control of Congress the Wilson administration would have received practically every cent of this money to squander," she emphasized.[32]

She used various arguments to illustrate the differences between the Democratic candidate and her choice, Senator Warren G. Harding, also of Ohio. Emma reported that he owned the *Dayton Daily News* and employed a pro-German editorial writer, who denounced Americans for questioning Germany's actions in the European campaign. Given the pro-German propaganda he published during the war, she asked readers if it was appropriate to elect Cox president of the United States. She appealed to those "who wore the khaki in defense of liberty" to think about giving their vote to a man who "prostituted his publication to the aid and comfort of the greatest and wickedest enemy the civilized world has ever known."[33]

In September, when the Democratic candidate traveled to Bellingham to speak, she telegraphed Governor Louis Hart and asked him to forward three questions to Cox. Emma explained that she simply wanted to learn where he stood on the issues. Newspapers across the country published these three questions, which were essentially issues of national importance. Did he favor the controversial Article X of Wilson's peace plan? Would he veto any congressional act that modified or repealed the Volstead Act? (The act established a Prohibition Bureau to enforce the Eighteenth Amendment, which went into effect in 1920 and prohibited the manufacturing, sale, and transportation of liquor within the United States.) Did he support the United States' assuming a mandate of Armenia?[34] Many believed that the mandate obligated the United States to spend years fighting for Armenian independence. Wilson proposed mandates as a postwar solution to territories that could not govern themselves. Governments would provide guidance to those nations outside of Europe that needed such aid.[35]

Emma asserted that the mandate would require the United States to commit military forces indefinitely to protect the new government of Armenia. Americans wanted peace after the Great War, not an extension of the fighting, she explained. "Let us assure Mr. Wilson that the mothers of our soldier boys have not forgotten the sacred blood that was shed on foreign soil. The minds of the American mothers do not run in harmony with the president, as does that of Mr. Cox, for their thoughts are continually centered on peace." Believing that all women were pacifists, she asked if mothers would vote to continue to support a policy that would place their sons in harm's way again. "No; a thousand times no," Emma repeated.[36]

The passage of the Volstead Act pleased Emma. She had supported temperance for many years, and now that the Eighteenth Amendment had passed, she had no desire to see it repealed or weakened in anyway. She feared that the election of Cox, who was a "wet" and favored light wines and beer, had the backing of the liquor industry.[37] They were counting on Cox to amend the act, she said. "Now! Will the women voters of America and other good citizens join hands with the liquor dealers' association and help to start a campaign for the re-establishing of the saloon?" she asked readers. "God forbid," she exclaimed.[38]

Cox failed to respond to her questions and instead made what Emma called "foolish attacks against the Republican campaign quotas." By contrast, she could proudly report that the Republican nominee stood in opposition to Article X, did not favor a U.S. mandate in Armenia, and believed that the Volstead Act should remain intact.[39]

As summer turned to fall, Emma took on additional duties to see that her party would seize victory at the polls. Calling upon the success of the various Woman's Days in 1910, she began planning Republican Day at the Western Washington Fair in Puyallup. Emma's work as president of Republican Day reflected her understanding of how to win the support of the people, and it served as an example of how women began to change party politics. She encouraged Republicans from all over the state to attend, where they could "touch elbows" with their friends and hear addresses from Raymond Robins, friend of Theodore Roosevelt and a progressive politician who fought against child labor and sweatshops. In addition, Emma planned for a GOP elephant and Uncle Sam to make appearances.[40]

After Republican Day had passed, Emma reported that Robins "opened the eyes of his audience" when he read from Wilson's League of Nations covenant, which permitted members of the League to oversee the implementation of agreements or contracts "with regard to the traffic in women and children and the traffic in opium and other dangerous drugs." Misreading Wilson's liberal plan, the speaker told fairgoers that the proposal would allow for the trafficking of human beings in the United States and elsewhere. The idea offended many, especially those who recalled the institution of slavery and the bloody Civil War. It is unknown, however, if Emma recognized the error of her speaker. If she did, she never questioned his logic. Instead, Emma asked readers to question their support of the Democratic candidate. "Ask yourselves if it is your wish that our government enter the slave trade and go across the seas into foreign lands to help enforce 'contracts' made to supply Moslem harems with innocent girls that are sold for a moneyed consideration into perpetual bondage."[41]

Aside from chipping away at the Cox campaign through her column and speeches across the state, Emma also played a small role in the 1920 gubernatorial campaign, even though the party had hoped that she would play a larger role. Reportedly, she had been urged to run for lieutenant governor that year, but declined.[42] She campaigned for Governor Hart. "Louis F. Hart has made good," she explained. He had achieved much during his first short term: he planted fruit trees and gardens at boys' and girls' training schools, reorganized the Industrial Welfare Commission, and reduced state employees by increasing efficiency. Also, he called a special session to ratify the Susan B. Anthony Amendment. "There was no dillydallying or piling up unnecessary expense to the taxpayers by a long drawn out session," she explained. The state legislature ratified the amendment quickly and without any visible quarrels.[43] Recognizing how parties operated, Emma probably thought that she owed a favor to Hart for calling the special session of the state legislature, and she therefore supported his reelection.

In November the Republicans swept the elections. Harding won in a landslide. He achieved the greatest victory in U.S. history up to that point in time by carrying every state in the Union except those in the South. His success could be linked to the increase in women voters at the polls in November; most of America's progressive women voted for Harding because he publicly supported many social justice programs that they favored, such as child labor and minimum wage laws.[44] Hart also won reelection, and Republican leaders credited Emma with winning over voters.

With the votes tallied and winners proclaimed, Emma still had some official duties remaining as a presidential elector. She was not the state's first female elector. That honor went to Helen J. Scott, who supported the Progressive Party candidate in 1912: Theodore Roosevelt. According to the *Ledger*, Scott's devotion to the party was "colossal." She penned eight hundred letters to friends, urging them to form Roosevelt clubs, and as a result of her hard work the Bull Moose campaign won Washington State's electoral votes. Roosevelt did not win the presidency, however; that honor went to Democrat Woodrow Wilson.

While Scott's ballot was not cast for the victor, Emma had the "distinction of voting for a president" in Olympia.[45] She and the six other electors gathered at the capital in the Temple of Justice on January 10, 1921, and unanimously voted in favor of Harding and his vice president, Calvin Coolidge. Although the clubwomen of the state hoped to have Emma take the ballots to Washington, DC, she nominated elector Arthur C. Rundle as the state's messenger. He would deliver Washington's seven votes to the president of the Senate.[46]

Emma's selection as a presidential elector reflected visible changes underway in politics. In the 1920s, women began to assume greater positions of power within local, state, and federal governments, but the political arena was slow to change. For instance, Georgia's governor appointed Rebecca Latimer Felton U.S. senator for only one day, in 1922. It would be ten more years before a woman would be elected to serve in the U.S. Senate. Two states out of forty-eight—Wyoming and Texas—had female governors in the 1920s. In 1922, Bertha Knight Landes ran for Seattle City Council using the language of municipal housekeeping, and four years later voters elected her the first female mayor of their city. Emma must have been particularly pleased with her selection, as Landes supported prohibition and forced Seattle police to conduct liquor raids on bootleggers.[47]

While many women had trouble integrating into the GOP, Emma made significant inroads into the state Republican Party, becoming vice chair of the Republican State Central Committee in the summer of 1922.[48] The party demanded that women display loyalty, and Emma had proven her allegiance again and again. Perhaps as a reward for her public support and devotion to the party, Republicans appointed her to this position. However, her appointment may have had more to do with a push for equal representation within the party. In the 1920s, the RNC encouraged states to place women in this slot. In response, many state Republican parties passed rules mandating the appointment of females as vice chairs of the state committees. Some state legislatures passed laws requiring parties to achieve equal representation within their committees, and in states where no bills had been passed, party leaders required half of the officers of the state committee to be female. Not all states supported equal representation.[49] At the time, Emma was the only woman to serve on the Washington State committee. Charles Hebberd of Spokane chaired the group, along with the assistance of secretary Frank W. Hull and treasurer J. D. Hoge.[50]

The *Tacoma News Tribune*, which announced Emma's new post,

emphasized her motto "Always be good natured and cheerful." Teachers and ministers had drilled the importance of such a virtue into their students and flocks, but it took "a woman to give a practical demonstration of its advantage in politics." Emma's strategies for success dramatically changed politics and the image of a politician, they asserted, as illustrated by the 1910 suffrage victory in Washington. The new vice chair was not the typical politician depicted by cartoonists, wearing a "wide-brimmed hat" and holding a "campaign cigar."[51] Emma's appointment indicated to the press that there were dramatic changes underway within the party. Women, through Emma's leadership, would bring civility and culture into the world of partisan politics.

Even though women had been voting in the Evergreen State for more than a decade and finally had female representation on the state executive committee, the Republican Party continued to treat women as second-class citizens. Most of Washington's women were not active within their state or local party committees. Instead, they joined women's Republican clubs across the state. The clubs were popular. There was reportedly so much interest that Emma issued a press release notifying newspaper readers across the country that she intended to hold the first state convention of Republican women after the 1922 election "if sentiment being manifested by women throughout the state continues." Then in Spokane, she told reporters, "The women all like to have a state convention and get into politics right."[52] She outlined the benefits of holding a statewide meeting in the *National Republican*: "It will be a means of getting better acquainted, laying plans for the future and emphasizing citizenship education features. Washington women are not in politics for the moment, but for life. They realize the immense responsibility and opportunity which suffrage meant to women."[53]

Emma dedicated much of her time over the next several years to organizing Washington's women, just as she had for the National American Woman Suffrage Association; this appeared to be her primary task as vice-chair and may have been the impetus for the party to appoint her to this position. She was well known throughout the state as the former president of the Washington Equal Suffrage Association and the National Council of Women Voters. If any woman could sway women to become Republican, Emma could; the *National Republican* reported that her influence over women was still "going strong" and she attracted many women into the Republican clubs she established.[54]

One of those was the Lewis County Republican Women's Club, which included women from Chehalis, Centralia, and Winlock. They were particularly active and frequently asked Emma to attend events sponsored by their organization. Following their vice chair's suggestion, they sponsored a summer picnic at the Lewis and Clark State Park in the summer of 1923, and they invited her to give an address, along with national committeeman Guy E. Kelly, Congressman Albert H. Johnson, Michigan Congressman John C. Ketcham, and other less well-known Republicans. As the principal speaker, Emma discussed the upcoming 1924 presidential election and her organizing work. Harding seemed to be the only Republican candidate, but the Democratic field was wide open, she asserted. William Jennings Bryan, an unsuccessful Democratic candidate for president in 1896, 1900, and 1908, "was ever 'willin' . . . but irrepressible," she kidded.[55]

Although Emma was the highest-ranking woman in the state party, she wanted a prominent place in the national party, a slot among the few women of the Republican National Executive Committee. She told fellow Republican Senator Wesley Jones, "For a long time I have desired to become a member of the Woman's Republican National Executive Board. It would help me greatly in my organizing work by broadening my influence with the women of this state." Emma believed that her appointment would help her battle the Democrats, who were "offering every possible inducement to the women of the state to cast their lot with them." She hoped that the senator could help with this request and pointed out that she had "never asked anything personal of the party before."[56]

Jones personally handled her request, writing to John T. Adams, chairman of the RNC, and Upton, a member of the executive committee. "I note that the Democratic women are getting active in connection with political matters and I think that we should not delay much longer enlisting our Republican women in political work," he explained to Adams. Emma was the perfect candidate for the committee, Jones asserted, as she had "rare tact and ability."[57] Disappointed to learn that all of the women's positions were filled, he told Emma that there were no openings. Jones hoped that she could fill a vacancy because, in his opinion, the current members of the executive committee were not doing "very good work."[58]

Several months later, however, Emma received her wish when Adams asked each member of the RNC to appoint a woman to serve as an associate member of the committee. The RNC unanimously adopted the plan, which President Harding, Chairman Adams, Upton, and Hamilton Kean of New Jersey approved.[59] Kelly, then the national committeeman, also from Tacoma, selected Emma. She finally received the national recognition she had been seeking but must have been disappointed to learn that the gesture meant little, as associate members had no voting rights within the committee.

Emma's popularity was one of the reasons Kelly selected her, calling her the "most widely known woman of the Northwest." She was the best choice for the post. Senator Poindexter, by contrast, said that she was "one of the very cleverest women workers" he had met and praised her organizational skills, tact, and ability to "interest the various kinds of women" in the work of the party. By 1923, she had organized twenty of Washington's counties, with plans to organize the remainder over the coming year and then hold a state women's Republican convention.[60]

That winter, Emma and the other associate members attended their first meeting of the RNC in Washington, DC, at the New Willard Hotel. The *National Republican*, which reported on the meeting, called the event a "new epoch in political history, in national history and in the history of the progress of women," but noted that the meeting seemed "less spectacular than might have been expected." A few days before the convention, the women attended teas and a luncheon at the Women's National Press Club, where they became acquainted with one another. Afterward, they discussed the possibility of changing the rules to allow women to be seated as full members on the RNC. On the first day of the convention, the associate members documented the historic moment by gathering for a photograph in front of the hotel.[61]

Henrietta L. Livermore of New York, appointed to the Republican National Executive Committee in 1920, addressed the committee, congratulating women upon their new status as associate members. She explained that the women did not ask to be added to the committee "that we might add something to our own dignity and honor. Quite the reverse. We have been asking it in order that we might better serve the Republican Party." Livermore explained that the Republicans had to challenge the idea "that there is something not quite so desirable among those [women] who have party loyalty and regularity as there is in those who exercise more independence" or nonpartisanship. The following day, the committee unanimously adopted a resolution to instruct the RNC Rules Committee to make women members full members, rather than associates, at the

1924 national convention. Emma received an appointment to the Committee on Policies and Platform.[62]

Awed by how easily they had been incorporated into the committee, one associate member noted that the men "accepted [the women] as equals." Another told the *National Republican* that she was struck by "how natural men acted" around the women. "They smoked and used man-language and didn't seem conscious that politics was different" with women on the committee.[63]

One of the highlights of the second day was a luncheon with President Harding and his wife, Florence. Held at the White House in the East Room, the committee members also had a chance to meet Vice President Coolidge and his wife, Grace. Later in the afternoon, Upton gathered the associate members together for a women's session, where they discussed numerous issues, and several of the women gave addresses. One woman from New York addressed "The Duty of an Associate Member," while a New Jersey woman gave a speech entitled "Women's Republican Clubs." They passed several resolutions, one of which thanked the RNC for supporting a resolution to make women full members of the committee.[64]

Upon returning home, Emma learned that Charles Hebberd had resigned as chairman of the Republican State Central Committee and would be replaced by Cecil B. Fitzgerald, a former Seattle councilman and mayor. Emma, fresh from her meeting with the associate members of the Republican Party, suggested that women also be given equal representation at the state level. The committee agreed with her proposal and unanimously passed a resolution directing every county committee to elect one woman to act as associate committee woman. These women would become honorary members of the Republican State Central Committee; Washington was reportedly the first state to take such action, and the press commended the plan, calling the decision "an epoch in modern politics."[65] The party must have delayed the issue, however, as Republicans continued to discuss the possibility of equal representation in June of that year.[66]

In the summer of 1923, Harding died, and Coolidge became president. He planned to run for president in the 1924 election. Although corruption and scandal had tainted the Harding administration, Coolidge managed to become the party's candidate, and Emma and the other Republican women in Washington supported his candidacy. A member of the Pierce County Women's Republican Club, Emma and more than two hundred women who belonged to the local chapter planned to actively campaign on behalf of the president.

In April 1924, the Washington Republicans held their state convention in Wenatchee, where they elected two female delegates-at-large and five women as alternate delegates. That same month, Louise M. Dodson of Iowa traveled to Washington to visit Republican women's clubs across the state. Then serving as national chair of field activities for the RNC, she began her tour in Tacoma and spoke at a meeting of the Pierce County Women's Republican Club. Emma, who had spent years traveling all over the state, consulted with Dodson on her itinerary and planned to accompany her on her trip across the state. Emma had successfully organized thriving clubs, and the Iowa leader concluded that the Evergreen State was "far above the average" in organization.[67]

Dodson and Emma worked together on the RNC Committee on Policies and Platform and must have had much to discuss. The appointment of twenty-nine women to the committee attracted the attention of many newspapers, who reported on the increasingly important role women would play in the upcoming 1924 national convention. The *Billings Gazette*, for example, reported, "Responsibility for victory or defeat in the coming presidential campaign is going to be nearly equal between men and women."[68]

In June, the Republicans held their national convention in Cleveland, and the number of female delegates jumped from 3 to 11 percent of the total number of attendees.[69] A reporter covering the convention noted that women "were *there* in force. They colored up the convention." Women had finally received equal representation on the RNC, although there was an abortive attempt by Thomas P. Fisk of Kelso, Washington, to challenge the decision to extend political equality to national committeewomen, which failed. A few delegates suggested Emma continue to serve as national committeewoman, but delegates, who had soured on Tacoma leadership, instead selected Mrs. John Lewis Hughes of Yakima.[70] Pleased by the outcome at the national convention, a delegate boasted, "Now the Democratic women have lost their best talking point."[71] As predicted, Coolidge became the party's nominee. Although she was not made a full member of the RNC in 1924, Emma remained loyal to her party.

When asked about the outcome at the convention, Emma was quite happy with the results. The selection of Hughes for national committeewoman pleased Emma, who had called upon her to organize the women of Yakima County. She told reporters that her successor was quite capable, as Hughes currently served as president of the Woman's Republican Club of Yakima County.

Upon hearing the news, the state chairman offered Emma her old position of vice-chair of the Republican State Central Committee, but again the position did not have much power. Emma was expected to establish women's clubs and to organize Republican women for the upcoming 1924 presidential campaign. Fitzgerald explained that there was great interest across the state in appointing Emma, "one of the most effective and popular workers of the party," to this position because of her work in the past—the 1910 suffrage campaign, for instance, and the 1920 presidential election.[72]

Over the next few months she gave many addresses on the upcoming election and the issue of women in politics. She spoke at a luncheon sponsored by the Lewis County Republican Woman's Club, where she explained the role she believed women should play in politics and how disinterested women "could be brought to the realization of their worth" to the party. Unfortunately, the press did not provide any specific examples from Emma's speech.[73] Later in the fall, she traveled to Whitman County, where she gave an address, and then she went back to western Washington, where she spoke at the Coolidge-Dawes Club in Seattle. She continued to stress the importance of reaching voters through Republican Days at state fairs. At some point that fall, Emma stepped down as vice chair of the state central committee, and Mabel Buland Campbell replaced her.[74]

Although she continued to dabble in politics over the next few years, she was less active. In 1927, Emma battled bladder cancer, and her condition gradually worsened. In August, she received radium treatment and finally underwent surgery, but she never recovered. She died at the age of seventy-nine on September 3, 1927, at Tacoma General Hospital. She left behind Henry, to whom she had been married for forty-seven years.[75]

In reporting her passing, local newspapers emphasized her strong ties to the national and state suffrage movements. Called Washington State's "mother of woman's suffrage," the *Tacoma News Tribune* reminded readers that Emma had been "an ardent worker for equal rights since girlhood." The papers reported that Emma had had served as president of the Washington Equal Suffrage Association, the National Council of Women Voters, and as vice chair of the state Republican Party.[76] More importantly, the *Tacoma Daily Ledger* noted that Emma was "largely responsible for passage of the woman's suffrage law in this state in 1910." Former national committeeman Guy Kelly and other Republican leaders attributed "much of the success in Republican organization in this state" to her hard work.[77]

Devastated by her death, Henry called her passing the "greatest sorrow" of his life.[78] He held his wife's funeral at the Buckley-King Funeral Church and asked Reverend Henry Victor Morgan to preside over the service. Members of the Custer Post of the Woman's Relief Corps, to which Emma belonged, also participated, as did four pall bearers: Guy Kelly, Burns Poe, E. Haakenson, and J. P. Swanson. Sarah Kendall, one of the attendees, noted "how lovely and peaceful she looked" at the viewing.[79] After the funeral, Henry had Emma's body cremated.

Upon hearing of her death, many people sent letters of condolence to Henry, including Washington Governor Roland Hartley. Fanny S. Cliff reminded Henry of his wife's "beautiful character, her fine mentality, [and] her wonderful *soul*."[80] Rex S. Roudebush, a Tacoma attorney, called her "a national figure and a woman of unusual and outstanding intellectual attainments," who "had culture and refinement to a high degree."[81]

Recalling Emma's accomplishments, Dr. Cora Smith King believed that someone—but not her—needed to compile the story of her involvement in the movement, which could be found in Emma's clippings and letters. King, who authored the Washington chapter in the final volume of the *History of Woman Suffrage*, believed that she did not do Emma justice in that piece. "There is so much more to tell of her," she wrote, "it would make a valuable contribution to the history of the state of Washington and to the country at large."[82]

Indeed, just ten years after the 1910 campaign, Emma had worried that Washington's women would never understand the challenges she faced in securing the ballot. On the eve of the ratification of the Nineteenth Amendment in Washington, Emma had told her friend Bernice Sapp that the "young women of our state will never know what it cost to secure the ballot for them. They will take it as a matter of course; that it is theirs because of some superiority they possess."[83] Suffragists toiled for many years to win that right. The securing of woman suffrage in Washington in 1910 was a tremendous feat, which reinvigorated the national movement, and it is Emma's primary legacy.

For most of Emma's life, from 1848 to 1920, American women struggled to secure the franchise. When the Nineteenth Amendment was finally ratified in 1920, disfranchised women evolved, as Catt said, from "wards of the nation" to "free and equal citizens," marking an end to the view that women were dependents.[84] By fighting for suffrage from Washington to New York and never doubting that male voters would extend the right to vote to women, Emma helped to forever end the idea of the "masculine monopoly of the public sphere."[85]

APPENDIX

Speech Delivered by Emma Smith DeVoe
to the Pomeroy Christian Church, June 1910

AT OUR NEXT GENERAL ELECTION, WHICH OCCURS IN NOVEMBER of this year, 1910, an amendment to the State constitution will be submitted to the voters of Washington, the substance of which is:

"The right of the citizen to vote shall not be denied or abridged by the United States or by any State, on account of sex."

This question was practically settled at the close of the Revolutionary War, so far as human beings in male form were concerned. Prior to this war, only tax-paying men voted in the colonies. The slogan at the time of the Revolutionary War was "Government without consent is unjust" and "Taxation without representation is tyranny." The logic of these two principles were then, as now, *unanswerable*. The reason that women did not vote at that time was because they were not tax-payers. When a woman married, all of her property passed into the possession of her husband. Then he became the tax-payer and voted. But conditions have changed. The law now permits woman to own property, hence she is a tax payer. What is taxation? It is the confiscation of private property for public purposes. Now can any one give a plausible excuse for men tax-payers to confiscate the private property of women tax-payers for any purpose whatever, and without her consent?

In the recent revolution in Finland, women shared with men the burdens of war, and when victory was won, their reward was political freedom equal with men. Not so with the loyal women in the American revolution. Our foremothers stood shoulder to shoulder with our forefathers, sharing with them all the burdens and privations of war, but when victory was won, they were denied political rights. They didn't agree with Lincoln, who said, "I go for all sharing the benefits and privileges of government, who assist in bearing its burdens, by no means excluding women."

Many persons, not realizing the hardships of the woman wage-earner, say, "Why do they not change their condition?" How like a certain foreign ruler, who during the food riots, when the people were crying for bread, asked, "Why do they not eat cake?"

But since no question is ever settled until it is settled right, we have this question ever before us. It may take on a new form, but it will not down.

We have, in America, an economic struggle, and it is the women who are in the throes of this warfare, because they form an important Brigade in the industrial army. Millions and millions of women are fellow workers and fellow sufferers with men. They are obliged to work, *if they live*, for less than a decent wage.

It has been conceded by all students of labor and expressed by the Hon. Carroll D. Wright, U.S. Commissioner of Labor, "that man's wages have not been raised for the reason that a woman's wage can be forced down."

Think of the thousands and thousands of poor, overworked women we have in our homes today, who receive no wage. They do not come to our back doors, asking for bread, neither do they drink nor gamble their money away, but they work late and early to keep their children together. Did you ever think of what an unusual thing it is to see a woman tramp? But someone will say, "All women do not wish to vote." Honorable John D. Long, ex-Secretary of the Navy, said, "If one man or woman wants to exercise the right to vote, what earthly reason is there for denying it, because other men and women do not wish to exercise it?"

The women of Wyoming, Colorado, Utah and Idaho vote, and the Governors of these States have accepted positions on the Advisory Board of our Campaign Committee. Governor Brady of Idaho says, "I know that if you can only get the information before the people, as to what the real benefits of equal suffrage are, that the intelligent citizens of Washington will not hesitate for a moment to grant the womanhood of your state that which is theirs by every natural right—the ballot."

Governor Brooks of Wyoming says, "Women vote as freely as men, and seem to possess an inborn intuition in political matters, which aids them materially in arriving at correct conclusions. Politics in Wyoming are discussed around the fireside, as they should be in every State."

Governor Spry of Utah says to the women of Washington: "If the men of your State will not let you vote, *come to Utah*. We will let you vote, and be glad to have you. With the experience Utah has had, we should not think for a moment of returning to the male suffrage system."

Governor Shafroth of Colorado says: "Do women want equal suffrage? Ask the women of Colorado. More than eighty percent of them voted at our last election. Submit the question to those who have tried it, and scarce a corporal's guard will be found to vote against it."

Judge Lindsey who was reelected last year as judge of the Juvenile Court of Denver on an independent ticket is a careful student on all such matters and his conclusions after fifteen years of experience are exceedingly valuable. He affirms that it has accomplished more good in Colorado than the fondest adherent ever predicted.

We ask that if you have a prejudice against it to free your mind of it at once, for the women in those four free states are no better and deserve no more than your wife or mother.

You know the employer cannot make suitable laws for the employed; neither can man make and execute just laws for women, because the rights of every human being are the same, because in each case the one in power fails to apply the unchanging principle of justice to any but those of his own class; because government without consent is unjust!

The burning question is *can we win in Washington*? The answer to that question largely depends upon what the *laboring man will do* for the cause. If he will make *this cause his very own* we *know we will win*.

Please do begin to discuss this question in your unions. Be sure that he understands the relation between woman suffrage and his needs.

If you are willing to assist please let us hear from you!

NOTES

INTRODUCTION

1   Ida Husted Harper, Anthony's biographer, does not place Susan B. Anthony in Illinois in 1856. At the time, Anthony was an agent for the American Anti-Slavery Society and spoke chiefly in New York. Emma's fictional story, however, says a great deal about her attempts to build her reputation by aligning herself with the canonized Anthony. *Seattle Star*, 4 November 1910, Scrapbook, vol. 11, Box 12, Emma Smith DeVoe Papers, Washington State Library, Tumwater, WA (hereafter cited as DeVoe Papers).

2   Jim and Tom Welch are descendants of the DeVoes, and they hold some of the couple's photos and letters. Emma is their great-great-aunt. Their maternal great-grandmother was one of Emma's sisters, Charity Anne Smith.

3   Such is the case for many of America's more famous suffragists, whose public careers have overshadowed their private lives. Jean H. Baker integrated the private lives and public work of five American suffragists in her book *Sisters: The Lives of America's Suffragists* (New York: Hill and Wang, 2005.)

4   The Illinois newspapers were much more difficult to search, as many of them are in tatters. Only a handful of newspapers from Washington, Illinois, from 1858 to 1880, have been microfilmed, making it difficult to locate information about the Smiths. A search of Warren County newspapers from 1848 to 1858 resulted in only one article featuring the name of Emma's father. See *Monmouth (IL) Atlas*, 4 April 1851.

5   There is some confusion about the spelling of her father's name. His probate records and the newspaper clippings I have found spell his name as Birdsey. An obituary held by Jim and Susan Welch spells it as Burdsey. I have chosen to follow the spelling in the legal records.

6   An application found at the Tacoma Public Library indicates that Emma did

attend college, but I did not uncover the specific details. Application, 12 April 1917, Pierce County World War One Service League Papers, Box 2, Northwest Room, Tacoma Public Library, Tacoma, Washington (hereafter cited as Pierce County Service League Papers).

7   For more information on Eureka College, see Harold Adams, *History of Eureka College* (Eureka, IL: Board of Trustees of Eureka College, 1982); Eureka College, *Eureka College, Eureka, Ill., 1855–1955: A Community of Learning in Search of Truth, Human and Divine* (Eureka, IL: Eureka College, 1955); *A History of Eureka College with Biographical Sketches and Reminiscences* (St. Louis: Christian Publishing Company, 1894), 203. An overview of her early life can be found in Frances E. Willard and Mary A. Livermore, eds., *American Women: Fifteen Hundred Biographies with over 1,400 Portraits: A Comprehensive Encyclopedia of the Lives and Achievements of American Women During the Nineteenth Century*, vol. 1 (New York: Mast, Crowell, and Kirkpatrick, 1897), 239.

8   *Washington (IL) Tazewell Independent*, 17 April 1879.

9   Ibid., 22 May 1879.

10 Alfred Seelye Roe, *The Ninth New York Heavy Artillery: A History of Its Organization, Services in the Defenses of Washington, Marches, Camps, Battles, and Muster-Out, with Accounts of Life in a Rebel Prison, Personal Experiences, Names and Addresses of Surviving Members, Personal Sketches, and a Complete Roster of the Regiment* (Worcester: Alfred Seelye Roe, 1899), 415–16.

11 *Washington (IL) Herald*, 5 February 1880, Scrapbook, vol. I, 1892–1894, Box 7, DeVoe Papers.

12 Jim Welch, e-mail to author, 13 June 2009.

13 Birdsey W. Smith Probate Records, Clerk of Circuit Court, Tazewell County, Pekin, Illinois.

14 Anne Firor Scott, "Epilogue," in *Votes for Women: The Struggle for Suffrage Revisited*, ed. Jean H. Baker (New York: Oxford University Press, 2002), 191.

15 Elizabeth Cady Stanton, Susan B. Anthony, Matilda Joslyn Gage, and Ida Husted Harper, eds., *The History of Woman Suffrage*, 6 vols. (Rochester, NY: Susan B. Anthony and Charles Mann, 1881-1922; repr., Salem, NH: Ayer, 1985).

16 Grace Farrell, *Lillie Devereux Blake: Retracing a Life Erased* (Amherst: University of Massachusetts Press, 2002), 164.

17 Quoted in Nancy F. Cott, "Across the Great Divide: Women in Politics Before and After 1920," in *Women, Politics and Change*, ed. Louise A. Tilly and Patricia Gurin (New York: Russell Sage Foundation, 1990), 156.

18 Baker's popular book also contended that the movement fostered "friendships that turned them into sisters with a cause" (*Sisters*, 4, 8). By contrast, many books in the suffrage literature emphasize the tensions apparent between reformers. For a sampling, see Farrell, *Lillie Devereux Blake;* G. Thomas Edwards, *Sowing Good Seeds: The Northwest Suffrage Campaigns of Susan B. Anthony* (Portland: Oregon Historical Society Press, 1990); Ruth Barnes Moynihan, *Rebel for Rights: Abigail Scott Duniway* (New Haven: Yale University Press, 1983); Abigail Scott Duniway, *Path Breaking: An Autobiographical History of the Equal Suffrage Movement in the*

Pacific Coast States, 2nd ed. (1914; reprinted with a new introduction by Eleanor Flexner, New York: Schocken Books, 1971); Rebecca J. Mead, *How the Vote Was Won: Woman Suffrage in the Western United States, 1868–1914* (New York: New York University Press, 2004).

19   The issue of money and woman suffrage is one of the key topics explored by historian Lisa Tetrault. She kindly sent me an advance copy of her unpublished article "The Incorporation of American Feminism: Suffragists and the Postbellum Lyceum." I thank her for sharing this essay, and I agree with her conclusion that "money, often big money, lies at the center of the suffrage story and was critical to its unfolding." She provides many examples of suffrage lecturers who, like Emma, worked in the movement to save their families from economic ruin. To read her recent publication with the same title, see the *Journal of American History* 96, no. 4 (March 2010): 1027–56.

20   In 1985, historian Nancy A. Hewitt argued that "diversity, discontinuity, and conflict were as much a part of the historical agency of women as of men." Hewitt, "Beyond the Search for Sisterhood: American Women's History in the 1980s," *Social History* 10, no. 3 (October 1985): 316.

21   May Arkwright Hutton to Ada L. James, 14 July 1911, Women's Suffrage in Wisconsin, part 2, the papers of Ada Lois James (microfilm edition), Wisconsin Historical Society, Madison, Wisconsin (hereafter cited as James Papers).

22   Jill Ker Conway, "Women Reformers and American Culture, 1870–1930," *Journal of Social History* 5, no. 2 (Winter 1971/1972): 166–67; Marlene LeGates, *In Their Time: A History of Feminism in Western Society* (New York: Routledge, 2001), 237.

23   See, for example, Nancy F. Cott, who writes, "Certainly not all women's activities in the political arena—not even all activities undertaken by women who claim to have 'women's interests' or 'women's needs' at heart—are by that token feminist." Cott, "What's in a Name? The Limits of 'Social Feminism'; or, Expanding the Vocabulary of Women's History," *The Journal of American History* 76, no. 3 (December 1989): 826.

24   Quoted in Karen J. Blair, *The Clubwoman as Feminist: True Womanhood Redefined, 1868–1914* (New York: Holmes & Meier Publishers, 1980), 11.

25   Expediency arguments are defined by historian Aileen S. Kraditor in her book, *The Ideas of the Woman Suffrage Movement, 1890–1920* (New York: Columbia University Press, 1965; reprint, New York: W. W. Norton and Company, 1981), 52–74.

26   My work is part of a recent trend exploring the importance of femininity and rhetoric as related to women speakers in the late nineteenth and early twentieth century. For examples of this approach among historians, see Carol Mattingly, *Well-Tempered Women: Nineteenth-Century Temperance Rhetoric* (Carbondale: Southern Illinois University Press, 1998); Carol Mattingly, *Appropriate[ing] Dress: Women's Rhetorical Style in Nineteen Century America* (Carbondale: Southern Illinois University Press, 2002); Nan Johnson, *Gender and Rhetorical Space in American Life, 1866–1910* (Carbondale: Southern Illinois University Press, 2002); Karlyn Kohrs Campbell, *Man Cannot Speak for Her: A Critical Study of Early Feminist Rhetoric*, vol. 1, Contributions in Women's Studies, no. 101 (New York:

Greenwood Press, 1989); Sara Hayden, "Negotiating Femininity and Power in the Early Twentieth Century West: Domestic Ideology and Feminine Style in Jeannette Rankin's Suffrage Rhetoric," *Communication Studies* 50, no. 2 (Summer 1999): 83–102. See also Ann Marie Nicolosi, "'The Most Beautiful Suffragette': Inez Milholland and the Political Currency of Beauty," *Journal of the Gilded Age and Progressive Era* 6, no. 3 (July 2007): 286–309; Lillian Faderman, "Acting 'Woman' and Thinking 'Man': The Ploys of Famous Female Inverts," *GLQ: A Journal of Lesbian and Gay Studies* 5, no. 3 (1999): 315–29.

27 Rebecca J. Mead's book is the leading source on the western suffrage movement. She is less convinced of the importance of the still hunt. See *How the Vote Was Won*, 28; by contrast, Holly J. McCammon and Karen E. Campbell argue that the larger "hurrah type" campaigns "were no more successful than small and less-active movements in winning the vote." McCammon and Campbell, "Winning the Vote in the West: The Political Successes of the Women's Suffrage Movements, 1866–1919," *Gender and Society* 15, no. 1 (February 2001): 75; see also Holly J. McCammon et al., "How Movements Win: Gendered Opportunity Structures and U.S. Women's Suffrage Movements, 1866 to 1919," *American Sociological Review* 66, no. 1 (February 2001): 64.

28 Emphasis in original. DeVoe to Carrie Chapman Catt, 23 November 1909, Box 1, Folder 15, DeVoe Papers.

29 DeVoe to Lucy B. Johnston, 21 June 1911, Box 3, Folder 12, Lucy B. Johnston Papers, Kansas State Historical Society, Topeka, Kansas (hereafter cited as Johnston Papers).

30 Ida Husted Harper, ed., *The History of Woman Suffrage*, vol. 6 (New York: J. J. Little and Ives Company, 1922), 676.

31 Emphasis in original. DeVoe to Johnston, 21 June 1911, Box 3, Folder 12, Johnston Papers.

32 Catt to Mrs. Stansbury, 23 June 1893, Ellis Meredith Papers, Box 1, Folder 1, Colorado Historical Society, Denver, Colorado (hereafter cited as Meredith Papers).

33 DeVoe to Johnston, 21 June 1911, Johnston Papers.

34 Emma quoted in *Spokane (WA) Evening Chronicle*, 22 February 1908, Scrapbook, vol. V, Box 8, DeVoe Papers. During Reconstruction, woman suffrage was not a popular idea, and suffragists living in the West were often portrayed as extremists. Mary Olney Brown, who lived in Washington Territory, believed that the women of Washington had been extended citizenship rights, and she encouraged women to vote in the 1868 elections. As she later recalled, "I was looked upon as a fanatic, and the idea of a woman voting was regarded as an absurdity"; Elizabeth Cady Stanton, Susan B. Anthony, and Matilda Joslyn Gage, *The History of Woman Suffrage*, vol. III (Rochester: Charles Mann Printing Co., 1886), 781. Later, in 1871, as Susan B. Anthony traveled across Washington, she found a similarly hostile reception in parts of the territory. Beriah Brown, editor of the *Seattle Territorial Dispatch*, warned readers, "It is a mistake to call Miss Anthony a Reformer, or the movement in which she is engaged as a reform; she is a Revolutionist, aiming at nothing less than the breaking up of the very foundations of

society and the overthrow of every social institution organized for the protection of the sanctity of the altar, the family circle, and the legitimacy of our offspring"; Edwards, *Sowing Good Seeds*, 101.

35   Kristi Andersen, *After Suffrage: Women in Partisan and Electoral Politics before the New Deal* (Chicago: University of Chicago Press, 1996), 25–27, 167.

36   Catt to Mary Smith Heyward, 27 November 1895, Clara Colby Papers, Wisconsin Historical Society, Madison, Wisconsin.

37   For more specific details on the tensions between East and West, see Mead, *How the Vote Was Won*.

38   DeVoe to Johnston, 6 February 1913, Box 5, Folder 11, Johnston Papers.

39   I am indebted to T. A. Larson for his brief studies on the National Council of Women Voters: "Wyoming's Contribution to the Regional and National Women's Rights Movement," *Annals of Wyoming* 52, no. 1 (Spring 1980): 2–15, and "Idaho's Role in America's Woman Suffrage Crusade," *Idaho Yesterdays* 18, no. 1 (Spring 1974): 2–15. I appreciate those authors who made brief references to the council in their work. They include Moynihan, *Rebel For Rights*, 216–18; Ellen Carol Dubois, *Harriot Stanton Blatch and the Winning of Woman Suffrage* (New Haven: Yale University Press, 1997), 192; Eleanor Flexner, *Century of Struggle: The Woman's Rights Movement in the United States*, rev. ed. (Cambridge: The Belknap Press of Harvard University Press, 1975), 312-13; Katherine H. Adams and Michael L. Keene, *Alice Paul and the American Suffrage Campaign* (Urbana: University of Illinois Press, 2008), 127; and Mead, *How the Vote Was Won*, 117–18. Suffragist Abigail Scott Duniway also discusses the council in her autobiography, *Path Breaking* (241–50).

40   Emphasis in original. DeVoe to Johnston, 6 February 1913, Box 5, Folder 11, Johnston Papers.

41   "Tacoma Woman Invited to Address World's Convention of Suffragists at Budapest," unidentified clipping, Scrapbook of Clara Watson Elsom, Box 5, DeVoe Papers.

1   MORAL REFORM AND STATEHOOD

1   Sherry H. Penney and James D. Livingston, *A Very Dangerous Woman: Martha Wright and Women's Rights* (Amherst: University of Massachusetts Press, 2004), 71–76, 225.

2   The first train to come into town that spring appeared on May 7. Dewayne Nelson, "Firsts in the History of Huron and Surrounding Area," Huron Public Library, South Dakota Collection, Huron, South Dakota. A description of the winter's impact on the people of South Dakota can be found in Doane Robinson's *History of South Dakota*, vol. 1 (Logansport, IN: B. F. Bowen & Co. Publishers, 1904), 306–9. According to the *Washington Republican*, Henry accepted a position with the G. B. & M. Railroad. I have found no such name for a railroad. *Washington (IL) Republican*, 3 March 1881.

3   The editors of the *Daily Huronite* later told readers, "Money is afraid of immoral-

ity. If you want to scare away investors just get the reputation of being a lawless town." *Daily Huronite (SD)*, 5 July 1887.

4   Ernest V. Sutton, *A Life Worth Living* (Pasadena, CA: Trail's End Publishing Co., 1948), 197.

5   See Beadle County Justice Court Records, 1882–1898, South Dakota State Historical Society, Pierre, South Dakota (hereafter cited as SDSHS).

6   *Huron (SD) Tribune*, 6 October 1881.

7   Henry had finished the home by January 1882, as reported in the daily newspaper. The land purchase was not officially dated until August 1882, though a payment of $37.50 was made on September 29, 1881. *The Huron Tribune and Dakota Huronite (SD)*, 5 January 1882; Indenture no. 428, 1 August 1882, Beadle County Register of Deeds, Beadle County Courthouse, Huron, South Dakota.

8   Receipt no. 870, 8 December 1882, Beadle County Register of Deeds, Beadle County Courthouse, Huron, South Dakota.

9   *Huron (SD) Tribune*, 24 November 1881.

10   *Proceedings of the Sixth Annual Session of the South Dakota Baptist Convention and the Ministerial Union Held with the Baptist Church at Dell Rapids Sept. 29 to Oct. 2, 1887* (Parker: The New Era Publishing House, 1887), 1, Baptist Church Records, 1872–1969, SDSHS (hereafter cited as Baptist Church Records).

11   Quoted in The *Daily Huronite (SD)*, 4 October 1886; for general attitudes towards the group, see Minutes of the Southern Baptist Dakota Baptist Association, 1872–1888, Baptist Church Records, SDSHS.

12   *Huron (SD) Tribune* and *Dakota Huronite*, 19 January 1882.

13   *Dakota Huronite (SD)*, 21 December 1882.

14   Ibid., 28 December 1882.

15   For a discussion of the naming of DeVoe, see J. H. DeVoe to Lawrence K. Fox, 12 August 1928, Lawrence Keith Fox Papers, SDSHS (hereafter cited as Fox Papers); C. H. Ellis, *History of Faulk County South Dakota: Together with Biographical Sketches of Pioneers and Prominent Citizens* (1909; reprint, Aberdeen: North Plains Press, 1973), 64–65; Faulk County Historical Society, *History of Faulk County, South Dakota, 1910–1982* (Faulkton: Moritz Publishing Company, 1982), 337, 339; Warranty Deed, 22 December 1885, Faulk County Register of Deeds, Faulk County Courthouse, Faulkton, South Dakota.

16   *Rapid City (SD) Daily Republican*, 20 July 1886.

17   *Dakota Huronite (SD)*, 3 May 1883.

18   Blair, *Clubwoman as Feminist*, 74.

19   An example of the duties of a municipal housekeeper and examples of how suffragists used municipal housekeeping to argue for the benefits of women suffrage can be found in Judith N. McArthur and Harold L. Smith, *Minnie Fisher Cunningham: A Suffragist's Life in Politics* (New York: Oxford University Press, 2003), 29–31.

20   Italics in original. Linda K. Kerber and Jane Sherron De Hart, eds., *Women's America: Refocusing the Past*, 4th ed. (New York: Oxford University Press, 1995), 229.

21   *Huronite (SD)*, 19 March 1885.

22 Ibid., 9 April 1885.

23 Ibid., 19 March 1885.

24 Ibid.

25 Ibid. 5 March 1885.

26 Ibid., 9 April 1885.

27 Capitalization in original. *Daily Huronite*, 1 April 1887.

28 Ibid.

29 Italics in original. Ibid., 4 April 1887.

30 Stephen B. Plummer, "Huron, South Dakota, 1880–1900: Economic and Political Determinants" (master's thesis, University of South Dakota, 1970), 45–46; Dorothy Huss et al., *Huron Revisited* (Huron: East Eagle Company, 1988), 276.

31 *Daily Huronite* (*SD*), 27 June 1887.

32 The council first passed the act in August 1887 and then passed the same act again in February 1888. The act appears in the *Charter and Ordinances of the City of Huron* in 1888. Huron City Council minutes, 30 August 1887 and 4 February 1888, Huron Municipal Building, Huron, South Dakota (hereafter cited as Huron City Council minutes); *Charter and Ordinances of the City of Huron* (Huron: City Council, n.d.), 58–59, Huron Public Library, South Dakota Collection, Huron, South Dakota.

33 Carol Leonard and Isidor Wallimann, "Prostitution and Changing Morality in the Frontier Cattle Towns of Kansas," *Kansas History* 2, no. 1 (Spring 1979): 50–51.

34 Paula Petrik, "Strange Bedfellows: Prostitution, Politicians, and Moral Reform in Helena, 1885–1887," *Montana: the Magazine of Western History* 35, no. 3 (Summer 1985): 5, 7.

35 *Daily Huronite* (*SD*), 5 July 1887.

36 Ibid., 7 November 1887.

37 Alvin John Brunn, "The History of the Temperance Movement in South Dakota to 1917" (master's thesis, University of South Dakota, 1948), 33.

38 This was a common trend in the American West. Richard White, *"It's Your Misfortune and None of My Own": A New History of the American West* (Norman: University of Oklahoma Press, 1991), 309.

39 *Daily Huronite* (*SD*), 20 December 1886.

40 Colleen McDannell, ed., *Religions of the United States in Practice*, vol. 1 (Princeton: Princeton University Press, 2001), 159; David Nicholls, ed., *The Cambridge History of American Music* (Cambridge: Cambridge University Press, 1998), 37.

41 *Proceedings of the Sixth Annual Session of the South Dakota Baptist Union*, 13, Baptist Church Records, SDSHS.

42 The statehood movement had always been popular in Huron, but this case made the issue even more urgent. The origins of the statehood movement can be traced to an 1879 Thanksgiving dinner in Yankton. John E. Miller, "The State of South Dakota Admitted to the Union as a State: November 2, 1889," in *The Uniting States: The Story of Statehood for the Fifty United States*, ed. Benjamin F. Shearer (Westport, CT: Greenwood Press, 2004), 1112.

43 *Daily Huronite* (*SD*), 25 June 1887.

44 Ibid., 27 June 1887.

45 Ibid., 29 June 1887.

46 Carrol Gardner Green, "The Struggle of South Dakota to Become a State," in *South Dakota Historical Collections*, vol. 12 (Pierre: Hipple Printing Company, 1924), 519–20; *Daily Huronite (SD)*, 24 February 1886.

47 *Daily Huronite (SD)*, 5 July 1887.

48 Weston Arthur Goodspeed, ed. *The Province and the States*, vol. 6 (Madison, WI: Western Historical Association, 1904), 311.

49 J. H. DeVoe to Fox, 12 August 1928, Fox Papers.

50 Miller, "The State of South Dakota," 1111–12.

51 John T. Woolley and Gerhard Peters, *The American Presidency Project* [online]. Santa Barbara, CA. Available from World Wide Web: http://www.presidency. ucsb.edu/ws/?pid=29627.

52 *Daily Huronite (SD)*, 31 May 1888.

53 Although the sheet music credits only Henry DeVoe for the composition of the statehood songs, W. C. Arnold, Chairman of the Campaign Committee, thanked both Emma and Henry for their "meritorious composition of both words and music." Therefore, both probably arranged, composed, and wrote lyrics to the songs. See Dakota Campaign Song Book for 1888, Scrapbook of Clara Watson Elsom, Box 5, DeVoe Papers.

54 The quartette was also known as the Statehood Glee Club or simply the Glee Club. *Daily Huronite (SD)*, 13 July 1888.

55 Ibid., 12 July 1888.

56 The sheet music differs from the lyrics printed in the *Daily Huronite*. In the sheet music, the DeVoes refer to Butler as "the old rebel sutler." *Daily Huronite (SD)*, 13 July 1888; Dakota Campaign Song Book for 1888, DeVoe Papers.

57 Ibid.

58 *Daily Huronite (SD)*, 5 October 1888.

59 Ibid., 7 November 1888.

60 Ibid., 10 November 1888.

61 John E. Miller, "More than Statehood on Their Minds: South Dakota Joins the Union, 1889," *Great Plains Quarterly* 10, no. 4 (Fall 1990): 206–17.

62 *Daily Huronite (SD)*, 14 March 1889.

63 *Minutes of the National Woman's Christian Temperance Union at the Sixteenth Annual Meeting, Chicago Illinois, November 8 to 13, 1889* (Chicago: Woman's Temperance Publication Association, 1889), lxxv–lxxvi.

64 *Evanston (IL) Union Signal*, 16 May 1889.

65 The *Daily Huronite* reported that she gave an address on woman suffrage. *Daily Huronite (SD)*, 3 July 1889.

66 I have not found a copy of Emma's speech in any newspaper. Willard and Livermore, *American Women*, 239.

67 Mattingly, *Well-Tempered Women*, 58–63.

68 *Daily Huronite (SD)*, 17 May 1889.

69 *Evanston (IL) Union Signal*, 8 August 1889.

70   Italics in original. *Minutes of the National Woman's Christian Temperance Union*, lxxvii; *Daily Huronite (SD)*, 20 June 1889.

71   *Minutes of the National Woman's Christian Temperance Union*, lxxviii.

72   Flaherty is also listed in the 1887 Police Magistrate, Police Justice Dockets, where he is charged with assault with attempt to shoot. For the murder summary, see *Daily Huronite (SD)*, 27 August 1888; the trial can be read about in the April 1889 edition of the newspaper. City of Huron Police Magistrate, Police Justice Dockets, March 1887, SDSHS.

73   *Evanston (IL) Union Signal*, 11 April 1889.

74   *Daily Huronite (SD)*, 3 September 1889.

75   Ibid., 23 August 1889 and 13 September 1889.

76   DeVoe to Julia W. Welles, 17 March 1912, Box 4, Folder 7, DeVoe Papers.

77   *Daily Huronite (SD)*, 1 October 1889.

78   Historian Rebecca Edwards also found that men began to accept women as voters during this period as both middle-class men and women wanted cleaner elections and less vulgar behavior at the polls. By the 1890s, the polls changed further as more women had school and municipal suffrage, which allowed women to vote for school boards, city council members, and mayors. Voters also accepted lunch and literature from women manning the polls. Rebecca Edwards, "Gender, Class, and the Transformation of Electoral Campaigns in the Gilded Age," in *We Have Come to Stay: American Women and Political Parties 1880–1960*, ed. Melanie Gustafson, Kristie Miller, and Elisabeth I. Perry (Albuquerque: University of New Mexico Press, 1999), 13, 16–18, 21; *Daily Huronite (SD)*, 1 October 1889.

79   *Evanston (IL) Union Signal*, 7 November 1889. Additional information about Putnam can be found in an article written by Lisa R. Lindell, "'Sowing the seeds of liberal thought': Unitarian Women Ministers in Nineteenth-century South Dakota," *South Dakota History* 38, no. 2 (Summer 2008): 148–80.

80   *Daily Huronite (SD)*, 4 October 1889.

81   Italics in original. Ibid., 9 October 1889.

82   Ibid.

83   Minutes, 4 October 1889, Box 6675, Folder 28, Pickler Family Papers, SDSHS. (hereafter cited as Pickler Family Papers).

84   Ida Husted Harper, *Life and Work of Susan B. Anthony*, vol. 2 (1898; reprint, New York: Arno and the New York Times, 1969), 656–57.

85   *Daily Huronite (SD)*, 22 October 1889; *Evanston (IL) Union Signal*, 19 December 1889; *Boston Woman's Journal*, 18 January 1890.

86   *Daily Huronite (SD)*, 23 October 1889.

87   Ibid., 26 October 1889.

88   Ibid., 2 and 6 November 1889; *Evanston (IL) Union Signal*, 19 December 1889.

2   THE SOUTH DAKOTA WOMAN SUFFRAGE CAMPAIGN

1   *Boston Woman's Journal*, 15 November 1890.

2   Many historians have studied the 1890 campaign. See Dorinda Riessen Reed, *The*

Woman Suffrage Movement in South Dakota, 2nd ed. (Pierre: South Dakota Commission on the Status of Women, 1975); Cecelia M. Wittmayer, "The 1889–1890 Woman Suffrage Campaign: A Need to Organize," *South Dakota History* 11, no. 3 (Summer 1981): 199–225; Mary Kay Jennings, "Lake County Woman Suffrage Campaign in 1890," *South Dakota History* 5, no. 4 (Fall 1975): 390–409; Dennis A. Norlin, "The Suffrage Movement and South Dakota Churches: Radicals and the Status Quo, 1890," *South Dakota History* 14, no. 4 (Winter 1984): 308–34.

3   Mary Gray Peck, *Carrie Chapman Catt: A Biography* (New York: The H. W. Wilson Company, 1944), 65.

4   Carol Mattingly studied the addresses of WCTU speakers and found that this rhetorical approach was very successful. See *Well-Tempered Women*.

5   *Huronite (SD)*, 13 November 1889.

6   *Daily Huronite (SD)*, 14 November 1889.

7   *Beatrice (NE) Woman's Tribune*, 28 December 1889.

8   Ibid., 7 December 1889.

9   *Evanston (IL) Union Signal*, 7 November 1889.

10   Harper, *Life and Work of Susan B. Anthony*, 681.

11   Members of the WCTU frequently wore a white ribbon bow as a sign of their commitment to consume no alcohol; white symbolized purity. By contrast, yellow was the color of the suffrage movement. Yellow became associated with woman suffrage in 1867, when Kansas suffragists adopted the sunflower as their symbol. *Beatrice (NE) Woman's Tribune*, 7 December 1889.

12   It appears that Emma initially worked under the WCTU because in a March 29th letter to the president, Anthony found the association guilty of holding meetings solely with the WCTU. The only meetings held were "W.C.T.U. county and district conventions." At the end of an extant speech from South Dakota, Emma asked for the ballot "in the name of the WCTU." Harper, *Life and Work of Susan B. Anthony*, 681; *Hecla (SD) Citizen*, 27 June 1890, Scrapbook, vol. 1, 1892–1894, Box 7, DeVoe Papers.

13   Mattingly, *Well-Tempered Women*, 67.

14   Frances E. Willard, *Woman and Temperance, or the Work and Workers of the Woman's Christian Temperance Union* (Hartford, CT: Park Publishing Company, 1883), 625.

15   Henry dedicated the song to the Woman's Relief Corps of South Dakota. When he and Emma returned to Illinois, he dedicated the song to the national WRC and changed Woman to Women. "A Soldier's Tribute to Woman," Scrapbook of Clara Watson Elsom, Box 5, DeVoe Papers; "A Soldier's Tribute to Women," Tom Welch Papers.

16   *Beatrice (NE) Woman's Tribune*, 4 January 1890.

17   *Boston Woman's Journal*, 4 January 1890.

18   Mary Dodge Woodward, *The Checkered Years*, ed. Mary Boynton Cowdrey (Caldwell, ID: The Caxton Printers, Ltd., 1937), 28.

19   *Boston Woman's Journal*, 4 January 1890.

20   *Beatrice (NE) Woman's Tribune*, 1 February 1890.

21   *Boston Woman's Journal*, 22 February 1890 and 5 April 1890.

22   *South Dakota State Journal* quoted in *Boston Woman's Journal*, 18 January 1890.

23   *Beatrice (NE) Woman's Tribune*, 4 January 1890.

24   Stephen T. Morgan, "Fellow Comrades: The Grand Army of the Republic in South Dakota," *South Dakota History* 36, no. 3 (Fall 2006): 235–36.

25   *Hecla (SD) Citizen*, 27 June 1890, Scrapbook, vol. 1, 1892–1894, Box 7, DeVoe Papers.

26   In the 1860s and 1870s, popular literature highlighted northern women's aid and assistance. This recognition faded quickly. By the 1880s recollections about the Civil War increasingly focused upon the battles and heroism of the soldiers, changing the perspective of the war and therefore its meaning. Alice Fahs, "The Feminized Civil War: Gender, Northern Popular Literature, and the Memory of the War, 1861–1900," *Journal of American History* 85, no. 4 (March 1999): 1461–94.

27   Jeannette Rankin used similar tactics when speaking. Hayden, "Negotiating Femininity and Power," 89–90.

28   *Hecla (SD) Citizen*, 27 June 1890.

29   Ibid.

30   Ibid.

31   *Boston Woman's Journal*, 1 October 1892. Carrie Lane Chapman had married George Catt in June 1890. Even though she had remarried, she continued to use her previous married name, Carrie Lane Chapman, in various suffrage campaigns, including in South Dakota and in the *Des Moines Woman's Standard*. To avoid any confusion, I refer to her as Carrie Chapman Catt in this and following chapters.

32   Olympia Brown, *Acquaintances, Old and New, Among Reformers* (Milwaukee: S. E. Tate Printing Co., 1911), 99.

33   *Beatrice (NE) Woman's Tribune*, 4 January 1890.

34   Carol S. Lomicky, "Frontier Feminism and the *Woman's Tribune*: The Journalism of Clara Bewick Colby," *Journalism History* 28, no. 3 (Fall 2002): 102–11.

35   There is a $50 discrepancy over the pledge of a Montana suffragist. The *Daily Huronite* reported she donated $200, while the suffrage newspaper, the *Woman's Journal*, reported a higher figure. *Daily Huronite (SD)*, 21 February 1890; *Boston (MA) Woman's Journal*, 1 March 1890.

36   *Daily Huronite (SD)*, 21 March 1890.

37   *Aberdeen (SD) Daily News*, 3 May 1890; Nancy Tystad Koupal, ed. and annotated, *Our Landlady/L. Frank Baum* (Lincoln: University of Nebraska Press, 1996), 11. For additional details about Marietta Bones, see Nancy Tystad Koupal, "Marietta Bones: Personality and Politics in the South Dakota Suffrage Movement," in *Feminist Frontiers: Women Who Shaped the Midwest*, ed. Yvonne J. Johnson (Kirksville, MO: Truman State University Press, 2010), 69-82.

38   The *Beatrice (NE) Woman's Tribune* printed a few snippets of a letter or two from Emma to Anthony, suggesting that they corresponded.

39   Julia Wiech Lief, "A Woman of Purpose: Julia B. Nelson," *Minnesota History* 47, no. 8 (Winter 1981): 302–14.

40 *Daily Huronite (SD)*, 1 April 1890.

41 Ibid., 8 April 1890.

42 *Dakota Ruralist* quoted in *Boston Woman's Journal*, 13 April 1890.

43 For more information, see Rosalind Urbach Moss, "The 'Girls' from Syracuse: Sex Role Negotiations of Kansas Women in Politics, 1887–1890," in *The Women's West*, ed. Susan Armitage and Elizabeth Jameson (Norman: University of Oklahoma Press, 1987), 253–64.

44 *Daily Huronite (SD)*, 29 April 1890.

45 Susan B. Anthony to Olympia Brown, 2 August 1890, Olympia Brown Papers, microfilm edition (hereafter cited as Brown Papers), The Schlesinger Library, Radcliffe Institute for Advanced Study, Harvard University, Cambridge, Massachusetts (hereafter cited as Schlesinger Library).

46 Suffragist Doris Stevens proclaimed that "Susan B. Anthony was the first militant suffragist" and that she had a "keen appreciation of the fact that the attention of the nation must be focused on minority issues by dramatic acts of protest." *Jailed for Freedom* (New York: Boni and Liveright Publishing Corporation, 1920) 3, 8.

47 Kathleen Barry, *Susan B. Anthony: A Biography of a Singular Feminist* (New York: New York University Press, 1988), 283, 300.

48 Harper, *Life and Work of Susan B. Anthony*, 918.

49 Farrell, *Lillie Devereux Blake*, 162.

50 Melanie Susan Gustafson, *Women and the Republican Party, 1854–1924* (Urbana: University of Illinois Press, 2001), 61.

51 Huron City Council minutes, 20 June 1890.

52 *Aberdeen (SD) Daily News*, 24 July 1890.

53 Harper, *Life and Work of Susan B. Anthony*, 684.

54 Emphasis in original. Anthony to Alice M. Pickler, 14 June 1890, Box 6674, Folder 37, Pickler Family Papers.

55 Herbert S. Schell and John E. Miller, *History of South Dakota*, rev. ed. (Pierre: South Dakota State Historical Society, 2004), 228.

56 *Daily Huronite (SD)*, 7 July 1890.

57 Ibid., 24 June 1890.

58 Helen M. Gougar to Pickler, 23 June 1890, Box 6674, Folder 40, Pickler Family Papers.

59 Harper, *Life and Work of Susan B. Anthony*, 683.

60 Anthony to Pickler, n.d., Box 6674, Folder 37, Pickler Family Papers ; S. A. Richards to Pickler, 23 June 1890, Box 6674, Folder 40, Pickler Family Papers.

61 *Aberdeen (SD) Weekly News*, 27 June 1890; *Aberdeen (SD) Weekly News*, 11 July 1890; *Aberdeen (SD) Daily News*, 1 July 1890.

62 The decision to select men for officers displeased Anthony, whose biographer wrote, "The Dakota people had made the mistake of electing a suffrage board entirely of men, except the treasurer and state organizer." Harper, *Life and Work of Susan B. Anthony*, 680.

63 *Boston Woman's Journal*, 6 September 1890.

64   Some of the committee members doubted Richards's loyalty to the new committee. She told Elizabeth Wardall, "As long as I maintain a position on this or any other committee, my position will be one of loyalty to the will of the majority. As questions come up for discussion *in the committee*, I shall state my views frankly and earnestly but I shall have no policy to maintain independent of, or outside of the committee." Emphasis in original. Richards to Wardall, 16 July 1890, Box 6674, Folder 9, Pickler Family Papers.

65   Suffrage newspapers disagreed over who was appointed to the music committee—Emma or Henry. I believe Henry was, as Anthony told Olympia Brown that he was in charge of putting together a suffrage campaign songbook. He also seemed the likely choice because Emma was busy organizing and speaking during these final months of the campaign. *Beatrice (NE) Woman's Tribune*, 19 July 1890; *Boston Woman's Journal*, 26 July 1890; Anthony to Brown, 2 August 1890, Brown Papers; *Des Moines (IA) Woman's Standard*, October 1890.

66   The organization handed an olive branch to Helen Barker. Irene G. Adams, vice president of the association, and Judge Thomas asked Barker to remain on the committee. Adams said, "Mrs. Barker we need your work for suffrage, won't you stay in the committee, if you can work in harmony with the rest of us, and speak for us." Adams also asked Anthony to extend an invitation to her, which she did. Adams to William F. Bailey, 18 August 1890, Box 6675, Folder 1, Pickler Family Papers.

67   *Daily Huronite (SD)*, 10 July 1890.

68   *Boston Woman's Journal*, 9 August 1890.

69   Brown, *Acquaintances*, 9, 98; E. S. R., "Olympia Brown," *American Reformers*, ed. Alden Whitman (New York: The H. W. Wilson Company, 1985), 132.

70   South Dakota Equal Suffrage Song Book, Box 6675, Folder 13, Pickler Family Papers; *Beatrice (NE) Woman's Tribune*, 13 September 1890.

71   *Boston Woman's Journal*, 6 September 1890.

72   *Aberdeen (SD) Weekly News*, 26 September 1890.

73   Laura M. Johns to Bailey, 3 September 1890, Box 6674, Folder 3, Pickler Family Papers.

74   In an article in the *Aberdeen Saturday Pioneer*, Frank L. Baum described the Guards as "a female band of Lancers." Koupal, *Our Landlady*, 193.

75   Information about the fair can be found in *Beatrice (NE) Woman's Tribune*, 11 October 1890; *Boston (MA) Woman's Journal*, 27 September 1890; Koupal, *Our Landlady*, 241.

76   "Press Notices of Emma Smith DeVoe, President of the Equal Suffrage Association of the First Congressional District, Illinois, and late State Lecturer of the South Dakota E.S.A.," Box 6677, Folder 28, Pickler Family Papers.

77   Emphasis in original. DeVoe to Bailey, 3 October 1890, Box 6674, Folder 2, Pickler Family Papers.

78   Ibid.; general information about Hager can be found in Jennings, "Lake County Woman Suffrage Campaign."

79   DeVoe to Bailey, 6 October 1890, Box 6674, Folder 2, Pickler Family Papers.

80   Ibid., 30 August 1890.

81   Harriet Taylor Upton, interview by Una R. Winter, 17 June 1940, Susan B. Anthony Papers, Box 1, Folder 3, Sophia Smith Collection, Smith College, Northampton, Massachusetts (hereafter cited as SSC).

82   Anna Howard Shaw, *The Story of a Pioneer* (New York: Harper & Brothers Publishers, 1915), 259–60.

83   Quoted in Mattingly, *Well-Tempered Women*, 65.

84   Press Notices of Emma Smith DeVoe, State Lecturer of South Dakota Equal Suffrage Association, Huron, S.D., Box 6674, Folder 43, Pickler Family Papers.

85   These themes are explored in Johnson, *Gender and Rhetorical Space in American Life*, 109–45; quotation 114.

86   Emphasis in original. DeVoe to Elizabeth Murray Wardall, 16 October 1890, Box 6674, Folder 2, Pickler Family Papers.

87   DeVoe to Bailey, October 1890, Box 6674, Folder 2, Pickler Family Papers.

88   Johns to "My dear friends," 25 October 1890, Box 6674, Folder 3, Pickler Family Papers.

89   Nettie C. Hall to Philena Johnson, 10 September 1890, Box 6674, Folder 3, Pickler Family Papers.

90   DeVoe to Bailey, 8 September 1890, Box 6674, Folder 2, Pickler Family Papers.

91   Ibid., 6 October 1890.

92   Ibid., 8 October 1890.

93   Alma Lutz, *Susan B. Anthony: Rebel, Crusader, Humanitarian* (Boston: Beacon Press, 1959), 254–55.

94   *Beatrice (NE) Woman's Tribune*, 7 June 1890.

95   DeVoe to Bailey, 12 October 1890, Box 6674, Folder 2, Pickler Family Papers.

96   Emphasis in original. Nelson to Bailey, 20 October 1890, Box 6674, Folder 4, Pickler Family Papers.

97   Nelson to unknown, 17 October 1890, Box 6674, Folder 4, Pickler Family Papers.

98   Hall to Wardall, 20 October 1890, Box 6674, Folder 6, Pickler Family Papers.

99   Andersen compared the differences between male and female politics in *After Suffrage*, 22–28; Johnson, *Gender and Rhetorical Space*, 123, 128–29.

100   I compiled these numbers by taking the figures in Emma's letters and those listed in Nelson's collections. Collections for Julia B. Nelson, October 1 to November 4, Box 6675, Folder 24, Pickler Family Papers; DeVoe to Bailey, October 1890, Box 6674, Folder 2, Pickler Family Papers.

101   DeVoe to Wardall, 4 November 1890, telegram, Box 6674, Folder 2, Pickler Family Papers.

102   *Yankton (SD) Daily Press and Dakotan*, 4 November 1890.

103   *Beatrice (NE) Woman's Tribune*, 1 November 1890.

3   BUILDING A NATIONAL REPUTATION

1   Italics in original. *Boston Woman's Journal*, 1 October 1892.

2   The exact date of her selection as national lecturer is unknown. Presumably

this occurred in November or December of 1890, after voters rejected the South Dakota woman suffrage amendment. See John William Leonard, ed., *Woman's Who's Who of America: A Biographical Dictionary of Contemporary Women of the United State and Canada, 1914–1915* (New York: The American Commonwealth Company, 1914), 243.

3   Doris Weatherford, *A History of the American Suffragist Movement* (Santa Barbara: ABC-Clio, 1998), 157; Farrell, *Lillie Devereux*, 164.

4   Ruth Bordin, *Frances Willard: A Biography* (Chapel Hill: University of North Carolina Press, 1986), 149–153.

5   Emphasis in original. DeVoe to Wardall, n.d., Box 6675, Folder 28, Pickler Family Papers.

6   Capitalization in original. Walter Thomas Mills and Co., "Harvey, Ill: The New Manufacturing Town 1 and ¼ Miles South of Chicago," Illinois State Library, Springfield, Illinois; James Gilbert explored Harvey in his book, *Perfect Cities: Chicago's Utopias of 1893* (Chicago: University of Chicago Press, 1991), 27.

7   Ray Hutchison, "Capitalism, Religion, and Reform: The Social History of Temperance in Harvey, Illinois," in *Drinking: Behavior and Belief in Modern History*, ed. Susanna Barrows and Robin Room (Berkeley: University of California Press, 1991), 190.

8   Alec C. Kerr, ed., *History: The City of Harvey 1890–1962* (Harvey: First National Bank in Harvey, 1962,) 32.

9   Interestingly enough, the *Huron (SD) Times* reported that Henry came to town with $800 and left town with $15,000. This statement of "fact" is erroneous and was simply an attempt to attract more financing and development in the area. Henry and Emma were not well off. Quoted in the *Daily Huronite (SD)*, 20 March 1891.

10   M. D. Sterling of the Chicago and Northwestern Railroad eventually rented the property from the DeVoes in August 1891. *Daily Huronite (SD)*, 25 August 1891.

11   Harvey Land Association, "The Town of Harvey," Illinois State Historical Library, Springfield, Illinois.

12   Quoted in Hutchison, "Capitalism, Religion, and Reform," 191.

13   Roe, *The Ninth New York Heavy Artillery*, 416.

14   Kerr, *History*, 28, 158.

15   Willard and Livermore, *American Women*, 239.

16   Paula M. Nelson, ed. *Sunshine Always: The Courtship Letters of Alice Bower & Joseph Gossage of Dakota Territory* (Pierre: South Dakota State Historical Society Press, 2006), 15.

17   *Boston Woman's Journal*, 30 January 1892.

18   *Beatrice (NE) Woman's Tribune*, 26 March 1892.

19   *Boston Woman's Journal*, 30 January 1892.

20   Ibid., 9 January 1892.

21   While the properties were foreclosed upon and sold in 1891, they were recorded later by the Register of Deeds. In Beadle the foreclosure and auction is documented in 1893; the Faulk County foreclosure and sale is documented in 1892.

Sheriff's Deeds, 1892, Book 9, pp. 328–30, Faulk County Register of Deeds, Faulk County Courthouse, Faulkton, South Dakota; Sheriff's Deeds, 1893, Book 83, pp. 597 and 598, Beadle County Register of Deeds, Beadle County Courthouse, Huron, South Dakota.

22   Warranty Deeds, 1893, Book 104, p. 90, Beadle County Register of Deeds, Beadle County Courthouse, Huron, South Dakota.

23   For an overview of the Alliance, see Nell Irvin Painter, *Standing at Armageddon: The United States 1877–1919* (New York: W. W. Norton & Company, 1987), 60–62, 68–71.

24   F. F. Keith, comp., *The Harvey Directory Company's Directory and Business Guide of the City of Harvey and the Village of North Harvey, Cook County, Illinois, with Descriptive and Historical Sketches of Harvey and Its Institutions* (Harvey: The Harvey Directory Company, 1895), 25.

25   Annie Diggs, "The Women in the Alliance Movement," *The Arena*, July 1892, 175; *Beatrice (NE) Woman's Tribune*, 5 September 1891.

26   Steven M. Buechler, *The Transformation of the Woman Suffrage Movement: The Case of Illinois, 1850–1920* (New Brunswick: Rutgers University Press, 1986), 149–50.

27   Susan B. Anthony and Ida Husted Harper, eds., *The History of Woman Suffrage, 1883–1900*, vol. 4 (Indianapolis: The Hollenbeck Press, 1902), 176.

28   *Sing Out!* 6, no. 4 (Winter 1957): 7, U.S. Suffrage Collection, Box 3, Folder 76, SSC.

29   The DeVoes sold the song from their home in Harvey. *Boston Woman's Journal*, 7 March 1891 and 25 July 1891.

30   Anthony and Harper, *History of Woman Suffrage*, 182.

31   *Washington Post*, 28 February 1891.

32   *Beatrice (NE) Woman's Tribune*, 14 March 1891; DeVoe gave this example in a speech she presented in Hecla, South Dakota. *Hecla (SD) Citizen*, 27 June 1890.

33   Jacqueline Van Voris, *Carrie Chapman Catt: A Public Life* (New York: The Feminist Press at the City University of New York, 1987), 30; Anthony and Harper, *History of Woman Suffrage*, 186.

34   *Boston Woman's Journal*, 30 January 1892.

35   Elisabeth S. Clemens explored the strategies debated in the 1893 and 1894 conventions in her book. Quoted in *The People's Lobby: Organizational Innovation and the Rise of Interest Group Politics in the United States, 1890–1925* (Chicago: University of Chicago Press, 1997), 84–86.

36   Quoted in Leila R. Brammer, *Excluded from Suffrage History: Matilda Joslyn Gage, Nineteenth-Century American Feminist* (Westport, CT: Greenwood Press, 2000), 16, 98–99.

37   *Beatrice (NE) Woman's Tribune*, 11 June 1892.

38   Olympia Brown, ed., *Democratic Ideals: A Memorial Sketch of Clara B. Colby* (Federal Suffrage Association, 1917), 66.

39   *Boston Woman's Journal*, 16 April 1892.

40   *Beatrice (NE) Woman's Tribune*, 11 June 1892.

41   Brown, *Democratic Ideals*, 68.

42   *Beatrice (NE) Woman's Tribune*, 11 June 1892.

43   *Boston Woman's Journal*, 16 April 1892.

44   Ibid., 30 July 1892.

45   General information about the FSA can be found in the Olympia Brown Papers.

46   Brown, *Democratic Ideals*, 71; Charles E. Neu, "Olympia Brown and the Woman's Suffrage Movement," *Wisconsin Magazine of History* 43, no. 4 (Summer 1960): 283.

47   *Des Moines (IA) Woman's Standard*, March 1891.

48   Ibid., May 1892.

49   Schell, *History of South Dakota*, 168.

50   *Beatrice (NE) Woman's Tribune*, 11 October 1890.

51   Ibid., 29 August 1891.

52   Iowa suffragists had been present at previous state fairs; they had built a Woman Suffrage Cottage at the state fairgrounds, but they had no specific day dedicated to women and their achievements. *Des Moines (IA) Woman's Standard*, January 1892; *Beatrice (NE) Woman's Tribune*, 13 February 1892.

53   *Beatrice (NE) Woman's Tribune*, 16 April 1892.

54   *Des Moines (IA) Woman's Standard*, Supplement, January 1892.

55   Nellie Flint to DeVoe, 20 March 1892, Box 2, Folder 12, DeVoe Papers.

56   Jeff Ostler, "Why the Populist Party Was Strong in Kansas and Nebraska, but Weak in Iowa," *Western Historical Quarterly* 23, no. 4 (November 1992): 460.

57   *Des Moines (IA) Woman's Standard*, May, June, July 1892.

58   Mary J. Coggeshall to DeVoe, 28 May 1892, Box 1, Folder 8, DeVoe Papers.

59   Van Voris, *Carrie Chapman Catt*, 31.

60   *Des Moines (IA) Woman's Standard*, October 1892.

61   Ibid., June 1888.

62   Brown, *Acquaintances*, 96.

63   The association elected Henry treasurer. Emphasis in original. C. Holt Flint to DeVoe, 28 May 1892, Box 2, Folder 12, DeVoe Papers; for details about the FSA officers and its lecturers, see *Boston Woman's Journal*, 28 May 1892; *Des Moines (IA) Woman's Standard*, July 1892.

64   Ellen Carol Dubois, ed., *Elizabeth Cady Stanton, Susan B. Anthony, Correspondence, Writings, Speeches* (New York: Schocken Books, 1981), 181.

65   "Programme of the 9th Annual Session of the Wisconsin Woman's Suffrage Association," Brown Papers.

66   Emma wrote these statements in February 1893 when the Eureka College Alumni Association asked her to pen a brief sketch of her life. *A History of Eureka College with Biographical Sketches*, 204.

67   *Des Moines (IA) Woman's Standard*, March 1893.

68   *Washington (DC) Woman's Tribune*, 24 June 1893.

69   *Topeka (KS) Farmer's Wife*, September 1893.

70   She raised $2,000 out of the $2,500 pledged to Kansas. Laura M. Johns thanked Emma for her "excellent work" which "is warmly appreciated." Unfortunately, a

majority of Kansans failed to pay their pledges. Harriet Taylor Upton, ed., *Proceedings of the Twenty-Sixth Annual Convention of the National-American Woman Suffrage Association Held in Washington, D.C., February 15, 16, 17, 18, 19 and 20, 1894* (Warren, Ohio: Chronicle Print, 1894), 145; Anthony and Harper, *History of Woman Suffrage*, 644; Catt to DeVoe, 3 June 1895, Box 1, Folder 12, DeVoe Papers.

71   *Boston Woman's Journal*, 4 November 1893.

72   Ibid., 21 April 1894.

73   Emphasis in original. DeVoe to Friends of Liberty, 16 September 1893, Box 6678, Folder 21, Pickler Family Papers.

74   *Boston Woman's Journal*, 11 November 1893.

75   Ibid., 3 February 1894.

76   Beverly Beeton, *Women Vote in the West: The Woman Suffrage Movement 1869–1896* (New York: Garland Publishing, 1986), 111–14.

77   Catt, however, was uncertain if DeVoe was a Populist, but in a later letter said she was. Catt to Mrs. Stansbury, 16 July 1893, Box 1, Folder 1, Meredith Collection; Catt to Mrs. Stansbury, 23 June 1893, Box 1, Folder 1, Meredith Collection.

78   Quoted in Painter, *Standing at Armageddon*, 117; Erik Larson, *The Devil in the White City: Murder, Magic, and Madness at the Fair That Changed America* (New York: Vintage Books, 2003), 334.

79   Quoted in Kerr, *History*, 33.

80   By 1894 a "border saloon" appeared in Harvey, and Henry heard a case involving the bar room in the spring. *Harvey (IL) Tribune Citizen*, 21 April 1894 and 12 May 1894.

81   Willis J. Abbot, "The Chicago Populist Campaign," *The Arena* 11 (February 1895): 330.

82   *Harvey (IL) Tribune Citizen*, 12 May 1894.

83   Chester McA. Destler, "Consummation of a Labor-Populist Alliance in Illinois, 1894," *Mississippi Valley Historical Review* 27, no. 4 (March 1941): 595.

84   *Topeka (KS) Farmer's Wife*, September 1893.

85   Anthony and Harper, *History of Woman Suffrage*, 173–74.

86   Harper, *Life and Work of Susan B. Anthony*, 777.

87   Ibid., 779, 781.

88   Emphasis in original. Elizabeth F. Hopkins to DeVoe, 21 April 1894, Box 4, Folder 56, DeVoe Papers.

89   Quoted in Michael Lewis Goldberg, *An Army of Women: Gender and Politics in Gilded Age Kansas* (Baltimore: Johns Hopkins University Press, 1997), 234.

90   Emphasis in original. Johns to DeVoe, 16 May 1894, Box 4, Folder 56, DeVoe Papers.

91   Harper, *Life and Work of Susan B. Anthony*, 785, 1020.

92   Anthony to Clara B. Colby, 26 May 1894, Clara B. Colby Papers, The Huntington Library, San Marino, California.

93   Quoted in Goldberg, *An Army of Women*, 235.

94   Ibid.

95   Harper, *Life and Work of Susan B. Anthony*, 785.

96   Emphasis in original. Johns to DeVoe, 19 June 1894, Box 4, Folder 56, DeVoe Papers.

97   Emphasis in original. Anthony to DeVoe, 21 August 1894, formerly of the DeVoe Papers. (This letter was stolen from the collection; fortunately, photocopies were made of the letter prior to its loss.)

98   Emphasis in original. Anthony to DeVoe, 25 August 1894, formerly of the DeVoe Papers. (This letter was stolen from the collection; fortunately, photocopies were made of the letter prior to its loss.)

99   Goldberg, *An Army of Women*, 256; Ann Birney and Joyce Thierer, "Shoulder to Shoulder: Kansas Women Win the Vote," *Kansas Heritage* 3, no. 4 (Winter 1995): 68.

100   DeVoe to Carrie M. Williams, 6 December 1897, Box 3, Folder 14, DeVoe Papers.

101   Harper, *Life and Work of Susan B. Anthony*, 798.

102   The 1896 NAWSA proceedings state that a production put on by Dr. Cora Smith Eaton raised over $300, which funded nearly all of DeVoe's expenses. Rachel Foster Avery, ed., *Proceedings of the Twenty-Eighth Annual Convention of the National-American Woman Suffrage Association Held in Washington, D.C., January 23d to 28th, 1896* (Philadelphia: Press of Alfred J. Ferris, 1896), 152.

103   *Grand Forks (ND) Daily Plainsdealer*, 11 February 1895.

104   *Fargo (ND) Daily Forum and Republican*, 21 February 1895.

105   *Buffalo (ND) Western Womanhood*, February 1895.

106   *Fargo (ND) Daily Forum and Republican*, 21 February 1895.

107   *Buffalo (ND) Western Womanhood*, February 1895.

108   Cora Smith Eaton to DeVoe, 2 March 1895, Box 2, Folder 2, DeVoe Papers.

109   Emma F. Bates to Flint, 21 March 1895, Box 3, Folder 1, DeVoe Papers.

110   Bates to DeVoe, 21 March 1895, Box 3, Folder 1, DeVoe Papers.

111   Peter H. Argersinger, "Ideology and Behavior: Legislative Politics and Western Populism," *Agricultural History* 58, no.1 (January 1984): 46.

112   Rebecca Edwards, *Angels in the Machinery: Gender in American Party Politics from the Civil War to the Progressive Era* (New York: Oxford University Press, 1997), 113.

113   Emphasis in original. Bates to DeVoe, 23 November 1895, Box 3, Folder 1, DeVoe Papers.

4   THE ORGANIZATION COMMITTEE

1   Harriet Taylor Upton, ed., *Proceedings of the Twenty-Seventh Annual Convention of the National-American Woman Suffrage Association Held in Atlanta, Ga., January 31st to February 5th 1895* (Warren, OH: W. M. Ritezel and Co. Printers, 1895), 21.

2   *Boston Woman's Journal*, 9 February 1895.

3   Upton, *Proceedings of the Twenty-Seventh Annual Convention*, 23–27.

4   Examples of these materials can be found in the Jane R. Breeden Papers, SDSHS (hereafter cited as Breeden Papers); Flexner, *Century of Struggle*, 244–45; a descrip-

tion of the committee's aid to local chapters can be found in Avery, *Proceedings of the Twenty-Eighth Annual Convention*, 41.

5   Clemens, *People's Lobby*, 89–90.

6   Ruth Bordin, *Woman and Temperance: The Quest for Power and Liberty, 1873–1900* (Philadelphia: Temple University Press, 1981), 72, 89–90, 94, 151; Jennie Cunningham Croly, *The History of the Woman's Club Movement in America* (New York: Henry G. Allen & Co., 1898), 169; Catt to Abigail Scott Duniway, 14 March 1895, Box 1 Folder 1, Abigail Scott Duniway Papers, University of Oregon, Special Collections and University Archives, Eugene, Oregon (hereafter cited as Duniway Papers).

7   When Ella Harrison, a Missouri suffragist, asked Catt about working as an organizer for the committee, Catt replied, "It has not been our custom to employ people for any length of time until they have been tested." Catt to Ella Harrison, 10 April 1896, Ella Harrison Papers, The Schlesinger Library (microfilm edition). In a letter to South Dakota women, Catt explained the type of workers she needed for the campaign. Each of the attributes listed in the text describe her organizers. Catt to Dear Friend, 15 December 1897, *National American Woman Suffrage Association Letters, 1897–1898* (Pierre, SD: South Dakota Status on the Commission of Women, 1970; microfilm edition).

8   Catt to DeVoe, 7 November 1895, Box 1, Folder 3, DeVoe Papers.

9   Catt to DeVoe, 9 February 1895, Box 1, Folder 10, DeVoe Papers.

10   Louise Avery Gillette to DeVoe, 24 March 1893, Box 2, Folder 9, DeVoe Papers.

11   T. A. Larson, "Woman's Rights in Idaho," *Idaho Yesterdays* 16, no. 1 (Spring 1972): 8–9.

12   The only mention of this orchard is found in a letter from Catt to Emma. Catt to DeVoe, 7 March 1895, Box 1, Folder 11, DeVoe Papers.

13   Ibid., 9 February 1895, Box 1, Folder 10.

14   Quoted in Doris Buck Ward, "The Winning of Woman Suffrage in Montana" (master's thesis, Montana State University, 1974), 46. T. A. Larson's study of the Montana woman suffrage movement provides a chronological overview of the battle for women's enfranchisement in that state, and a few pages are devoted to Emma's work there; see T. A. Larson, "Montana Women and the Battle for the Ballot," *Montana: the Magazine of Western History* 23, no. 1 (January 1973): 24–41. Two Montana women also wrote brief essays on the history of woman suffrage in Montana. See "A Half Century of Progress for Montana Women," SC 122, Mary Long Alderson Papers, Montana Historical Society, Helena, Montana (hereafter cited as MHS); "Woman Suffrage in Montana," Box 5, Folder 9, MC 78, Martha Edgerton Plassmann Papers, MHS.

15   Catt to DeVoe, 7 March 1895, Box 1, Folder 11, DeVoe Papers.

16   Avery, *Proceedings of the Twenty-Eighth Annual Convention*, 40.

17   Numerous studies have addressed this issue, including Beeton, *Women Vote in the West*; T. A. Larson, "Emancipating the West's Dolls, Vassals and Hopeless Drudges: The Origins of Woman Suffrage in the West," in *Essays in Western History in Honor of T. A. Larson*, ed. Roger Daniels (Laramie: University of Wyo-

ming Publications, 1971), 1–16; Mead, *How the Vote Was Won.*

18   Patricia Easton, "A Brief Custer County History," Miles City.com http://www.milescity.com/History/stories/bcch/.

19   *Billings (MT) Gazette*, 18 May 1895.

20   *Boston Woman's Journal*, 13 July 1895.

21   For a discussion of how and why state suffrage associations were formed, see Holly J. McCammon, "Stirring Up Suffrage Sentiment: The Formation of the State Woman Suffrage Organizations, 1866–1914," *Social Forces* 80, no. 2 (December 2001): 449–80.

22   *Boston Woman's Journal*, 13 July 1895.

23   Catt to DeVoe, 3 June 1895, Box 1, Folder 12, DeVoe Papers.

24   DeVoe to Catt, 11 June 1895, Box 1, Folder 12, DeVoe Papers.

25   *Boston Woman's Journal*, 13 July 1895.

26   Ibid.

27   Ibid.

28   Sara Hunter Graham, *Woman Suffrage and the New Democracy* (New Haven: Yale University Press, 1996), 36–38.

29   Beverly Beeton and G. Thomas Edwards, "Susan B. Anthony's Woman Suffrage Crusade in the American West," *Journal of the West* 21, no. 2 (April 1982): 13.

30   Ward, "Winning of Woman Suffrage in Montana," 47.

31   *Bozeman New Issue* quoted in *Boston Woman's Journal*, 13 July 1895.

32   Emphasis in original. DeVoe to Catt, 11 June 1895, Box 1, Folder 12, DeVoe Papers.

33   Emphasis in original. Catt to DeVoe, 11 June 189[5], Box 1, Folder 10, DeVoe Papers.

34   Ibid., 15 June 1895, Box 1, Folder 12

35   Details about Waite's loss can be found in Mead, *How the Vote Was Won*, 71.

36   Emphasis in original. Catt to DeVoe, 9 February 1895, Box 1, Folder 10, DeVoe Papers.

37   Duniway, *Path Breaking*, 210.

38   Roberta O. McKern, "The Woman Suffrage Movement in Oregon and the Oregon Press" (master's thesis, University of Oregon, 1975), 36–37.

39   T. A. Larson, "The Woman Suffrage Movement in Washington," *Pacific Northwest Quarterly* 67, no. 2 (April 1976): 53.

40   Upton, *Proceedings of the Twenty-Seventh Annual Convention*, 23.

41   Catt to DeVoe, 19 March 1895, Box 1, Folder 11, DeVoe Papers.

42   Ibid., 7 March 1895.

43   Ibid., 19 March 1895.

44   Catt to Duniway, 14 March 1895, Box 1, Folder 1, Duniway Papers.

45   *Boston Woman's Journal*, 13 July 1895.

46   Catt to DeVoe, 3 June 1895, Box 1, Folder 12, DeVoe Papers.

47   Ibid., 189[5], Box 1, Folder 10

48   Ibid., 1 April 1895, Box 1, Folder 11

49   Ibid., 11 June 189[5], Box 1, Folder 10

50   Emma's accusation offended Catt, who said that was one of the "meanest" things

she said. "Don't you think it is a little too much responsibility for one poor individual?" Ibid., 9 July 1895, Box 1, Folder 12.

51   *Boise Idaho Daily Statesman*, 3 July 1895.

52   Catt to DeVoe, 9 July 1895, Box 1, Folder 12, DeVoe Papers.

53   Emma visited the state prison to accurately count the number of men and female inmates. She found 330 men and five women imprisoned. *Boston (MA) Woman's Journal*, 10 August 1895.

54   Ibid., 3 August 1895.

55   Catt to DeVoe, 8 August 1895, Box 1, Folder 12, DeVoe Papers.

56   Ibid.

57   Wilder Nutting to DeVoe, 12 July 1895, Box 3, Folder 2, DeVoe Papers.

58   Catt to DeVoe, 8 August 1895, Box 1, Folder 12, DeVoe Papers.

59   Emphasis in original. Sarepta Sanders to DeVoe, 7 August 1895, Box 4, Folder 58, DeVoe Papers.

60   For more information on Utah and woman suffrage, see Carol Cornwall Madsen, ed., *Battle for the Ballot: Essays on Woman Suffrage in Utah, 1870–1896* (Logan: Utah State University Press, 1997).

61   Catt to DeVoe, 8 August 1895, Box 1, Folder 12, DeVoe Papers.

62   Ibid.

63   Ibid., 21 October 1895, Box 1, Folder 3.

64   Emphasis in original. Henry DeVoe to Catt, 4 November 1895, Box 4, Folder 54, DeVoe Papers.

65   Catt to DeVoe, 7 November 1895, Box 4 Folder 53, DeVoe Papers.

66   DeVoe to Catt, n.d., Box 4, Folder 53, DeVoe Papers.

67   Catt to DeVoe, 5 November 1895, Box 1, Folder 3, DeVoe Papers.

68   Ibid., 7 November 1895, Box 4, Folder 53.

69   Ibid; Flint to DeVoe, 24 November 1895, Box 2, Folder 12, DeVoe Papers. Mrs. C. Holt Flint told Emma that Susan B. Anthony was the one who "said you were jealous, and we both know that for some reason you were not one of her pets. When I told her last winter that I had just come from your house, she said, 'Ain't Henry a good fellow?' and not a word about you." This statement is contrary to an 1894 letter typed by Carrie Chapman Catt, which said that Anthony thought highly of Emma.

70   Emphasis in original. Flint to DeVoe, 16 November 1895 and n.d., Box 2, Folder 12, DeVoe Papers.

71   Catt to DeVoe, 7 November 1895, Box 1, Folder 3, DeVoe Papers; *National Suffrage Bulletin*, November 1895, Schlesinger Library; Catt to Isabel Howland, 16 December 1895, Box 1, Folder 30, Isabel Howland Papers, SSC.

72   Catt to DeVoe, 3 December 1895, Box 1, Folder 14, DeVoe Papers. An example of Catt's begging style can be found in Catt to friend, 19 December 1895, George and Phoebe Apperson Hearst Papers, Bancroft Library, Berkeley, California.

73   Flint to DeVoe, 10 January 1896, Box 2, Folder 12, DeVoe Papers.

74   The press reported the title as "The Elevation of the Woman Means the Elevation of the Race." Unidentified clipping, n.d., Scrapbook, vol. 5, Box 8, DeVoe Papers.

75   Avery, *Proceedings of the Twenty-Eighth Annual Convention*, 48, 56–57.

76   Ibid., 45–46.

77   Catt to DeVoe, 28 February 1896, Box 1, Folder 14, DeVoe Papers.

78   Ibid.

79   The women of Virginia City refused to communicate with the committee because their club had dissolved a week after Emma left in 1895. They did so because men of the community "threatened to boycott all lady members," and the women believed that the club would "destroy" their chances at marriage. Even some of the husbands of the married women threatened their wives with divorce and a strike. Helen M. Reynolds to DeVoe, n.d., Box 3, Folder 5, DeVoe Papers; "A Glorious End," unidentified newspaper clipping, n.d., SC 45, George E. Morse Papers, MHS.

80   Catt to DeVoe, 15 April 1896, Box 1, Folder 15, DeVoe Papers.

81   *Billings (MT) Gazette*, 24 April 1896; Catt to DeVoe, 11 April 1896, Box 1, Folder 15, DeVoe Papers.

82   Catt to DeVoe, 22 April 1896, Box 1, Folder 15, DeVoe Papers.

83   *Butte (MT) Miner*, 24 May 1896.

84   Catt to DeVoe, 25 June 1896, Box 1, Folder 15, DeVoe Papers.

85   Minutes of the Helena Business Women's Suffrage Club, 13 and 18 June 1896, Helena Business Women's Suffrage Club Records, MHS.

86   Henry to Emma, 5 June 1896, Box 1, Folder 19, DeVoe Papers.

87   Ibid.

88   Michael P. Malone, Richard B. Roeder, and William L. Lang, *Montana: A History of Two Centuries*, rev. ed (Seattle: University of Washington Press, 1991), 215–18.

89   Catt to DeVoe, 25 June 1896, Box 1, Folder 15, DeVoe Papers; Reynolds to DeVoe, 16 June 1896, Box 3, Folder 5, DeVoe Papers.

90   Catt to DeVoe, 25 June 1896, Box 1, Folder 15, DeVoe Papers.

91   Ibid.

92   Ibid., 24 July 189[6], Box 1, Folder 10.

93   *Boston Woman's Journal*, 6 February 1897.

94   Ibid., 6 March 1897.

95   Catt to DeVoe, 20 February 1897, Box 4, Folder 52, DeVoe Papers.

96   Emphasis in original. Flint to DeVoe, 4 April 1897, Box 2, Folder 12, DeVoe Papers.

97   Ibid., 17 April 1897.

98   Emphasis in original. Catt to DeVoe, 11 April 1897, Box 4, Folder 52, DeVoe Papers.

99   Flint to DeVoe, 4 May 1897, Box 2, Folder 12, DeVoe Papers.

100 Rachel Foster Avery, ed., *Proceedings of the Thirtieth Annual Convention of the National American Woman Suffrage Association and the Celebration of the Fiftieth Anniversary of the First Woman's Rights Convention at the Columbia Theatre, Twelfth and F Streets, Washington, D.C. February 13, 14, 15, 16, 17, 18, 19, 1898* (Philadelphia: Press of Alfred J. Ferris, 1898), 94–95.

101 For example, Helen Reynolds told Jane R. Breeden that Emma and Mrs. Flint were encouraged to go to South Dakota because they were "enemies of Mrs. Catt and her methods." Reynolds to Breeden, 14 February 1898, Box 1, Folder 1, Jane R. Breeden Papers, SDSHS.

102 Clare M. Williams must have written to Emma earlier than December 30, as Emma responded on 6 December. Williams to DeVoe, 30 December 1897, Box 6678, Folder 22, Pickler Family Papers.

103 DeVoe to Williams, 6 December 1897, Box 3, Folder 14, DeVoe Papers.

104 Emma no longer owned this farm, and it is unknown why she told South Dakotans that she did. Ibid.

105 Emphasis in original. Ibid.

106 Ibid.

107 Anna R. Simmons to DeVoe, 13 January 189[8], Box 3, Folder 15, DeVoe Papers.

108 DeVoe to Simmons, 28 January 1898, Box 3, Folder 15, DeVoe Papers.

109 Emphasis in original. Simmons to Williams and Mrs. Judge Bennett, 3 February 1898, Box 6676, Folder 21, Pickler Family Papers.

110 Simmons to Williams, 9 February 1898, Box 6676, Folder 23, Pickler Family Papers.

111 Simmons to DeVoe, [illegible date] February 1898, Box 3, Folder 15, DeVoe Papers.

112 Simmons to Bennett, 28 February 1898, Box 6676, Folder 21, Pickler Family Papers.

113 Catt to Simmons, 28 February 1898, Box 6676, Folder 22, Pickler Family Papers.

114 Emma's letter quoted by Simmons in Simmons to Flint, 6 April 1898, Box 3, Folder 15, DeVoe Papers.

115 Graham, *Woman Suffrage and the New Democracy*, 8.

116 *Boston Woman's Journal*, 15 April 1899.

117 DeVoe to brother and sisters, 1 January 1906, Box 1, Folder 19, DeVoe Papers.

5 THE NORTHWEST CAMPAIGNS

1 *Milwaukee (WI) Free Press*, 7 July 1911.

2 Graham, *Woman Suffrage and the New Democracy*, 33–52.

3 Larson, "Woman Suffrage Movement in Washington," 52, 54–56; C. H. Baily, "How Washington Women Regained the Ballot," *Pacific Monthly* 26, no. 1 (July 1911): 4–7.

4 Harper, *History of Woman Suffrage*, 673.

5 Edwards, *Sowing Good Seeds*, 210–12.

6 Emphasis in original. DeVoe to Catt, 23 November 1909, Box 1, Folder 15, DeVoe Papers.

7 Frances M. Björkman, "Women's Political Methods," *Collier's*, 20 August 1910, 22.

8 Mead, *How the Vote Was Won*, 118–19.

9 In 1884, immigrants who worked on the Northern Pacific Railroad line opposed the measure because they feared that women would vote in favor of prohibition.

Each worker voting against suffrage received $2.50. Moynihan, *Rebel for Rights*, 180–81, 207–8.

10   Edwards, *Sowing Good Seeds*, 203–10.

11   *Portland Woman's Tribune*, 15 June 1907.

12   Ibid., 29 January 1906.

13   Ibid., 31 March 1906.

14   Ibid., 3 February 1906.

15   Ibid., 28 April 1906.

16   Laura Gregg to DeVoe, 14 March 1906, Box 3, Folder 2, DeVoe Papers.

17   Suffragists believed that immigrants overwhelmingly rejected suffrage, but there was no proof that this was the case.

18   Emma called Astoria the "second sized city in Oregon" in a letter to Clara B. Colby. Anna Howard Shaw to DeVoe, 20 April, 21 April, 4 May 1906, Box 3, Folder 11, DeVoe Papers; *Portland Woman's Tribune*, 26 May 1906.

19   *Portland Woman's Tribune*, 26 May 1906.

20   Ibid., 9 June 1906.

21   Ibid., 26 May 1906.

22   *Boston Woman's Journal*, 2 June 1906.

23   Shaw to DeVoe, 2 June 1906, Box 3, Folder 12, DeVoe Papers.

24   G. Thomas Edwards attributes the failure to hostility from the liquor industry, apathy among women, and general opposition to woman suffrage. See *Sowing Good Seeds*, 279, 296–97.

25   DeVoe to brother and sisters, 1 January 1906, Box 1, Folder 19, DeVoe Papers.

26   Clara Colby mentioned their move in 1908, though they had moved earlier. *Portland Woman's Tribune*, 23 May 1908.

27   Ibid., 8 December 1906, Scrapbook, vol. 5, Box 8, DeVoe Papers.

28   DeVoe to Shaw, 14 December 1907, Box 3, Folder 13, DeVoe Papers.

29   *Proceedings of the Thirty-Ninth Annual Convention of the National-American Woman Suffrage Association Held at Chicago February 14th to 19th, inclusive, 1907* (Warren, OH: Press of Wm. Ritezel & Co., 1907), 94.

30   Duniway explained her mistake in *Path Breaking*, 224–25.

31   By January 1908, WESA had 800 members. Ellen S. Leckenby to J. H. DeVoe, 24 October 1907, Box 2, Folder 16, DeVoe Papers; Harriet Taylor Upton to DeVoe, 7 January 1908, Box 3, Folder 18, DeVoe Papers.

32   Cora Smith Eaton to J. H. DeVoe, 6 November 1907, Box 2, Folder 2, DeVoe Papers.

33   As an example of Eaton's devotion, she once told Emma, then commanding the bill through the legislature, you "are the state general, or 'boss.' You speak and I obey." Eaton to DeVoe, 15 January 1909, Box 2, Folder 3, DeVoe Papers.

34   DeVoe to Shaw, 14 December 1907, Box 3, Folder 13, DeVoe Papers.

35   Shaw to DeVoe, 18 January 1908, Box 3, Folder 13, DeVoe Papers.

36   Eaton to Friend, 20 September 1907, Box 2, Folder 2, DeVoe Papers.

37   As Rebecca J. Mead argued, support of what she termed the "progressive-farmer-labor" coalition was crucial to securing suffrage in the western United States, and

one of the reasons women secured woman suffrage in Washington. *How the Vote Was Won*, 112–15.

38 *Des Moines Woman's Standard*, March 1908.

39 As suffragists sought the aid of laborers, labor leaders also looked for their aid. Emphasis in original. Luema G. Johnson to DeVoe, 11 January 1908, Box 2, Folder 15, DeVoe Papers; John Putnam, "A 'Test of Chiffon Politics': Gender Politics in Seattle, 1897–1917," *Pacific Historical Review* 69, no. 4 (November 2000): 596.

40 For examples on the discussion of Progressive coalitions, see John D. Buenker, "Essay," in *Progressivism* (reprint, 1977; Rochester, VT: Schenkman Books, Inc., 1986), 31–69.

41 By summer, she had secured the support of clubwomen and the WCTU. Meeting privately with the WCTU, Emma probably told its leaders of her South Dakota experience, which showed that temperance and woman suffrage could not be wedded without fracturing the movement. To avoid antagonizing the liquor industry, WCTU leadership agreed to "let the work of their unions"—training women and speaking on behalf of woman suffrage—"go unheralded." Upton to DeVoe, 1 June 1908, Box 3, Folder 18, DeVoe Papers; Harper, *History of Woman Suffrage*, 680.

42 *Spokane (WA) Evening Chronicle*, 22 February 1908, Scrapbook, vol. 5, Box 8, DeVoe Papers.

43 Patricia Voeller Horner, "May Arkwright Hutton: Suffragist and Politician," in *Women in Pacific Northwest History: An Anthology*, ed. Karen J. Blair (Seattle: University of Washington Press, 1988), 27, 33.

44 James W. Montgomery, *Liberated Woman: A Life of May Arkwright Hutton* (Fairfield, WA: Ye Galleon Press, 1974), 102, 105.

45 Hutton to DeVoe, 20 March 1908, Box 2, Folder 11, DeVoe Papers.

46 Eaton to J. H. DeVoe, 12 March 1908, Box 2, Folder 2, DeVoe Papers.

47 Leckenby to DeVoe, 15 March 1908, Box 2, Folder 16, DeVoe Papers.

48 Ida N. McIntire to DeVoe, 15 July 1908, Box 2, Folder 18, DeVoe Papers.

49 Eaton to DeVoe, 28 August 1908, Box 2, Folder 4, DeVoe Papers.

50 Hutton to DeVoe, 21 August 1908, Box 2, Folder 11, DeVoe Papers.

51 Upton to DeVoe, 6 October 1908, Box 3, Folder 19, DeVoe Papers.

52 Their help was immeasurable. The president of the club, Lucy Kangley, and her sisters actively worked for suffrage across the state, and in the summer of 1908, they traveled to Mount Vernon, Anacortes, Burlington, and the islands that dotted the Puget Sound, where they polled local residents on the issue of woman's enfranchisement and spoke in favor of equal suffrage. They showed older suffragists in Skagit County how to canvass voters and did the same in Anacortes and Burlington. DeVoe to Elsie Wallace Moore, 21 September 1908, Box 2, Folder 20, DeVoe Papers.; *Boston Woman's Journal*, 8 August 1908; Björkman, "Women's Political Methods," 23.

53 "Equal Suffrage Advocates in Session," 2 October 1908, Scrapbook, vol. 6, Box 8, DeVoe Papers.

54 Harper, *History of Woman Suffrage*, 675.

55 At the time, some New York suffragists used more militant methods like open-air meetings, but the newspapers in Washington overwhelmingly focused their attention upon the British women and so, too, did Washington suffragists. La Reine Baker compared the American and English movements in the *Spokesman-Review*; the women of Washington intended to win the ballot with "winning smiles." *Spokane (WA) Spokesman-Review*, 27 June 1909.

56 "Women Planning Suffrage Lobby," unidentified clipping, n.d., Scrapbook, vol. 6, Box 8, DeVoe Papers.

57 Baily, "How Washington Women Regained the Ballot," 9.

58 DeVoe to Kate M. Gordon, 15 January 1909. Box 2, Folder 10, DeVoe Papers.

59 *Seattle Post-Intelligencer*, 22 January 1909, Scrapbook, vol. 6, Box 8, DeVoe Papers.

60 *Seattle Daily Times*, 30 January 1909, Scrapbook, vol. 6, Box 8, DeVoe Papers.

61 "Too Aggressive, Hurt Cause of the Women," unidentified clipping, n.d., Scrapbook, vol. 8, Box 9, DeVoe Papers.

62 Eaton to Catt, 24 October 1909, Box 2, Folder 5, DeVoe Papers.

63 *Boston Woman's Journal*, 20 March 1909.

64 Ibid., 6 March 1909.

65 Kate M. Gordon to Eaton and DeVoe, 29 March 1909, Box 2, Folder 4, DeVoe Papers.

66 Ibid., 19 April 1909, Box 2, Folder 10, DeVoe Papers.

67 Hutton to Baker, 3 May 1909, Box 1, Folder 5, May Arkwright Hutton Papers, Northwest Museum of Arts and Culture/Eastern Washington Historical Society, Spokane, Washington (hereafter cited as Hutton Papers).

68 As an example, Hutton and Baker purchased more than $200 worth of clothing for Emma. See "Bought her gowns," unidentified clipping, n.d., Scrapbook, vol. 8, Box 9, DeVoe Papers.

69 Hutton to Leona W. Brown, 28 May 1909, Box 1, Folder 6, Hutton Papers. Leona Brown's name is also sometimes spelled Leonia Browne.

70 *Seattle Post-Intelligencer*, 5 May 1909, Scrapbook, vol. 6, Box 8, DeVoe Papers.

71 *Seattle Times*, 23 May 1909.

72 Henry was referring to a series of articles run in the *Seattle Times* dated 23 May 1909, 26 May 1909, and 28 May 1909.

73 Emphasis in original. J. H. DeVoe to Eaton, 29 May 1909, Box 2, Folder 5, DeVoe Papers.

74 Hutton to Carrie Hill, 4 June 1909, Box 1, Folder 7, Hutton Papers.

75 Eaton to DeVoe, 4 June 1909, Box 2, Folder 5, DeVoe Papers.

76 Eaton to Hutton, 17 June 1909, Box 2, Folder 5, DeVoe Papers.

77 Hutton to Eaton, 19 June 1909, Box 2, Folder 5, DeVoe Papers.

78 Katherine M. Smith to Hutton, 26 December 1910, May Arkwright Hutton Papers, Washington State Library, Tumwater, Washington (hereafter cited as Hutton WSL Papers).

79 *Ellensburg Localizer*, 29 June 1909; *Walla Walla (WA) Statesman*, 29 June 1909,; *Seattle Post-Intelligencer*, 30 June 1909, Scrapbook, vol. 3, Box 9, DeVoe Papers.

80 *Seattle Post-Intelligencer*, 30 June 1909, Scrapbook, vol. 3, Box 9, DeVoe Papers.

81   See, for example, *Oakland (CA) Tribune*, 1 July 1909.

82   Numerous state newspapers covered the events: *Ellensburg (WA) Record*, 1 July 1909; *Seattle Star*, 1 July 1909; *Seattle Post-Intelligencer*, 1 July 1909, Scrapbook, vol. 3, Box 9, DeVoe Papers.

83   *Seattle Post-Intelligencer*, 4 July 1909, Scrapbook, vol. 3, Box 9, DeVoe Papers.

84   *Seattle Times*, 5 July 1909, Scrapbook, vol. 3, Box 9, DeVoe Papers.

85   Upton to Catt, 17 November 1909, Box 3, Folder 18, DeVoe Papers.

86   Maud C. Stockwell to DeVoe, 8 April 1911, Box 4, Folder 21, DeVoe Papers. Shaw's comments must have hurt Emma, who had loved Shaw and admitted that she had "implicit confidence and trust" in her. Emma promised that if she served another term as WESA president that there would not be "such wicked stuff published in the papers about Eastern women as was published in the Oregon campaign. I shall come down so hard on any such thing." DeVoe to Shaw, 30 March 1909, Box 3, Folder 12, DeVoe Papers.

87   *Seattle Times*, 4 July 1909.

88   Björkman, "Women's Political Methods," 22.

89   "Too Aggressive, Hurt Cause of the Women," unidentified clipping, n.d., Scrapbook, vol. 8, Box 9, DeVoe Papers.

90   Björkman, "Women's Political Methods," 23–24.

91   This advertising style is explored by Michael McGerr in his essay "Political Style and Women's Power, 1830–1930," *Journal of American History* 77, no. 3 (December 1990): 870–74.

92   Björkman, "Women's Political Methods," 22–23.

93   *Boston Woman's Journal*, 7 May 1910 and 12 November 1910.

94   Dr. Cora Smith Eaton, "How Washington Women Won the Vote," 351, Scrapbook, Box 10, DeVoe Papers.

95   *Seattle Town Crier*, 4 February 1911.

96   Harper, *History of Woman Suffrage*, 677.

97   A biography of the senator can be found in Koupal, *Our Landlady*, 237; *Boston Woman's Journal*, 28 August 1909.

98   Linda J. Lumsden, *Rampant Women: Suffragists and the Right of Assembly* (Knoxville: University of Tennessee Press, 1997), 75.

99   When newspapers reported that Tacoma suffragists would be marching in a Labor Day parade in 1910, Dr. Johnson, WESA state superintendent of work among the labor unions, informed the press that the information was erroneous. "Tacoma suffragists are not London suffragettes, and we never intended to march in the Labor Day parade. . . . The women are going to take part in the parade, however, and have declared themselves decisively in favor of having a float and riding in it." *Tacoma (WA) Ledger*, 30 August 1910, Scrapbook, vol. 10, Box 11, DeVoe Papers. For more on how divisive marching tactics were, see Lumsden, *Rampant Women*, 75–76.

100   Suffragists increasingly used the automobile as a political tool after 1910, although some conservative women questioned the value of the technology to promote their ideas. They feared that motor tours and other brash techniques suffragists

used to call attention to the cause were not respectable. Virginia Scharff, *Taking the Wheel: Women and the Coming of the Motor Age* (Albuquerque: University of New Mexico Press, 1999), 79–83.

101 Margaret Finnegan describes the significance of color in suffrage spectacles in her book, *Selling Suffrage: Consumer Culture and Votes for Women* (New York: Columbia University Press, 1999), 93.

102 *Boston Woman's Journal*, 30 October 1909; *Seattle Votes for Women*, January 1910.

103 For example, a quote from an Aberdeen, Washington, newspaper indicates that DeVoe effectively gauged public opinion. "It may require a few dum dum bullets to drive an idea into an Englishman's head, but aren't there other methods just as efficacious?" *Aberdeen (WA) World*, 30 October 1909, Scrapbook, vol. 8, Box 9, DeVoe Papers.

104 *Spokane (WA) Evening Chronicle*, 30 October 1909, Scrapbook, vol. 8, Box 9, DeVoe Papers.

105 *Seattle Times*, 23 February 1910. Claudius O. Johnson reported that May Arkwright Hutton took credit for Borah's introduction of the resolution in the U.S. Senate on February 21, 1910. Claudius O. Johnson, *Borah of Idaho* (Seattle: University of Washington Press, 1967), 180.

106 According to J. Anthony Lukas, Borah "pursued women voraciously, soon gaining a reputation as Boise's 'town bull'" in the 1890s. His office was located near the capitol's red-light district. He also found that May Arkwright Hutton believed that Borah was "very susceptible to the charms of young women." Later, he had an affair with Alice Roosevelt Longworth. J. Anthony Lukas, *Big Trouble: A Murder in a Small Western Town Sets Off a Struggle for the Soul of America* (New York: Simon & Schuster, 1997), 290, 329; for details of the affair, see Stacy A. Cordery, *Alice: Alice Roosevelt Longworth, from White House Princess to Washington Power Broker* (New York: Viking, 2007).

107 *Seattle Votes for Women*, February 1910. The *Tacoma Tribune* reported only four women attended, while the *Boston Woman's Journal* noted eight. *Tacoma (WA) Tribune*, 2 March 1910, Scrapbook, vol. 9, Box 11, DeVoe Papers; *Boston Woman's Journal*, 5 February 1910.

108 Ibid.

109 DeVoe to Harriet France, 19 March 1910, Box 2, Folder 8, DeVoe Papers.

110 *Seattle Votes for Women*, March 1910.

111 Ibid., April 1910.

112 James H. Brady to DeVoe, 10 September 1910, Box 1, Folder 3, DeVoe Papers.

113 *Seattle Post-Intelligencer*, 10 May 1910, Scrapbook, vol. 9, Box 11, DeVoe Papers; *Boston Woman's Journal*, 22 October 1910.

114 DeVoe to France, 13 September 1910, Box 2, Folder 8, DeVoe Papers; *Yakima (WA) Morning Herald*, 28 September 1910, Scrapbook, vol. 10, Box 11, DeVoe Papers.

115 Speech/Article, n.d., Box 1, Folder 20, DeVoe Papers.

116 Detailed information on the canvass plan can be found in DeVoe to Suffrage Co-Worker, 22 July 1910, Box 1, Folder 21, DeVoe Papers; DeVoe to Suffrage Co-Workers, 17 August 1909, Box 1, Folder 21, DeVoe Papers.

117   Augusta Kegley to DeVoe, 21 September 1909, Box 3, Folder 21, DeVoe Papers.

118   C. B. Kegley to DeVoe, 16 February 1910, Box 3, Folder 21, DeVoe Papers.

119   "Resolution No. 62—-Subject, Equal Suffrage," Introduced by Dr. Luema G. Johnson, of Tacoma, Box 3, Folder 17, DeVoe Papers.

120   DeVoe to Catt, 23 November 1909, Box 4, Folder 54, DeVoe Papers.

121   *Tacoma (WA) Daily News*, 30 August 1910, Scrapbook, vol. 10, Box 11, DeVoe Papers.

122   *Boston Woman's Journal*, 22 October 1910.

123   *Tacoma Ledger* quoted in ibid., 26 November 1910.

124   *Tacoma News* quoted in Eaton, "How Washington Women Won the Vote," 353, DeVoe Papers.

125   *Tacoma (WA) Daily News*, 11 November 1910, Scrapbook, vol. 11, Box 12, DeVoe Papers.

126   Bessie I. Savage to DeVoe, August 1910, Box 3, Folder 10, DeVoe Papers.

127   Dr. Cora Smith King, "The National Council of Women Voters: What It Stands for and How It Was Organized by Governor James H. Brady of Idaho, Now U.S. Senator," *National Review*, 6 March 1914, 10, 12. National Woman's Party Papers, the Suffrage Years (microfilm edition; hereafter cited as NWP Papers), Library of Congress, Washington, DC (hereafter cited as LOC).

128   Ibid. Susa Young Gates is sometimes listed as Susan Young Gates in the press.

129   Smith to Hutton, 26 December 1910, Hutton WSL Papers.

130   Ibid.

131   *Tacoma (WA) Tribune*, 13 January 1911.

132   A short biography of Mason can be found in Leonard, *Woman's Who's Who of America*, 548.

133   *Tacoma (WA) Sunday Tribune*, 15 January 1911; *Seattle Post Intelligencer*, 15 January 1911, Scrapbook, vol. 4, Box 13, DeVoe Papers.

134   Information on the Nesika club can be found in Sandra Haarsager, *Organized Womanhood: Cultural Politics in the Pacific Northwest, 1840–1920* (Norman: University of Oklahoma Press, 1997), 217; Leonard, *Woman's Who's Who of America*, 548.

135   *Tacoma (WA) Tribune*, 18 January 1911, "Tacoma Women thru 1949," Vertical Files, Northwest Room, Tacoma Public Library, Tacoma, Washington.

136   *Tacoma (WA) Daily News*, 14 January 1911.

6   THE NINETEENTH AMENDMENT

1   *Tacoma (WA) News Tribune*, 23 March 1920.

2   Ibid., 2 April 1920.

3   Eleanor Flexner believed it was nearly impossible to differentiate between the Congressional Committee and Congressional Union. "No one could really tell where the activities of one began and the other left off, especially where finances were concerned." *Century of Struggle*, 274.

4   Ibid., 257, 266.

5   Emphasis in original. Bernice A. Sapp to DeVoe, 24 January 1911, Box 3, Folder 8, DeVoe Papers.

6   Cornelia Templeton Jewett gives a hint of what the NCWV faced in February 1911 in a letter. Jewett to Alice Park, 21 February 1911, Alice Park Papers, Box 3, Folder 11, The Huntington Library, San Marino, California (hereafter cited as Park Papers.)

7   Letters to Minerva Goodman hint at Emma's involvement and interest in the California campaign. DeVoe to Minerva Goodman, 11 and 20 February 1911, Minerva Goodman Papers, Holt-Atherton Special Collections, University of the Pacific Library, Stockton, California (hereafter cited as Goodman Papers).

8   "Woman To-Day," *Collier's*, 29 April 1911, 20; for information the PEL and its members, see Gayle Gullett, *Becoming Citizens: The Emergence and Development of the California Women's Movement, 1880–1911* (Urbana: University of Illinois Press, 2000), 182–83; Mead, *How the Vote Was Won*, 132.

9   DeVoe to Goodman, 23 May 1911, Goodman Papers.

10   Brady to DeVoe, 19 August 1911, Box 4, Folder 3, DeVoe Papers.

11   Brown to DeVoe, 16 May 1911, telegram, Box 1, Folder 4, DeVoe Papers.

12   *Racine Wisconsin Citizen*, October 1911, U.S. Suffrage Collection, Box 14, Folder 214, SSC.

13   Catherine Waugh McCulloch to James, 29 May 1911, James Papers.

14   This is the same Katherine Smith that sided with Hutton against Emma in Washington. She signed her name with a C, rather than a K, in this letter. Catherine M. Smith to James, 26 November 1911, James Papers.

15   Brown to Emma, 25 October 1911, Box 1, Folder 5, DeVoe Papers.

16   After the Washington campaign, Henry and Emma began looking for a permanent home in Washington. Eventually, they purchased a house in Parkland. Deed, 1911, Book 361, p. 189, Office of the Pierce County Auditor, Pierce County Annex, Tacoma, Washington.

17   "New Laws in Suffrage States: Acts Passed by 1911 Legislatures of Colorado, Idaho, Utah, Washington and Wyoming," U.S. Suffrage Collection, Box 12, Folder 176, SSC.

18   Emphasis in original. DeVoe to Johnston, 31 December 1912, Box 5, Folder 10, Johnston Papers.

19   William L. O'Neill, *Everyone Was Brave: A History of Feminism in America* (Chicago: Quadrangle Books, 1971), 128; Flexner, *Century of Struggle*, 271.

20   *Tacoma (WA) Daily News*, 8 April 1913, Scrapbook, 1913, DeVoe Papers; *Washington Times*, 31 March 1913; *Washington (DC) Herald*, 1 April 1913.

21   Inez Haynes Irwin, *The Story of the Woman's Party* (1921; repr., New York: Kraus Reprint Co., 1971), 34.

22   Ibid., 35; *Washington Post*, 6 April 1913.

23   Christine A. Lunardini credits only Paul and her organization, but western women voters also participated, and they deserve to be included in this victory. Christine A. Lunardini, *From Equal Suffrage to Equal Rights: Alice Paul and the National Woman's Party, 1910–1928* (New York: New York University Press, 1986), 36–37.

24   Alice Paul to DeVoe, 24 June 1913, NWP Papers.

25   DeVoe to Paul, 13 July 1913, NWP Papers.

26   Summary of organization of the Olympia Branch of the NCWV, n.d., Box 4, Folder 8, DeVoe Papers.

27   Call to Conference, 28 July 1913, Scrapbook, 1913, DeVoe Papers.

28   National Council of Women Voters flyer, n.d., Box 6, National Woman's Party Papers, Group IV, Addition I, 1884–1963, LOC.

29   King to DeVoe, 22 July 1913, telegram, NWP Papers.

30   *Tacoma (WA) Daily News*, 2 August 1913, Scrapbook, 1913, DeVoe Papers.

31   Beverly Beeton kindly shared this cartoon with me as I was writing my dissertation. It came from Colleen Morris' master's thesis: "An Herstorical View of the Alaskan Territorial Legislature's 1913 Vote to Emancipate Women," (master's thesis, Harvard University, 1995).

32   "Bombarded by Petitions of Women," unidentified clipping, n.d., Scrapbook, 1913, DeVoe Papers.

33   Irwin, *The Story of the Woman's Party*, 38–39.

34   Amelia R. Fry, *Conversations with Alice Paul: Woman Suffrage and the Equal Rights Amendment*, an oral history conducted 24–26 November 1972 and 10–12 May 1973, Regional Oral History Office, The Bancroft Library, University of California, Berkeley, 1976, 115.

35   *Charleston (WA) Navy Yard America*, 29 August 1913, Scrapbook, 1913, DeVoe Papers.

36   *Washington Times*, 14 August 1913.

37   Formation of the Olympia Council of Women Voters, n.d., Box 4, Folder 8, DeVoe Papers.

38   DeVoe to Marion E. Hay, 27 September 1913, Box 5, Folder 1, Marion E. Hay Papers, Northwest Museum of Arts and Culture/Eastern Washington State Historical Society, Spokane, Washington.

39   Victoria Bissell Brown, "Jane Addams, Progressivism, and Woman Suffrage: An Introduction to 'Why Women Should Vote,'" in *One Woman, One Vote: Rediscovering the Woman Suffrage Movement*, ed. Marjorie Spruill Wheeler (Troutdale, OR: NewSage Press, 1995), 182.

40   Shaw saw NCWV as NAWSA's rival, and when asked about the council by Frances Munds of Arizona, she advised her to avoid the association, whose members had not been loyal to NAWSA. Initially, Munds followed Shaw's advice, but she eventually joined NCWV, as her name appears on the stationary after 1913. Frances W. Munds to Park, 7 March 1913, Park Papers; Mead, *How the Vote Was Won*, 118, 211n115.

41   Fry, *Conversations with Alice Paul*, 334.

42   Paul to Anna Howard Shaw, 17 August 1913, NWP Papers.

43   Emma was scheduled to meet with President Woodrow Wilson on the final day of the convention, but it is unknown if this meeting took place. *Tacoma (WA) News*, 12 August 1913, Scrapbook, 1913, DeVoe Papers.

44   Paul to Jeannette Rankin, 23 August 1913, NWP Papers.

45   *Washington Post*, 19 August 1913.

46   DeVoe to Jessie Hardy Stubbs, 27 September 1913, NWP Papers.

47   DeVoe to Margaret S. Roberts, 2 October 1913, Margaret S. Roberts Papers (microfilm edition), Schlesinger Library (hereafter cited as Roberts Papers).

48   DeVoe to Paul, 25 September 1913, NWP Papers.

49   Lucy Burns to DeVoe, 19 January 1914, NWP Papers.

50   Lunardini, *From Equal Suffrage to Equal Rights*, 49.

51   DeVoe to Mrs. Thomas Hepburn, 10 February 1914, Box 1, Folder 22, Duniway Papers.

52   Nancy F. Cott, *The Grounding of Modern Feminism* (New Haven: Yale University Press, 1987), 54–57.

53   For example, NAWSA came to support the Shafroth-Palmer Amendment over the Susan B. Anthony Amendment in 1914. The Shafroth-Palmer Amendment would have required states to place woman suffrage on their ballots as a referendum issue if 8 percent of voters in the previous election signed a petition to do so. If Congress passed this amendment, woman suffrage would become exclusively a state's rights issue and thus removed from Congress and the national agenda. The decision was strategic, designed to placate state's rights suffragists, who opposed the passage of a federal amendment enfranchising women. Paul opposed the amendment and so did Emma. If suffrage became a state's rights issue, it would be years before women outside of the West would become full citizens.
     The debate over the amendment interested many western women who were already voters. Virginia Arnold of Portland, Oregon, asked Emma which amendment the NCWV supported. She replied, "I will tell you that we support the Susan B. Anthony amendment first, last and all the time." As a sign of her commitment, she even offered to have the delegates of the 1915 NCWV conference pass a resolution written by Paul which stated that they favored the Anthony Amendment and objected to the NAWSA supported Shafroth-Palmer Amendment. Lunardini, *From Equal Suffrage to Equal Rights*, 55–57; DeVoe to Virginia Arnold, 8 April 1915, NWP Papers; DeVoe to Paul, 19 May 1915, NWP Papers.

54   DeVoe to Duniway, 12 February 1914, Box 1, Folder 22, Duniway Papers.

55   DeVoe to Burns, 11 January 1914, NWP Papers.

56   Mead, *How the Vote Was Won*, 118.

57   Roberts to Paul, 18 February 1914, telegram, NWP Papers; *Boise Idaho Daily Statesman*, 17 February 1914; *Boise (ID) Evening Capitol News*, 16 February 1914.

58   Executive Secretary to Edna A. Stone, 24 February 1914, NWP Papers.

59   Emphasis in original. DeVoe to Paul, 16 April 1914, NWP Papers; not all were opposed, however, and several Idaho women wrote letters to their senator, hoping he might consider national action on the issue. See for instance, Georgia Swann to William E. Borah, 7 March 1914, Box 16, Folder "Woman Suffrage Feb. 3-March 26, 1914," William E. Borah Papers, Library of Congress, Washington, DC (hereafter cited as Borah Papers).

60   *Tacoma (WA) Daily News*, April 1914, NWP Papers.

61   Emphasis in original. DeVoe to Paul, 16 April 1914, NWP Papers.

62   *Washington (DC) Suffragist*, 9 and 16 May 1914.

63   Irwin, *Story of the Woman's Party*, 67.

64   For example, the Boise NCWV repudiated the work of the CU in October of 1914. Helena Hill Weed to Paul, 22 October 1914, NWP Papers; Paul to Weed, 16 October 1914, NWP Papers, King to Weed, 30 October 1914, NWP Papers.

65   Duniway to Paul, n.d., NWP Papers.

66   DeVoe to King, 27 September 1914, NWP Papers.

67   *Washington (DC) Suffragist*, 10 October 1914.

68   For examples of DeVoe's unwillingness to help the CU, see, Anna T. McCue to Paul, 23 September 1914; 2 and 10 October 1914, NWP Papers.

69   Someone wrote on the top of the letter: "Not for publication, you rogue." King to Paul, 6 October 1914, NWP Papers.

70   DeVoe to Paul, 3 May 1914, NWP Papers.

71   "Women Advised to Return Home," unidentified clipping, n.d., NWP Papers.

72   Wesley L. Jones to DeVoe, 28 September 1914, Box 3, Folder 12, Wesley L. Jones Papers (hereafter cited as Jones Papers), Special Collections Division, University of Washington Libraries, Seattle, Washington (hereafter cited as UW).

73   Brady told Roberts of his plan in a letter. See, Brady to Roberts, 14 September 1914, Roberts Papers.

74   Lunardini, *From Equal Suffrage to Equal Rights*, 67.

75   DeVoe to Jones, 8 October 1914, Box 8, Folder 29, Jones Papers.

76   For more specific information about Emma's work in New York, see Helen Barten (Brewster) Owens Papers (microfilm edition), Schlesinger Library.

77   Catt to DeVoe, 17 September 1914, Tom Welch Papers.

78   Details about the auxiliary could not be found. DeVoe to King, 25 October 1914, Box 5, Folder 24, DeVoe Papers.

79   DeVoe to Anne Martin, 24 March 1915, Anne Martin Papers, Bancroft Library, University of California, Berkeley, California (hereafter cited as Martin Papers).

80   Paul to Margaret F. Whittemore, 13 March 1915, NWP Papers.

81   DeVoe to Mrs. Ernest Lister, 18 February 1915, Box 2H-2-94, Folder "Women's Suffrage," Ernest Lister Papers (hereafter cited as Lister Papers) Washington State Archives, Olympia, Washington (hereafter cited as WSA).

82   "Tacoma Man Tells Boston People Suffrage Is Failure in This State," unidentified clipping, n.d., Box 2H-2-94, Folder "Woman Suffrage," Lister Papers.

83   DeVoe to Roberts, 8 April 1915, Roberts Papers.

84   Lister to DeVoe, 12 April 1915, Box 2H-2-94, "Folder Women's Suffrage," Lister Papers.

85   "Testimony of Governors Concerning Woman Suffrage in Their Respective States," Box 1, Folder 46, Duniway Papers.

86   DeVoe to Duniway, 11 June 1915, Box 1, Folder 41, Duniway Papers.

87   Roberts to Carrie Chapman Catt, 10 September 1915, Roberts Papers; Roberts obviously changed her mind or talked out of both sides of her mouth, because Paul reported that Roberts helped their cause in Idaho. Paul to King, 2 September 1915, NWP Papers.

88 Munds to Martin, 26 March 1915, Martin Papers.

89 For information about the national convention, see folders 38 and 39 in the Duniway Papers; DeVoe to Martin, 25 February 1915, Martin Papers.

90 *The Phoenix Arizona Republican*, 2 September 1915, NWP Papers.

91 "To the Woman Voters of America," 1915, NWP Papers.

92 Roberts to Catt, 18 July 1916, Roberts Papers.

93 Qualified Voters to Borah, 1 May 1916, Box 36, Folder "Woman Suffrage 1915–1916," Borah Papers.

94 Emphasis in original. DeVoe to Sapp, 10 May 1916, Box 4, Folder 7, DeVoe Papers. Irritation ran high in 1916, with the eastern women coming west to tell women which candidates to support, including Republican women. They favored presidential Republican candidate Charles Evans Hughes, who ran against President Woodrow Wilson. These women found western women hostile to their efforts. The wife of Montana's governor said, "It is ridiculous for these women, who haven't a vote, to come all the way out here to tell women who can vote how to do it." Portland women also repudiated the "Eastern women's vote-getting invasion." Quotes about the Hughes campaign can be found in Molly M. Wood, "Mapping a National Campaign Strategy: Partisan Women in the Presidential Election of 1916," in *We Have Come to Stay: American Women and Political Parties 1880–1960*, ed. Melanie Gustafson, Kristie Miller, and Elisabeth I. Perry (Albuquerque: University of New Mexico Press, 1999), 82.

95 A summary of the convention can be found in Olympia Brown's papers and the local newspaper. She disagreed with the press, saying that the association did not intend to oppose the CU. Brown to Editor, 5 August 1916, Brown Papers; *Cheyenne (WY) State Leader*, 27 and 28 July 1916.

96 Executive board minutes, 1916, National American Woman Suffrage Association Papers (microfilm edition), LOC (hereafter cited as NAWSA Papers).

97 DeVoe to Lister, 14 September 1916, Woman Suffrage Special Collection, Box 1, WSA.

98 Lister to R. W. Clarke, 2 October 1916, Box 1, Woman Suffrage Special Collection.

99 *Tacoma (WA) Vanguard*, 1 October 1916, Pearl Tyer Papers, Idaho State Historical Society, Boise, Idaho.

100 Reed, *Woman Suffrage Movement in South Dakota*, 95, 117.

101 DeVoe to Mamie Shields Pyle, 18 November 1918, Box 4, Folder "Correspondence November 1918, 15–30," Mamie Shields Pyle Papers, Richardson Collection, Archives and Special Collections, University of South Dakota, Vermillion, South Dakota.

102 In 1918 Emma also wrote a letter to Catt detailing how Senator Borah might be persuaded to vote for woman suffrage. Catt to Board of Officers, 13 March 1917, Maud Wood Park Papers (microfilm edition), Schlesinger Library; Letter to Park, 1 June 1918, Catt Papers, Box 2, Folder 5, SSC.

103 Unidentified sheet listing state congressional chairman and the congressional aides, n.d., NAWSA Papers.

104   Sara Hunter Graham outlines the duties of congressional aides in *Woman Suffrage and the New Democracy*, 98.

105   "Prominent Suffragist Visitor in Salt Lake," unidentified clipping, n.d., Scrapbook, Emma Elizabeth Lindsey Thomas Papers, Manuscripts Division, University of Utah, Marriott Library, Salt Lake City, Utah.

106   Van Voris, *Carrie Chapman Catt*, 137–38; Peck, *Carrie Chapman Catt*, 267–68.

107   Application, 12 April 1917, Pierce County Service League Papers.

108   Examples of the DeVoe's war work can be found in the *Tacoma (WA) Tribune*, 15 May 1918; *Tacoma (WA) News Tribune*, 30 August 1918.

109   Marjorie Spruill Wheeler, "Introduction: A Short History of the Woman Suffrage Movement in America," in *One Woman, One Vote: Rediscovering the Woman Suffrage Movement*, ed. Marjorie Spruill Wheeler (Troutdale, OR: NewSage Press, 1995), 16–17; Ronald Schaffer, *America in the Great War: The Rise of the War Welfare State* (New York: Oxford University Press, 1991), 93–94.

110   Mead made this assertion much more strongly in her dissertation than in her book. "How the Vote Was Won: Woman Suffrage in the Western United States, 1868–1914" (PhD diss., University of California-Los Angeles, 1999), 182.

111   Catt to Jeannette Rankin, 3 December 1917, Box 9, Folder 14, MC 147, Jeannette Rankin Papers, MHS.

112   Roberts to DeVoe, 13 March 1919, Roberts Papers.

113   *New York Woman Citizen*, 5 April 1919; Justina Leavitt Wilson, *Minutes of the Jubilee Convention (1869–1919) of the National American Woman Suffrage Association Including the Regular Sessions of Convention and Conferences of Women Voters, St. Louis, Missouri, March 24–29, 1919* (New York: National Woman Suffrage Publishing Co., 1919), 15, 35–36, NAWSA Papers.

114   Although the Washington State NCWV officially became a part of the League of Women Voters on January 6th, the local Tacoma club did not disband until the ratification of the Nineteenth Amendment in August 1920, and Emma continued to use her NCWV title well into September 1920. Harper, *History of Woman Suffrage*, 683; for examples of the NCWV's continuation, see *Tacoma (WA) News Tribune*, 24 August 1920, Scrapbook, vol. 12, Box 12, DeVoe Papers; *Galveston (TX) Daily News*, 11 September 1920.

115   *Tacoma (WA) Daily Ledger*, 2 July 1919; Graham, *Woman Suffrage and the New Democracy*, 131.

116   Ibid., 19 August 1919; for general information about the fight, see Woman Suffrage Files, Louis F. Hart Papers, WSA (hereafter cited as Hart Papers).

117   *Tacoma (WA) Daily Ledger*, 15 January 1920.

118   DeVoe to Sapp, 14 January 1920, Box 4, Folder 8, DeVoe Papers.

119   Sapp to DeVoe, 17 January 1920, Box 4, Folder 21, DeVoe Papers.

120   Carrie Chapman Catt and Nettie Rogers Shuler, *Woman Suffrage and Politics: The Inner Story of the Suffrage Movement* (1923; reprint with an introduction by T. A. Larson, Seattle: University of Washington Press, 1969), 384.

121   Harper, *History of Woman Suffrage*, 684–85.

122   DeVoe to Sapp, 4 March 1920, Box 4, Folder 8, DeVoe Papers.

123   Harper, *History of Woman Suffrage*, 685–86.

7   PARTY WOMAN

1   *Tacoma (WA) News Tribune*, 17 August 1922, Tacoma Women thru 1949, Vertical File, Northwest Room, Tacoma Public Library, Tacoma, Washington.

2   Those continuities have been addressed in Cott, "Across the Great Divide," 153–76.

3   Arthur S. Link, *Woodrow Wilson: Revolution, War, and Peace* (Arlington Heights: Harlan Davidson, 1979), 72–103.

4   Margaret MacMillan, *Paris 1919: Six Months that Changed the World* (New York: Random House Trade Paperbacks, 2003), 15.

5   *Tacoma (WA) News Tribune*, 13 August 1920, Scrapbook, vol. 12, Box 12, DeVoe Papers.

6   DeVoe to Miles Poindexter, 29 July 1919, Box 350, Folder "George E. deSteiguer-Dirks Jno. L.," Miles Poindexter Papers, UW (hereafter cited as Poindexter Papers).

7   *Centralia (WA) Daily Chronicle*, 28 March 1919.

8   Link, *Woodrow Wilson*, 104.

9   DeVoe to Poindexter, 29 July 1919, Poindexter Papers. Other notable Republican women, such as Alice Roosevelt Longworth (daughter of Teddy Roosevelt), fought against the League. Known as the "Colonel of Death," Longworth worked in conjunction with Senator William E. Borah to lobby senators to join their cause, called the Battalion of Death. For Longworth's part in the League's defeat, see Cordery, *Alice*, 281–86; and Carol Felsenthal, *Alice Roosevelt Longworth* (New York: G.P. Putnam's Sons, 1988), 141–42.

10   *Tacoma (WA) News Tribune*, 27 August 1920, Scrapbook, vol. 12, Box 12, DeVoe Papers.

11   Other suffrage leaders became drawn into party leadership after the passage of the Nineteenth Amendment. For examples, see Gustafson, *Women and the Republican Party*, 181; Andersen, *After Suffrage*, 95–96.

12   According to the press, Emma had a ribbon from the campaign that had belonged to her father. *Tacoma (WA) Daily Ledger*, 13 April 1924.

13   Ibid., 10 February 1920.

14   Ibid., 21 February 1920.

15   Andersen, *After Suffrage*, 81.

16   *Tacoma (WA) Daily Ledger*, 26 April 1920.

17   Ibid., 27 April 1920.

18   Ibid., 26 April 1920.

19   *Tacoma (WA) News Tribune*, 27 April 1920.

20   Haskell had been named member of the state executive committee in the summer of 1919 and pushed for the consolidation of men and women's Republican clubs, but the merger in Pierce County did not last long. In 1920, Sarah Flannigan was made a member of the executive committee and the steering committee for

the state convention. Elizabeth Meyers was made county treasurer for Adams County, and Birdie Campbell was made vice chair of the state finance committee. *Tacoma (WA) Daily Ledger*, 25 January 1920, 26 April 1920, 27 April 1920.

21 Ibid., 27 April 1920.

22 Ibid., 27 April 1920.

23 The women selected included Frances M. Haskell, Sarah Weedin, Sarah Flannigan, Mrs. Joseph Latham, and Mrs. W. E. Brown. *Official Report of the Proceedings of the Seventeenth Republican National Convention Held in Chicago, Illinois, June 8, 9, 10, 11, and 12, 1920* (New York: The Tenny Press, 1920), 68; *Tacoma (WA) Daily Ledger*, 28 April 1920.

24 Gustafson, *Women and the Republican Party*, 181; Andersen, *After Suffrage*, 81–83.

25 Quoted in Catherine E. Rymph, *Republican Women: Feminism and Conservatism from Suffrage Through the Rise of the New Right* (Chapel Hill: University of North Carolina Press, 2006), 18.

26 *Proceedings of the Seventeenth Republican National Convention*, 81.

27 *Tacoma (WA) News Tribune*, 3 August 1920, Scrapbook, vol. 12, Box 12, DeVoe Papers.

28 Ibid., 10 August 1920.

29 By September 1920, Democrats believed that Cox had lost the campaign, and to win over supporters, he began speaking more about the League. James E. Cebula, *James M. Cox: Journalist and Politician* (New York: Garland Publishing, 1985), 114.

30 *Tacoma (WA) News Tribune*, 13 August 1920, Scrapbook, vol. 12, Box 12, DeVoe Papers.

31 Ibid.

32 Ibid., 17 August 1920.

33 Ibid., 24 August 1920.

34 *Fresno (CA) Morning Republican*, 11 September 1920; *Galveston (TX) Daily News*, 11 September 1920.

35 MacMillan, *Paris 1919*, 98–99.

36 *Tacoma (WA) News Tribune* 17 August 1920, Scrapbook, vol. 12, Box 12, DeVoe Papers.

37 Cebula, *James Cox*, 102.

38 *Tacoma (WA) News Tribune*, 3 September 1920, Scrapbook, vol. 12, Box 12, DeVoe Papers.

39 Ibid., 14 September 1920.

40 Ibid., 2 October 1920.

41 Ibid, 12 October 1920.

42 A search of Louis F. Hart's papers in Olympia did not make mention of this discussion, nor do the few Republican Party papers I have examined from this period. I suspect that this was either an error in her obituary or that there were simply discussions between Emma and the party. *Tacoma (WA) Daily Ledger*, 4 September 1927, "Tacoma Women thru 1949," Vertical Files, Northwest Room, Tacoma Public Library, Tacoma, Washington.

43   *Tacoma (WA) News Tribune*, 30 October 1920.

44   Blanche Wiesen Cook, *Eleanor Roosevelt*, vol. 1: 1884–1933 (New York: Penguin Books, 1992), 275.

45   *Tacoma (WA) Sunday Ledger*, 9 January 1921.

46   Minutes of Meeting of Presidential Electors of the State of Washington, Box 2J-1-11, Folder "Elections 1918–25," Hart Papers.

47   For information about Landes, see Doris H. Pieroth, "Bertha Knight Landes: The Woman Who Was Mayor," in *Women in Pacific Northwest History: An Anthology*, ed. Karen J. Blair (Seattle: University of Washington Press, 1988), 83–106.

48   Rymph explores the idea of integration versus separatism in *Republican Women.*

49   Rymph, *Republican Women*, 27–28; Jo Freeman, *A Room at a Time: How Women Entered Party Politics* (Lanham, MD: Rowman and Littlefield Publishers, 2000), 115.

50   *Chehalis (WA) Bee-Nugget*, 6 October 1922.

51   *Tacoma (WA) News Tribune*, 17 August 1922.

52   *Helena (MT) Independent*, 24 August 1922; *Davenport (IA) Democrat and Leader*, 24 August 1922; *Oshkosh (WI) Daily Northwestern*, 24 August 1922.

53   *Washington (DC) National Republican*, 7 October 1922.

54   Ibid., 9 September 1922.

55   Ibid, 18 August 1923; *Chehalis (WA) Bee-Nugget*, 20 July 1923.

56   DeVoe to Jones, 18 January 1923, Box 3, Folder 12, Jones Papers.

57   Jones to John T. Adams, 8 February 1923, Box 3, Folder 12, Jones Papers.

58   Jones to DeVoe, 8 February 1923, Box 3, Folder 12, Jones Papers.

59   *New York Times*, 26 June 1923.

60   *Washington (DC) National Republican*, 8 September 1923.

61   Ibid., 22 December 1923.

62   Minutes of Meeting of the Republican National Committee held at Washington, DC, December 11–12, 1923, Papers of the Republican Party (microfilm edition), Republican National Committee Headquarters, Washington, DC.

63   *Washington (DC) National Republican*, 26 January 1924.

64   Ibid., 22 December 1923.

65   *Tacoma (WA) Daily Ledger*, 13 February 1924; *Tacoma (WA) News Tribune*, 13 February 1924.

66   *Tacoma (WA) News Tribune*, 28 June 1924.

67   Reports of Dodson's trip can be found in *Tacoma (WA) News Tribune*, 8 April 1924; *Washington (DC) National Republican*, 26 April 1924; *Tacoma (WA) Daily Ledger*, 8 April 1924.

68   *Billings (MT) Gazette*, 7 May 1924.

69   Andersen, *After Suffrage*, 82–83.

70   *Tacoma (WA) Daily Ledger*, 13 June 1924.

71   Italics in original. *New York Woman Citizen*, 28 June 1924.

72   *Tacoma (WA) Daily Ledger*, 13 June 1924; *Tacoma (WA) News Tribune*, 28 June 1924.

73   *Chehalis (WA) Bee-Nugget*, 11 July 1924.

74   *Tacoma (WA) Daily Ledger*, 21 October 1924.

75   Emma's probate records provide a brief overview of her medical condition at the time. Emma Smith DeVoe Probate records, 11 June 1928, Pierce County Clerk's Office, County-City Building, Tacoma, Washington.

76   *Tacoma (WA) News Tribune*, 5 September 1927, Vertical Files, "Tacoma-Biography DE-DM," Northwest Room, Tacoma Public Library, Tacoma, WA.

77   *Tacoma (WA) Daily Ledger*, 4 September 1927, Vertical Files, "Tacoma-Women thru 1949," Northwest Room, Tacoma Public Library, Tacoma, WA.

78   John Henry DeVoe to Governor Hartley, 3 October 1927, Jim and Susan Welch Papers (hereafter cited as Welch Papers).

79   Sarah Kendall to Henry DeVoe, 24 September 1927, Welch Papers.

80   Emphasis in original. Fanny S. Cliff to Henry DeVoe, 14 November 1927, Welch Papers.

81   Rex S. Roudebush to Henry DeVoe, 20 September 1927, Welch Papers.

82   King to Henry DeVoe, 1 September 1927, Welch Papers.

83   DeVoe to Bernice Sapp, 4 March 1920, Box 4, Folder 8, DeVoe Papers.

84   *New York Woman Citizen*, 4 September 1920.

85   Ellen Carol Dubois, *Feminism and Suffrage: The Emergence of an Independent Women's Movement in America, 1848–1869* (Ithaca: Cornell University Press, 1999), 46.

BIBLIOGRAPHY

Primary Sources

GOVERNMENT RECORDS

Beadle County Register of Deeds, Beadle County Courthouse, Huron, South Dakota
    Indentures, 1882
    Receipts, 1882
    Sheriff's Deeds, 1893
    Warranty Deeds, 1893

Faulk County Register of Deeds, Faulk County Courthouse, Faulkton, South Dakota
    Warranty Deeds, 1885
    Sheriff's Deeds, 1892

Huron Municipal Building, Huron, South Dakota
    City Council Minutes, 1887–1890

Office of the Pierce County Auditor, Pierce County Annex, Tacoma, Washington
    Deeds, 1911

Pierce County Clerk's Office, County-City Building, Tacoma, Washington
    Emma Smith DeVoe Probate Records

Tazewell Clerk of Circuit Court, Pekin, Illinois
    Birdsey W. Smith Probate Records

INTERVIEWS

Fry, Amelia R. *Conversations with Alice Paul: Woman Suffrage and the Equal Rights Amendment.* An oral history conducted 24–26 November 1972 and 10–12 May

1973, Regional Oral History Office, The Bancroft Library, University of California, Berkeley, 1976, 648 pp.

MANUSCRIPT COLLECTIONS

Bancroft Library, University of California, Berkeley, California
George and Phoebe Apperson Hearst Papers
Anne Martin Papers

Colorado Historical Society, Denver, Colorado
Ellis Meredith Papers

The Huntington Library, San Marino, California
Clara B. Colby Papers
Alice Park Papers

Huron Public Library, Huron, South Dakota
Charter and Ordinances of the City of Huron
Dewayne Nelson, "Firsts in the History of Huron and the Surrounding Area," South Dakota Collection

Idaho State Historical Society, Boise, Idaho
Pearl Tyer Papers

Illinois State Library, Springfield, Illinois
Harvey Land Association, "The Town of Harvey"
Walter Thomas Mills and Co., "Harvey, Ill: The New Manufacturing Town 1 and ¼ Miles South of Chicago"

Kansas State Historical Society, Topeka, Kansas
Lucy B. Johnson Papers

Library of Congress, Washington, DC
William E. Borah Papers
National American Woman Suffrage Association Papers (microfilm edition)
National Woman's Party Papers, Group IV: Addition I, 1884–1963
National Woman's Party Papers, the Suffrage Years (microfilm edition)

Montana Historical Society, Helena, Montana
Mary Long Alderson Papers
Helena Business Women's Suffrage Club Records
George E. Morse Papers
Martha Edgerton Plassmann Papers
Jeannette Rankin Papers

Northwest Museum of Arts and Culture/Eastern Washington
Historical Society, Spokane, Washington
Marion E. Hay Papers
May Arkwright Hutton Papers

Northwest Room, Tacoma Public Library, Tacoma, Washington
Pierce County World War One Service League Papers
Vertical Files

Republican National Committee Headquarters, Washington, DC
Papers of the Republican Party (microfilm edition)

The Schlesinger Library, Radcliffe Institute for Advanced Study,
Harvard University, Cambridge, Massachusetts
Olympia Brown Papers (microfilm edition)
Ella Harrison Papers (microfilm edition)
National Suffrage Bulletin
Helen Barten (Brewster) Owens Papers (microfilm edition)
Maud Wood Park Papers (microfilm edition)
Margaret S. Roberts Papers (microfilm edition)

Sophia Smith Collection, Smith College, Northampton, Massachusetts
Susan B. Anthony Papers
Isabel Howland Papers
U.S. Suffrage Collection

South Dakota State Historical Society, Pierre, South Dakota
Baptist Church Records, 1872–1969
Beadle County Justice Court Records, 1882–1898
Jane R. Breeden Papers
City of Huron Police Magistrate, Police Justice Dockets, 1884–1909
Lawrence Keith Fox Papers
Pickler Family Papers

University of the Pacific Library, Holt-Atherton Special Collections, Stockton, California
Minerva Goodman Papers

University of Oregon, Special Collections and University Archives, Eugene, Oregon
Abigail Scott Duniway Papers

University of South Dakota, Archives and Special Collections, Vermillion, South Dakota
Mamie Shields Pyle Papers, Richardson Collection

University of Utah, Marriott Library, Manuscripts Division, Salt Lake City, Utah
Emma Elizabeth Lindsey Thomas Papers

University of Washington Libraries, Special Collections Division, Seattle, Washington
Wesley L. Jones Papers
Miles Poindexter Papers

Washington State Archives, Olympia, Washington
Louis F. Hart Papers
Ernest Lister Papers
Woman Suffrage Special Collection

Washington State Library, Tumwater, Washington
 Emma Smith DeVoe Papers
 May Arkwright Hutton Papers

Wisconsin Historical Society, Madison, Wisconsin
 Clara Colby Papers
 Ada L. James Papers (microfilm edition)

Jim and Susan Welch Papers, private collection

Tom Welch Papers, private collection

NEWSPAPERS

Aberdeen (SD) Daily News
Aberdeen (SD) Weekly News
Beatrice (NE) Woman's Tribune
Billings (MT) Gazette
Boise (ID) Evening Capitol News
Boise Idaho (ID) Daily Statesman
Boston Woman's Journal
Buffalo (ND) Western Womanhood
Butte (MT) Miner
Centralia (WA) Daily Chronicle
Chehalis (WA) Bee-Nugget
Cheyenne (WY) State Leader
Daily Huronite (SD)
Dakota Huronite (SD)
Davenport (IA) Democrat and Leader
Des Moines (IA) Woman's Standard
Evanston (IL) Union Signal
Fargo Daily Forum (ND) and Republican
Fresno (CA) Morning Republican
Galveston (TX) Daily News
Grand Forks (ND) Daily Plainsdealer
Harvey (IL) Tribune Citizen
Helena (MT) Independent
Huron (SD) Tribune
Huron (SD) Tribune and Dakota Huronite
Huronite (SD)
Milwaukee (WI) Free Press
Monmouth (IL) Atlas
New York Times
New York Woman Citizen
Oakland (CA) Tribune
Oshkosh (WI) Daily Northwestern

Portland Woman's Tribune
Rapid City (SD) Daily Republican
Seattle Times
Seattle Town Crier
Seattle Votes for Women
Spokane (WA) Spokesman-Review
Tacoma (WA) Daily Ledger
Tacoma (WA) Daily News
Tacoma (WA) News Tribune
Tacoma (WA) Sunday Ledger
Tacoma (WA) Sunday Tribune
Tacoma (WA) Tribune
Topeka (KS) Farmer's Wife
Washington (DC) National Republican
Washington (DC) Suffragist
Washington (DC) Woman's Tribune
Washington (IL) Republican
Washington (IL) Tazewell Independent
Washington Times
Washington (DC) Herald
Washington Post
Yankton (SD) Daily Press and Dakotan

Secondary Sources

Abbot, Willis J. "The Chicago Populist Campaign." *The Arena* 11 (February 1895): 330–37.

Adams, Harold. *History of Eureka College*. Eureka, IL: Board of Trustees of Eureka College, 1982.

Adams, Katherine H., and Michael L. Keene. *Alice Paul and the American Suffrage Campaign*. Urbana: University of Illinois Press, 2008.

Andersen, Kristi. *After Suffrage: Women in Partisan and Electoral Politics before the New Deal*. Chicago: University of Chicago Press, 1996.

Anthony, Susan B., and Ida Husted Harper, eds.. *The History of Woman Suffrage, 1883–1900*. Vol. 4. Indianapolis: The Hollenbeck Press, 1902.

Argersinger, Peter H. "Ideology and Behavior: Legislative Politics and Western Populism." *Agricultural History* 58, no. 1 (January 1984): 43–58.

Avery, Rachel Foster, ed. *Proceedings of the Thirtieth Annual Convention of the National American Woman Suffrage Association and the Celebration of the Fiftieth Anniversary of the First Woman's Rights Convention at the Columbia Theatre, Twelfth and F Streets, Washington, D.C., February 13, 14, 15, 16, 17, 18, 19, 1898*. Philadelphia: Press of Alfred J. Ferris, 1898.

———. *Proceedings of the Twenty-Eighth Annual Convention of the National-American Woman Suffrage Association Held in Washington, D.C., January 23d to 28th, 1896*. Philadelphia: Press of Alfred J. Ferris, 1896.

Baily, C. H. "How Washington Women Regained the Ballot." *Pacific Monthly* 26, no. 1 (July 1911): 1–11.

Baker, Jean H. *Sisters: The Lives of America's Suffragists*. New York: Hill and Wang, 2005.

Barry, Kathleen. *Susan B. Anthony: A Biography of a Singular Feminist*. New York: New York University Press, 1988.

Beeton, Beverly. *Women Vote in the West: The Woman Suffrage Movement 1869–1896*. New York: Garland Publishing, 1986.

Beeton, Beverly, and G. Thomas Edwards. "Susan B. Anthony's Woman Suffrage Crusade in the American West." *Journal of the West* 21, no. 2 (April 1982): 5–15.

Birney, Ann, and Joyce Thierer. "Shoulder to Shoulder: Kansas Women Win the Vote." *Kansas Heritage* 3, no. 4 (Winter 1995): 64–68.

Björkman, Frances M. "Women's Political Methods." *Collier's*, 20 August 1910, 22–24.

Blair, Karen J. *The Clubwoman as Feminist: True Womanhood Redefined, 1868–1914*. New York: Holmes and Meier, 1980.

Bordin, Ruth. *Frances Willard: A Biography*. Chapel Hill: University of North Carolina Press, 1986.

———. *Woman and Temperance: The Quest for Power and Liberty, 1873–1900*. Philadelphia: Temple University Press, 1981.

Brammer, Leila R. *Excluded from Suffrage History: Matilda Joslyn Gage, Nineteenth-Century American Feminist*. Westport: Greenwood Press, 2000.

Brown, Olympia. *Acquaintances, Old and New, Among Reformers*. Milwaukee: S. E. Tate Printing Co., 1911.

———, ed. *Democratic Ideals: A Memorial Sketch of Clara B. Colby*. Federal Suffrage Association, 1917.

Brown, Victoria Bissell. "Jane Addams, Progressivism, and Woman Suffrage: An Introduction to 'Why Women Should Vote.'" In *One Woman, One Vote: Rediscovering the Woman Suffrage Movement*, edited by Marjorie Spruill Wheeler, 182–95. Troutdale, OR: NewSage Press, 1995.

Brunn, Alvin John. "The History of the Temperance Movement in South Dakota to 1917." Master's thesis, University of South Dakota, 1948.

Buechler, Steven M. *The Transformation of the Woman Suffrage Movement: The Case of Illinois, 1850–1920*. New Brunswick: Rutgers University Press, 1986.

Buenker, John D. "Essay." In *Progressivism*. Reprint, 1977. Rochester, VT: Schenkman Books, Inc., 1986.

Campbell, Karlyn Kohrs. *Man Cannot Speak for Her: A Critical Study of Early Feminist Rhetoric*. Vol. 1. Contributions in Women's Studies, no. 101. New York: Greenwood Press, 1989.

Catt, Carrie Chapman, and Nettie Rogers Shuler. *Woman Suffrage and Politics: The Inner Story of the Suffrage Movement*. Seattle: University of Washington Press, 1969. First published 1923 by Scribner.

Cebula, James E. *James M. Cox: Journalist and Politician*. New York: Garland Publishing, 1985.

Clemens, Elisabeth S. *The People's Lobby: Organizational Innovation and the Rise of*

Interest Group Politics in the United States, 1890–1925. Chicago: University of Chicago Press, 1997.

Conway, Jill Ker. "Women Reformers and American Culture, 1870–1930." *Journal of Social History* 5, no. 2 (Winter 1971/1972): 164–177.

Cook, Blanche Wiesen. *Eleanor Roosevelt.* Vol. 1: 1884–1933. New York: Penguin Books, 1992.

Cordery, Stacy A. *Alice: Alice Roosevelt Longworth, from White House Princess to Washington Power Broker.* New York: Viking, 2007.

Cott, Nancy F. "Across the Great Divide: Women in Politics Before and After 1920." In *Women, Politics and Change,* edited by Louise A. Tilly and Patricia Gurin, 153–76. New York: Russell Sage Foundation, 1990.

———. *The Grounding of Modern Feminism* (New Haven: Yale University Press, 1987).

———. "What's in a Name? The Limits of 'Social Feminism'; or Expanding the Vocabulary of Women's History." *Journal of American History* 76, no. 3 (December 1989): 809–29.

Croly, Jennie Cunningham. *The History of the Woman's Club Movement in America.* New York: Henry G. Allen & Co., 1898.

Destler, Chester McA. "Consummation of a Labor-Populist Alliance in Illinois, 1894." *Mississippi Valley Historical Review* 27, no. 4 (March 1941): 589–602.

Diggs, Annie. "The Women in the Alliance Movement." *The Arena,* July 1892, 160–79.

Dubois, Ellen Carol, ed. *Elizabeth Cady Stanton, Susan B. Anthony, Correspondence, Writings, Speeches.* New York: Schocken Books, 1981.

———. *Feminism and Suffrage: The Emergence of an Independent Women's Movement in America, 1848–1869.* Ithaca: Cornell University Press, 1999.

———. *Harriot Stanton Blatch and the Winning of Woman Suffrage.* New Haven: Yale University Press, 1997.

Duniway, Abigail Scott. *Path Breaking: An Autobiographical History of the Equal Suffrage Movement in the Pacific Coast States.* 2nd ed., 1914. Reprinted with a new introduction by Eleanor Flexner. New York: Schocken Books, 1971.

Easton, Patricia. "A Brief Custer County History." Miles City.com http://www.milescity.com/History/stories/bcch/

Edwards, Rebecca. *Angels in the Machinery: Gender in American Party Politics from the Civil War to the Progressive Era.* New York: Oxford University Press, 1997.

———. "Gender, Class, and the Transformation of Electoral Campaigns in the Gilded Age." In *We Have Come to Stay: American Women and Political Parties, 1880–1960,* edited by Melanie Gustafson, Kristie Miller, and Elisabeth I. Perry, 13–22. Albuquerque: University of New Mexico Press, 1999.

Edwards, G. Thomas. *Sowing Good Seeds: The Northwest Suffrage Campaigns of Susan B. Anthony.* Portland: Oregon Historical Society Press, 1990.

Ellis, C. H. *History of Faulk County South Dakota: Together with Biographical Sketches of Pioneers and Prominent Citizens.* 1909. Reprint, Aberdeen: North Plains Press, 1973.

Eureka College. *Eureka College, Eureka, Ill., 1855–1955: A Community of Learning in Search of Truth, Human and Divine.* Eureka, IL: Eureka College, 1955.

Faderman, Lillian. "Acting 'Woman' and Thinking 'Man': The Ploys of Famous Female

Inverts," *GLQ: A Journal of Lesbian and Gay Studies* 5, no. 3 (1999): 315–29.

Fahs, Alice. "The Feminized Civil War: Gender, Northern Popular Literature, and the Memory of the War, 1861–1900." *Journal of American History* 85, no. 4 (March 1999): 1461–94.

Farrell, Grace. *Lillie Devereux Blake: Retracing a Life Erased.* Amherst: University of Massachusetts Press, 2002.

Faulk County Historical Society. *History of Faulk County, South Dakota, 1910–1982.* Faulkton: Moritz Publishing Company, 1982.

Felsenthal, Carol. *Alice Roosevelt Longworth.* New York: G.P. Putnam's Sons, 1988.

Finnegan, Margaret. *Selling Suffrage: Consumer Culture and Votes for Women.* New York: Columbia University Press, 1999.

Flexner, Eleanor. *Century of Struggle: The Woman's Rights Movement in the United States.* Rev. ed. Cambridge: Belknap Press of Harvard University Press, 1975.

Freeman, Jo. *A Room at a Time: How Women Entered Party Politics.* Lanham, MD: Rowman and Littlefield Publishers, 2000.

Gilbert, James. *Perfect Cities: Chicago's Utopias of 1893.* Chicago: University of Chicago Press, 1991.

Goldberg, Michael Lewis. *An Army of Women: Gender and Politics in Gilded Age Kansas.* Baltimore: The Johns Hopkins University Press, 1997.

Goodspeed, Weston Arthur, ed. *The Province and the States.* Vol. 6. Madison, WI: Western Historical Association, 1904.

Graham, Sara Hunter. *Woman Suffrage and the New Democracy.* New Haven: Yale University Press, 1996.

Green, Carrol Gardner. "The Struggle of South Dakota to Become a State." In *South Dakota Historical Collections.* Vol. 12. Pierre: Hipple Printing Company, 1924, 503–33.

Gullett, Gayle. *Becoming Citizens: The Emergence and Development of the California Women's Movement, 1880–1911.* Urbana: University of Illinois Press, 2000.

Gustafson, Melanie Susan. *Women and the Republican Party, 1854–1924.* Urbana: University of Illinois Press, 2001.

Haarsager, Sandra. *Organized Womanhood: Cultural Politics in the Pacific Northwest, 1840–1920.* Norman: University of Oklahoma Press, 1997.

Harper, Ida Husted, ed. *The History of Woman Suffrage.* Vol. 6. New York: J. J. Little and Ives Company, 1922.

———. *Life and Work of Susan B. Anthony.* Vol. 2, 1898. Reprint, New York: Arno and the New York Times, 1969.

Hayden, Sara. "Negotiating Femininity and Power in the Early Twentieth Century West: Domestic Ideology and Feminine Style in Jeannette Rankin's Suffrage Rhetoric." *Communication Studies* 50, no. 2 (Summer 1999): 83–102.

Hewitt, Nancy A. "Beyond the Search for Sisterhood: American Women's History in the 1980s," *Social History* 10, no. 3 (October 1985): 299–321.

History of Eureka College with Biographical Sketches and Reminiscences, A. St. Louis: Christian Publishing Company, 1894.

Horner, Patricia Voeller. "May Arkwright Hutton: Suffragist and Politician." In *Women in Pacific Northwest History: An Anthology*, edited by Karen J. Blair, 25–42. Seattle: University of Washington Press, 1988.

Huss, Dorothy, et al. *Huron Revisited*. Huron: East Eagle Company, 1988.

Hutchison, Ray. "Capitalism, Religion, and Reform: The Social History of Temperance in Harvey, Illinois." In *Drinking: Behavior and Belief in Modern History*, edited by Susanna Barrows and Robin Room, 184–216. Berkeley: University of California Press, 1991.

Irwin, Inez Haynes. *The Story of the Woman's Party*. 1921. Reprint, New York: Kraus Reprint Co., 1971.

Jennings, Mary Kay. "Lake County Woman Suffrage Campaign in 1890." *South Dakota History* 5, no. 4 (Fall 1975): 390–409.

Johnson, Claudius O. *Borah of Idaho*. Seattle: University of Washington Press, 1967.

Johnson, Nan. *Gender and Rhetorical Space in American Life, 1866–1910*. Carbondale: Southern Illinois University Press, 2002.

Keith, F. F. comp. *The Harvey Directory Company's Directory and Business Guide of the City of Harvey and the Village of North Harvey, Cook County, Illinois, with Descriptive and Historical Sketches of Harvey and Its Institutions*. Harvey: The Harvey Directory Company, 1895.

Kerber, Linda K. and Jane Sherron De Hart, eds. *Women's America: Refocusing the Past*. 4th ed. New York: Oxford University Press, 1995.

Kerr, Alec C., ed. *History: The City of Harvey 1890–1962*. Harvey: First National Bank in Harvey, 1962.

Koupal, Nancy Tystad. "Marietta Bones: Personality and Politics in the South Dakota Suffrage Movement." In *Feminist Frontiers: Women Who Shaped the Midwest*, edited by Yvonne J. Johnson, 69-82. Kirksville, MO: Truman State University Press, 2010.

———, ed. and annotated. *Our Landlady/L. Frank Baum*. Lincoln: University of Nebraska Press, 1996.

Kraditor, Aileen S. *The Ideas of the Woman Suffrage Movement, 1890–1920*. New York: Columbia University Press, 1965. Reprint, New York: W. W. Norton and Company, 1981.

Larson, Erik. *The Devil in the White City: Murder, Magic, and Madness at the Fair That Changed America*. New York: Vintage Books, 2003.

Larson, T. A. "Emancipating the West's Dolls, Vassals and Hopeless Drudges: The Origins of Woman Suffrage in the West." In *Essays in Western History in Honor of T. A. Larson*, edited by Roger Daniels, 1–16. Laramie: University of Wyoming Publications, 1971.

———. "Idaho's Role in America's Woman Suffrage Crusade." *Idaho Yesterdays* 18, no. 1 (Spring 1974): 2–15.

———. "Montana Women and the Battle for the Ballot." *Montana: The Magazine of Western History* 23, no. 1 (January 1973): 24–41.

———. "The Woman Suffrage Movement in Washington" *Pacific Northwest Quarterly* 67, no. 2 (April 1976): 49–62.

———. "Woman's Rights in Idaho." *Idaho Yesterdays* 16, no. 1 (Spring 1972): 2–15, 18–19.

———. "Wyoming's Contribution to the Regional and National Women's Rights Movement." *Annals of Wyoming* 52, no. 1 (Spring 1980): 2–15.

LeGates, Marlene. *In Their Time: A History of Feminism in Western Society*. New York: Routledge, 2001.

Leonard, Carol, and Isidor Wallimann. "Prostitution and Changing Morality in the Frontier Cattle Towns of Kansas." *Kansas History* 2, no. 1 (Spring 1979): 34–53.

Leonard, John William, ed. *Woman's Who's Who of America: A Biographical Dictionary of Contemporary Women of the United State and Canada, 1914–1915*. New York: The American Commonwealth Company, 1914.

Lief, Julia Wiech. "A Woman of Purpose: Julia B. Nelson." *Minnesota History* 47, no. 8 (Winter 1981): 302–14.

Lindell, Lisa R. "'Sowing the seeds of liberal thought': Unitarian Women Ministers in Nineteenth-century South Dakota." *South Dakota History* 38, no. 2 (Summer 2008): 148–80.

Link, Arthur S. *Woodrow Wilson: Revolution, War, and Peace*. Arlington Heights: Harlan Davidson, 1979.

Lomicky, Carol S. "Frontier Feminism and the *Woman's Tribune*: The Journalism of Clara Bewick Colby." *Journalism History* 28, no. 3 (Fall 2002): 102–11.

Lukas, J. Anthony. *Big Trouble: A Murder in a Small Western Town Sets Off a Struggle for the Soul of America*. New York: Simon & Schuster, 1997.

Lumsden, Linda J. *Rampant Women: Suffragists and the Right of Assembly*. Knoxville: University of Tennessee Press, 1997.

Lunardini, Christine A. *From Equal Suffrage to Equal Rights: Alice Paul and the National Woman's Party, 1910–1928*. New York: New York University Press, 1986.

Lutz, Alma. *Susan B. Anthony: Rebel, Crusader, Humanitarian*. Boston: Beacon Press, 1959.

MacMillan, Margaret. *Paris 1919: Six Months that Changed the World*. New York: Random House Trade Paperbacks, 2003.

Madsen, Carol Cornwall, ed. *Battle for the Ballot: Essays on Woman Suffrage in Utah, 1870–1896*. Logan: Utah State University Press, 1997.

Malone, Michael P., Richard B. Roeder, and William L. Lang. *Montana: A History of Two Centuries*. Rev. ed. Seattle: University of Washington Press, 1991.

Mattingly, Carol. *Appropriate[ing] Dress: Women's Rhetorical Style in Nineteenth-Century America*. Carbondale: Southern Illinois University Press, 2002.

———. *Well-Tempered Women: Nineteenth-Century Temperance Rhetoric*. Carbondale: Southern Illinois University Press, 1998.

McArthur, Judith N. and Harold L. Smith. *Minnie Fisher Cunningham: A Suffragist's Life in Politics*. New York: Oxford University Press, 2003.

McCammon, Holly J. "Stirring Up Suffrage Sentiment: The Formation of the State Woman Suffrage Organizations, 1866–1914." *Social Forces* 80, no. 2 (December 2001): 449–80.

McCammon, Holly J., and Karen E. Campbell. "Winning the Vote in the West: The Political Successes of the Women's Suffrage Movements, 1866–1919." *Gender and Society* 15, no. 1 (February 2001): 55–82.

McCammon, Holly J. et al. "How Movements Win: Gendered Opportunity Structures and U.S. Women's Suffrage Movements, 1866 to 1919." *American Sociological Review* 66, no. 1 (February 2001): 49–70.

McDannell, Colleen, ed. *Religions of the United States in Practice*. Vol. 1. Princeton: Princeton University Press, 2001.

McGerr, Michael. "Political Style and Women's Power, 1830–1930," *Journal of American History* 77, no. 3 (December 1990): 864–85.

McKern, Roberta O. "The Woman Suffrage Movement in Oregon and the Oregon Press." Master's thesis, University of Oregon, 1975.

Mead, Rebecca J. *How the Vote Was Won: Woman Suffrage in the Western United States, 1868–1914*. New York: New York University Press, 2004.

———. "How the Vote Was Won: Woman Suffrage in the Western United States, 1868–1914." PhD diss., University of California-Los Angeles, 1999.

Miller, John E. "More than Statehood on Their Minds: South Dakota Joins the Union, 1889." *Great Plains Quarterly* 10, no. 4 (Fall 1990): 206–17.

———. "The State of South Dakota Admitted to the Union as a State: November 2, 1889." In *The Uniting States: The Story of Statehood for the Fifty United States*, edited by Benjamin F. Shearer, 1103–28. Westport, CT: Greenwood Press, 2004.

Minutes of the National Woman's Christian Temperance Union at the Sixteenth Annual Meeting, Chicago Illinois, November 8 to 13, 1889. Chicago: Woman's Temperance Publication Association, 1889.

Montgomery, James W. *Liberated Woman: A Life of May Arkwright Hutton*. Fairfield, WA: Ye Galleon Press, 1974.

Morgan, Stephen T. "Fellow Comrades: The Grand Army of the Republic in South Dakota." *South Dakota History* 36, no. 3 (Fall 2006): 229–59.

Morris, Colleen. "An Herstorical View of the Alaskan Territorial Legislature's 1913 Vote to Emancipate Women." Master's thesis, Harvard University, 1995.

Moss, Rosalind Urbach. "The 'Girls' from Syracuse: Sex Role Negotiations of Kansas Women in Politics, 1887–1890." In *The Women's West*, edited by Susan Armitage and Elizabeth Jameson, 253–64. Norman: University of Oklahoma Press, 1987.

Moynihan, Ruth Barnes. *Rebel for Rights, Abigail Scott Duniway*. New Haven: Yale University Press, 1983.

National American Woman Suffrage Association Letters, 1897–1898. Pierre, SD: South Dakota Status on the Commission of Women, 1970. Microfilm edition.

Nelson, Paula M., ed. *Sunshine Always: The Courtship Letters of Alice Bower & Joseph Gossage of Dakota Territory*. Pierre: South Dakota State Historical Society Press, 2006.

Neu, Charles E. "Olympia Brown and the Woman's Suffrage Movement." *Wisconsin Magazine of History* 43, no. 4 (Summer 1960): 277–87.

Nicholls, David, ed. *The Cambridge History of American Music*. Cambridge: Cambridge University Press, 1998.

Nicolosi, Ann Marie. "'The Most Beautiful Suffragette': Inez Milholland and the Political Currency of Beauty," *Journal of the Gilded Age and Progressive Era* 6, no. 3 (July 2007): 286–309.

Norlin, Dennis A. "The Suffrage Movement and South Dakota Churches: Radicals and the Status Quo, 1890." *South Dakota History* 14, no. 4 (Winter 1984): 308–34.

Official Report of the Proceedings of the Seventeenth Republican National Convention Held in Chicago, Illinois, June 8, 9, 10, 11, and 12, 1920. New York: The Tenny Press, 1920.

O'Neill, William L. *Everyone Was Brave: A History of Feminism in America.* Chicago: Quadrangle Books, 1971.

Ostler, Jeff. "Why the Populist Party Was Strong in Kansas and Nebraska, but Weak in Iowa." *Western Historical Quarterly* 23, no. 4 (November 1992): 451–74.

Painter, Nell Irvin. *Standing at Armageddon: The United States 1877–1919.* New York: W. W. Norton & Company, 1987.

Peck, Mary Gray. *Carrie Chapman Catt: A Biography.* New York: The H. W. Wilson Company, 1944.

Penney, Sherry H., and James D. Livingston. *A Very Dangerous Woman: Martha Wright and Women's Rights.* Amherst: University of Massachusetts Press, 2004.

Petrik, Paula. "Strange Bedfellows: Prostitution, Politicians, and Moral Reform in Helena, 1885–1887." *Montana: the Magazine of Western History* 35, no. 3 (Summer 1985): 2–13.

Pieroth, Doris H. "Bertha Knight Landes: The Woman Who Was Mayor." In *Women in Pacific Northwest History: An Anthology*, edited by Karen J. Blair, 83–106. Seattle: University of Washington Press, 1988.

Plummer, Stephen B. "Huron, South Dakota, 1880–1900: Economic and Political Determinants." Master's thesis, University of South Dakota, 1970.

Proceedings of the Thirty-Ninth Annual Convention of the National-American Woman Suffrage Association Held at Chicago February 14th to 19th, inclusive, 1907. Warren, OH: Press of Wm. Ritezel & Co., 1907.

Putnam, John. "A 'Test of Chiffon Politics': Gender Politics in Seattle, 1897–1917." *Pacific Historical Review* 69, no. 4 (November 2000): 595–616.

R., E. S. *"Olympia Brown."* In *American Reformers*, edited by Alden Whitman. New York: The H. W. Wilson Company, 1985.

Reed, Dorinda Riessen. *The Woman Suffrage Movement in South Dakota.* 2nd ed. Pierre: South Dakota Commission on the Status of Women, 1975.

Robinson, Doane. *History of South Dakota.* Vol. 1. Logansport, IN: B. F. Bowen & Co. Publishers, 1904.

Roe, Alfred Seelye. *The Ninth New York Heavy Artillery: A History of Its Organization, Services in the Defenses of Washington, Marches, Camps, Battles, and Muster-Out, with Accounts of Life in a Rebel Prison, Personal Experiences, Names and Addresses of Surviving Members, Personal Sketches, and a Complete Roster of the Regiment.* Worcester: Alfred Seelye Roe, 1899.

Rymph, Catherine E. *Republican Women: Feminism and Conservatism from Suffrage Through the Rise of the New Right.* Chapel Hill: University of North Carolina, 2006.

Schaffer, Ronald. *America in the Great War: The Rise of the War Welfare State.* New York: Oxford University Press, 1991.

Scharff, Virginia. *Taking the Wheel: Women and the Coming of the Motor Age.* Albuquerque: University of New Mexico Press, 1999.

Schell, Herbert S. *History of South Dakota*. Rev. ed. John E. Miller. Pierre: South Dakota State Historical Society, 2004.

Scott, Anne Firor. "Epilogue." In *Votes for Women: The Struggle for Suffrage Revisited*, edited by Jean H. Baker, 189–96. New York: Oxford University Press, 2002.

Shaw, Anna Howard. *The Story of a Pioneer*. New York: Harper & Brothers Publishers, 1915.

Stanton, Elizabeth Cady, Susan B. Anthony, Matilda Joslyn Gage, and Ida Husted Harper, eds. *The History of Woman Suffrage*. 6 vols. Rochester, N.Y.: Susan B. Anthony and Charles Mann, 1881–1922. Reprint, Salem, NH: Ayer, 1985.

Stanton, Elizabeth Cady, Susan B. Anthony, and Matilda Joslyn Gage, eds. *The History of Woman Suffrage*. Vol. 3. Rochester: Charles Mann Printing Co., 1886.

Stevens, Doris. *Jailed for Freedom*. New York: Boni and Liveright Publishing Corporation, 1920.

Sutton, Ernest V. *A Life Worth Living*. Pasadena, CA: Trail's End Publishing Co., 1948.

Tetrault, Lisa. "The Incorporation of American Feminism: Suffragists and the Postbellum Lyceum." Unpublished essay.

———. "The Incorporation of American Feminism: Suffragists and Postbellum Lyceum." *Journal of American History* 96, no. 4 (March 2010): 1027–56.

Upton, Harriet Taylor, ed. *Proceedings of the Twenty-Seventh Annual Convention of the National-American Woman Suffrage Association Held in Atlanta, Ga., January 31st to February 5th 1895*. Warren, OH: W. M. Ritezel and Co. Printers, 1895.

———. *Proceedings of the Twenty-Sixth Annual Convention of the National-American Woman Suffrage Association Held in Washington, D.C., February 15, 16, 17, 18, 19 and 20, 1894*. Warren, OH: Chronicle Print, 1894.

Van Voris, Jacqueline. *Carrie Chapman Catt: A Public Life*. New York: The Feminist Press at the City University of New York, 1987.

Ward, Doris Buck. "The Winning of Woman Suffrage in Montana." Master's thesis, Montana State University, 1974.

Weatherford, Doris. *A History of the American Suffragist Movement*. Santa Barbara: ABC-CLIO, 1998.

Wheeler, Marjorie Spruill. "Introduction: A Short History of the Woman Suffrage Movement in America." In *One Woman, One Vote: Rediscovering the Woman Suffrage Movement*, edited by Marjorie Spruill Wheeler, 9–19. Troutdale, OR: NewSage Press, 1995.

———. Introduction to "Carrie Chapman Catt, Strategist," by Robert Booth Fowler. In *One Woman, One Vote: Rediscovering the Woman Suffrage Movement*, edited by Marjorie Spruill Wheeler, 295–98. Troutdale, OR: NewSage Press, 1995.

White, Richard. *"It's Your Misfortune and None of My Own": A New History of the American West*. Norman: University of Oklahoma Press, 1991.

Willard, Frances E. *Woman and Temperance, or the Work and Workers of the Woman's Christian Temperance Union*. Hartford, CT: Park Publishing Company, 1883.

Willard, Frances E., and Mary A. Livermore, eds. *American Women: Fifteen Hundred Biographies with over 1,400 Portraits: A Comprehensive Encyclopedia of the Lives and Achievements of American Women during the Nineteenth Century*. Vol. 1. New York: Mast, Crowell, and Kirkpatrick, 1897.

Wittmayer, Cecelia M. "The 1889–1890 Woman Suffrage Campaign: A Need to Organize." *South Dakota History* 11, no. 3 (Summer 1981):199–225.

"Woman To-Day." *Collier's*, 29 April 1911, 20.

Woodward, Mary Dodge. *The Checkered Years.* Edited by Mary Boynton Cowdrey. Caldwell, ID: The Caxton Printers, Ltd., 1937.

Wood, Molly M. "Mapping a National Campaign Strategy: Partisan Women in the Presidential Election of 1916." In *We Have Come to Stay: American Women and Political Parties 1880–1960,* edited by Melanie Gustafson, Kristie Miller, and Elisabeth I. Perry, 77–86. Albuquerque: University of New Mexico Press, 1999.

Woolley, John T., and Gerhard Peters. *The American Presidency Project* [online]. Santa Barbara, CA. Available from World Wide Web: http://www.presidency.ucsb.edu/ ws/?pid=29627.

INDEX

The initials ESD and JHD indicate Emma Smith DeVoe and John Henry DeVoe.

A

court case approach, 68–69
Covington, Kentucky, 108
Cox, James M., 172, 173–75, 226n29
Coxey, Jacob Sechler, 77
Cranmer, Emma, 53, 110
Cressey, George A., 15, 16
CU. See Congressional Union (CU)

D

Daily Huronite: elections, 25–26, 45–46;
    girls school, 34; Huron's lawlessness,
    193n3; statehood movement, 22, 23,
    24, 25, 31; Woman's Day activities, 32
Dakota Huronite, 17, 18, 19
Dakota Ruralist, 46
"The Dakotas Are Coming" (song), 25
Dakota Territory: county liquor option,
    20–22; statehood movement, 22–25,
    26. *See also* Huron; South Dakota,
    suffrage campaign
The Dalles, Oregon, 118
Davis, Augustine, 19–20
Dayton Daily News, 173
Deadwood Pioneer, 53
Deer Lodge, Montana, 97
Deming, Zell Hart, 136, 137
Demmon, Mrs., 68
Democrats: Congressional Union
    opposition, 154–56, 159, 160–61;
    Dakota statehood movement, 22–25,
    29; national elections, 172–73; and
    National Woman's Party, 223n94; in
    Senate suffrage consideration, 148,
    151; Washington state, 121. *See also*
    Republicans
demonstrations/parades, 52, 131, 143–44,
    153–54, 216n99
Des Moines Woman's Standard, 70, 71, 72,
    74, 104
DeVoe, Dakota Territory (town), 17
DeVoe, Emma Smith: overviews, 3–12,
    13–14, 60–62; appreciation/monetary
    conflicts, 100–104, 106–8, 212n101;

campaign philosophy, 61, photo section; death and obituaries, 182–83;
Flint relationship, 73–74, 102; girls
school formation, 33–34; in Harvey
community, 61–62, 63–64, 77, 111–12;
in Huron community, 14–17, 21–22,
46; League of Nations opposition,
168–69; Mexico visit, photo section;
national opposition to, 101–2; in
National Woman's Alliance, 64–65;
newspaper column, 171–74; portraits,
photo section; Republican National
Committee positions, 178–80; statehood movement, 23, 24–25, 196n53;
suffrage activity beginnings, 28–34;
in Tacoma/Parkland communities,
112, 142, 162, 219n16, photo section;
temperance movement, 26–28; World
War I support activity, 162. *See also*
National American Woman Suffrage
Association (NAWSA); National
Council of Women Voters (NCWV);
Washington State Republican Committee
DeVoe, Emma Smith (state campaigns):
Arizona, 100–101, 102; Florida, 88–89;
Iowa, 70–73, 74, 108; Kansas, 75–76,
79–80, 81–82; Montana, 89–93,
97–98, 103, 104–7, 210n53; Nevada, 99,
100, 103; New Mexico, 100–101, 102;
North Dakota, 82–83, 84; Oregon,
116–18; Utah, 99; Wisconsin, 104. *See
also* Idaho, suffrage campaign; South
Dakota, suffrage campaign; Washington (territory and state)
DeVoe, John Henry: overview, 4–5;
Anthony letter, 33; Civil War service,
23, photo section; defenses/support
of ESD, 100–101, 122, 126; economic
activity, 105, 118; on ESD's death,
183; farm investments, 15, 17, 48, 64,
88, 203n21; and free love rumor, 56;
in Harvey community, 61–64, 77,
89, 105–6, 206n80; health, 111–12; in

Huron community, 14–19, 20, 48, 59, 194n7, 203nn9–10; Independent Party, 49, 50; Mexico visit, photo section; Populist Party, 77–78; portrait, photo section; Red Cross work, 162; state-hood movement, 23, 24–25, 196n53; suffrage campaigns, 39–40, 50, 65–66, 69, 201n65, 205n63; in Washington communities, 118–19, 142, 219n16, photo section

Dickinson, A. J., 16, 17

Diggs, Annie L., 65, 78, 88

divorce rate accusation, 149

Dodson, Louise M., 181

Douglas County, Oregon, 116–17

Duniway, Abigail Scott: Catt communication, 88; Congressional Union conflicts, 154, 158; on ESD's speaking tour, 97; Federal Suffrage Association, 69; Idaho campaign, 93–96; Oregon campaign, 115–16

E

Eaton, Cora Smith (later King): on conciliatory tactics, 8; on ESD's accomplishments, 84, 119–20, 122–23, 183; federal campaign, 143–44, 146–47; Hutton conflict, 125, 126, 127, 129; mountain climbing publicity, 115; partisan campaigns, 154, 155; Washington campaign, 115, 131

economic conditions: Colorado, 76–77; Illinois, 5, 77–78; impact on pledge campaigns, 97; Iowa, 72; Kansas, 75; Montana, 104; and Populist Party growth, 76–78; South Dakota, 36, 48, 52, 59

Edmunds-Tucker Act, 99

Edwards, G. Thomas, 213n24

Edwards, Mr., 84

Edwards, Rebecca, 197n78

Elk Point, South Dakota, 57

Emerson, Ralph Waldo, 103

Emory speech, ESD's, 54

England, 123, 127, 128, 132, 147, 150, 215n55

English, Elisha, 16, 21

Eureka College, 4

Evans, Dora A., 28

F

farmers, 120–21, 134

Farmers' Alliance, 28, 37, 40–41, 48, 64

Faulk County, Dakota Territory/South Dakota, 17, 64, 203n21

federal amendment campaigns: Anthony's early work, 65, 67, 69; conflicting amendments, 221n53; CU's role, 147–48, 152–54, 158, 159–60, 161, 162; FSA-led, 61, 68–70, 73–74, 205n63; Idaho-based activity, 136, 152–53, 158, 159, 221n59, 222n87; NCWV-led, 143–44, 145–50, 152–54, 156–57, 221n53, 223n102; ratification process, 13, 139, 164–65, 175, 183–84. *See also* Congress, U.S. (suffrage legislation)

Federal Suffrage Association, 61, 68–70, 73–74, 205n63

Felton, Rebecca Latimer, 176

femininity quality, ESD's use, 55. *See also* conciliatory tactics

feminist label, 8, 191n23. *See also* conciliatory tactics

Fielder, William, 27, 33

Finland, 120, 185–186

First Baptist Church, Huron, 14, 15–16, 21

Fish, Ellen S., 136–37

Fisk, Thomas P., 181

Fitzgerald, Cecil B., 180

Flaherty, John, 29

Flandreau, South Dakota, 56–57, 72

Flannigan, Sarah, 170, 225n20, 226n23

Flexner, Eleanor, 218n3

Flint, Mrs. C. Holt, 73–74, 88–89, 97, 102, 103, 108, 210n69, photo section

Florida, 88–89

Forest City, Iowa, 72

Kegley, Augusta, 134
Kegley, C. B., 134
Kelley, Florence, 61, 128
Kelly, Guy, 178–79, 183
Kendall, Sarah, 183
Kendrick, John, 159
Kentucky, 108
Ketcham, John C., 178
Ketchum, Frank, 18, 19–20
King, Cora Smith. *See* Eaton, Cora Smith (later King)
Kitchen Contest, *Tacoma Daily News,* 134
Knights of Labor, 48

L

labor unions, 37, 89, 93–94, 120–21, 134, 216n99
La Follette, Robert M., 142
Lake, Illinois, 64
Landes, Bertha Knight, 176
Latham, Mrs. Joseph, 226n23
Latter Day Saints, 99
League of Nations, 168–69, 172, 174–75, 225n8
League of Women Voters, 162–64, 165, 224n114
Leckenby, Ellen S., 119, 122, 124–25
legal argument strategy, 68–69
Lewis County Republican Women's Club, 178, 182
"The Liberty of the Mother Means the Liberty of the Race" (DeVoe speech), 103
Lindsey, Ben, 133, 187
Lister, Ernest, 155, 157, 161
Lister, Mary Alma, 157
literary association, Huron, 16–17
literature, suffrage, 37, 40–41, 49, 133
Livermore, Henrietta L., 179
Livermore, Mary, 63
Livingston, Montana, 91, 104–5
Long, John D., 186
Longworth, Alice Roosevelt, 225n8

Los Angeles, California, 141, 159
Loucks, Henry L., 48, 53
Lukas, J. Anthony, 217n106

M

Marion County, Oregon, 117
marriage, ESD's, 4–5
Martin, Anne, 156, 158
Maryland, 147–48
Mason, Virginia, 136, 137, 138, 154
May 2 demonstration, 153–54
McCammon, Holly J., 192n27
McCarter, Margaret Hill, 171
McCaslin, D. S., 21
McCormick, Ruth Hanna, 171
McCredie, Mrs. R. C., 170
McCulloch, Catherine Waugh, 142
McCumber, Porter James, 149
McIntire, Ida N., 122
McIntosh, Alex, 46
Mead, Rebecca J., 192n27, 213n37
Mellette, Arthur C., 29
Mendenhall, Estella G., 170
Methodist Episcopalian Church, Faulk County, 17
Meyers, Elizabeth, 225n20
Michigan, 143
Milburn, Judge, 90
Miles City, Montana, 90, 104–5
Minnesota, 45, 129
Minor, Virginia T., 69
Mississippi Valley Suffrage Conference, 60, 73
Mitchell, Rebecca, 88
Mitchell convention, South Dakota, 51–52
Mondell, Frank W., 144–45, 156
Montana: Populist Party, 89, 105–6; statehood, 26
Montana, suffrage campaign: Catt-ESD conflicts, 97–98, 100–101, 106–7; ESD's speaking tours, 89–93, 97, 103–5, 107, 210n53; organizational challenges, 90–91, 104, 211n79; outside

speaker problem, 223n94; pledge system outcome, 102; vote outcome, 156
moral reform campaigns, 16–21. *See also* temperance movement
Morgan, Henry Victor, 183
Mormons, 99
Morton, Levi P., 26
Mott, Lucretia, 73
Mount Rainier, 115, 130
Mouser, I. J., 16
"Mr. Carpetbagger" (DeVoe song), 24
Munds, Frances, 158, 220n40
municipal housekeeping philosophy, 17–18, 21–22, 42–43, 90, 135–36, 197n78
music: community activities, 15, 17; ESD's talent, 4–5; fundraising impact, 42; statehood movement, 23, 24–25, 196n53; suffrage movement, 39–40, 42, 50, 51, 65–66, 201n65, photo section; temperance movement, 21–22, 31
Myers, Annice F. Jeffreys, 114
Myers, Jefferson, 114

N

National American Woman Suffrage Association (NAWSA): and Congressional Union, 151–52; federal campaign, 132, 139, 143–45, 160, 221n53, 223n102; finances, 86–87, 106–8, 143; Kansas campaign, 78–80; leadership changes, 67, 113–14, 160; and League of Women Voters, 162–63; national conventions, 43, 65–68, 86–87, 103, 107, 114–15, 119, 127–28; North Dakota campaign, 84–85; Oregon campaign, 116, 117–18; partisan politics policy, 78; peace activism decision, 162; reorganizations, 44, 86–87; schisms/factionalism, 61, 68–70, 140, 142, 148–49, 220n40; state-by-state approach, 35–36; unification dispute, 68; Washington campaign and con-

flicts, 119, 120, 125, 128–29; Wisconsin campaign, 142. *See also* Catt, Carrie Chapman
National Council of Women Voters (NCWV): overview, 11–12; benefit-oriented pamphlet, 142–43; California campaign, 140–41; Congressional Union relationship, 139–40, 150–52, 154–55, 156–57, 158; federal campaign, 143–44, 145–50, 152–54, 156–57, 221n53, 223n102; formation of, 115, 136–38; League of Women Voters merger, 163–65, 224n114; national conventions, 148–49, 157, 158–59; and National Woman's Party, 159–60; NAWSA relationship, 148–49, 160, 220n40; New York campaign, 156; presidential change, 148; Wisconsin campaign, 141–42
National League for Woman's Service, 162
National Republican, 177, 179, 180
National Suffrage Bulletin, 87
National Woman's Alliance (NWA), 64–65
National Woman's Party (NWP), 159–60, 161, 162, 223n94
National Woman Suffrage Association (NWSA), 44, 45, 68, 69
NAWSA. *See* National American Woman Suffrage Association (NAWSA)
NCWV. *See* National Council of Women Voters (NCWV)
Neblett, Viola, 88
Nebraska Woman Suffrage Association, 44
Nelson, Julia B., 45, 57–58
Nevada, 99, 100, 156
New Mexico, 113, 165
New Northwest, 94
newspaper-oriented strategies: ESD's columns, 171–74; suffrage campaign, 92, 134
New York, 74, 147, 156, 215n55

Nicholl, Thomas F., 15
Nineteenth Amendment, ratification process, 13, 139, 164–65, 175, 183–84. *See also* federal amendment campaigns
Non-Partisan Constitutional Prohibition Organization, 26, 29
North, James, 147
North Dakota, 26, 82–85
North Dakota House Journal, 85
Northern Pacific Railroad, 118–19
Norway, 120
Nutting, Wilder, 90, 91, 97, 98
NWA (National Woman's Alliance), 64–65
NWP (National Woman's Party), 159–60, 162
NWSA (National Woman Suffrage Association), 44, 45, 68, 69

O

Ohio, 143
Oklahoma, 107
Onida Journal, 55
Order of Good Templars, 17
Oregon, 94, 114–18, 143, 153–54, 165, 213n24
Organization Committee, NAWSA's: dissolution, 111; finance problems, 97; state association conflicts, 95; structure of, 86–88

P

Palmer, Thomas W., 40–41
Pankhurst, Emmeline G., 128, 132
parades/demonstrations, 52, 131, 143–44, 153–54, 216n99
Park, Maud Wood, 161
Parker, Adella, 130
Parton, Sara Willis, 8
Paul, Alice: background, 143; demonstrations/parades, 143–44, 148, 159–60, 162; federal campaign, 143, 145–46,

149, 162, 221n53, 222n87; partisan orientation, 150–51, 154; portrait, photo section. *See also* Congressional Union (CU)
Paulhamus, William H., 131
PEL (Political Equality League), 130, 141, 142
Pennsylvania, 74
People's Party, 64
Perkins, Sidney A., 134
petitions, 123, 144, 147–48, 159
physical appearances, role in campaigns, 9, 54–55, 96
Pickler, Alice, 29, 30, 44, 51, 110
Pickler, John, 29, 44, 49
Pierce, Gilbert A., 23
Pierce County Women's Republican Club, 180–81
Piper, George U., 124
Plankinton, South Dakota, 57
pledge system, NAWSA's, 87, 99, 102
Plummer, W. C., 83–84
Poe, Burns, 183
Poindexter, Miles, 168–69, 179
Political Equality League (PEL), 130, 141, 142
Pomeroy Christian Church, ESD speech, 185–87
Populist Party, 76–78, 81, 85, 94, 105–6
Portland convention, NAWSA's, 114–15
Portland Woman's Tribune, 116, 118
presidential elector position, ESD's, 170–71, 175–76
Preston, Elizabeth, 83, 84
Prim, Judge, 94
Prineville, Oregon, 118
prohibition. *See* temperance movement
prostitution, 18, 19, 20, 29–30, 195n32
publicity-oriented tactics, Washington campaign, 115, 130, 131–32. *See also* parades/demonstrations
Pullman, Illinois, 64
Putnam, Helen G., 32
Puyallup Valley Fair, 131

R

radicalism, 77–78

railroads, 5, 14, 100, 118–19

Rainier, Oregon, 118

Ramsey, Samuel A., 33, 45, 49

Rankin, Jeannette, 162, 163

ratification process, Nineteenth Amendment, 13, 139, 164–65, 175, 183–84. *See also* federal amendment campaigns

Red Cross, 162

Red Lodge, Montana, 91

Reno, Nevada, 100

Republican Day events, 174

Republican National Committee (RNC), 170, 178–80

Republicans: clubs, 177–78, 180–81; congressional elections, 154–55; Dakota statehood movement, 22–25, 26, 29; and Independent Party, 48–49; national conventions, 171, 181–82; national elections, 25–26, 108, 172–75; and National Woman's Party, 223*n*94; Nineteenth Amendment ratification, 165

Republicans, suffrage planks: California, 141; Idaho, 88; Kansas, 78–81, 82–83; Montana, 89; national level, 153; North Dakota, 84; South Dakota, 48, 52

Reynolds, Helen M., 104, 212*n*101

Rice, Harvey J., 19

Richards, Frances, 97

Richards, James H., 96, 97

Richards, Sarah A., 33, 50, 201*n*64

Rickards, J. E., 92

RNC (Republican National Committee), 170, 178–80

Roberts, Margaret S., 136, 150, 158, 159, 163, 222*n*87

Robins, Raymond, 174

Robinson, Hanson, 68

Roosevelt, Theodore, 175

Roseburg, Oregon, 116

Roudebush, Rex S., 183

Rundle, Arthur C., 176

S

salaries, ESD's, 69, 70, 83, 88, 97, 104, 106–8, 109

Salt Lake City, Utah, 159

Sanders, Harriet P., 106

Sanders, Sarepta, 98

Sanders, Wilbur F., 92

San Francisco conference, NCWV's, 157, 158–59

Sapp, Bernice A., 140, 165, 183

Savage, Mr., 127

schoolhouse speeches, 57–58

school suffrage, 65, 82

Scott, Helen J., 175

Seaside, Oregon, 117–18

Seattle, Washington, 119, 127–28, 176

Seattle Federation of Women's Clubs, 136–37

Seattle Post-Intelligencer, 128, 133, 134

Seattle Times, 126, 129

Senate, U.S. *See* Congress *entries*

Seneca Falls convention, 13

"Severance of Church and State, or Lewis K's Lamentation" (DeVoe song), 25, 26

Shafroth, John F., 133, 187

Shafroth-Palmer Amendment, 221*n*53

Shaw, Anna Howard: background, 30, 45; NAWSA leadership positions, 67, 140, 160; NCWV opposition, 148–49, 156; portrait, 55, photo section

Shaw, Anna Howard (state campaigns): California, 99; Idaho, 96; Kansas, 79, 81, 82; Nevada, 99; Oregon, 117–18; South Dakota, 45, 49, 52–55, 66; Washington, 120, 128, 129, 216*n*86

shoe stores, JHD's, 5, 20, 34, 48, 62, 63–64

Simmons, Anna R., 109–11

Sixteenth Amendment, 41, 67, 68

Taft, William H., 132
temperance movement: Baptist leadership, 15–16, 21–22; county option, 20–22; Harvey community, 62–63, 77, 206n80; Huron conflicts, 18–20; municipal housekeeping perspective, 17–18, 21–22; and statehood movement, 26–29, 31; and suffrage movement, 30–33, 38, 116, 212n9, 213n24, 214n41. *See also* Woman's Christian Temperance Union (WCTU)
Tennessee, 165
Tetrault, Lisa, 191n19
Texas, 107, 176
The Dalles, Oregon, 118
Thomas, D. C., 50, 201n66
Tillman, Benjamin R., 149
Todd, Hugh C., 155
trains, campaign-oriented, 115, 127–28, 159
Trout, Grace Wilbur, 163
Turner, George, 155
"Two State Injine" (song), 24

U

Union Signal, 37
unity/harmony facade, overview, 6–7. *See also* National American Woman Suffrage Association (NAWSA); National Council of Women Voters (NCWV)
Upton, Harriet Taylor, 54, 97, 129, 171, 179
Utah, 99, 133–34, 136, 159, 186, 187

V

Vermillion, South Dakota, 57
Vernon, Mabel, 158
Vest, George G., 22–23
"The Viewpoint of a Republican Woman" (DeVoe), 171–72
Virginia City, Montana, 211n79
Volstead Act, 173–75

W

Waite, Davis, 94
Walsh, Thomas J., 149
Wardall, Alonzo, 33, 43–44, 48, 50, 119
Wardall, Elizabeth Murray, 56–57, 58, 62, 119, 201n64
Wardall, R. R., 34
Washington, D.C.: NAWSA conventions, 43, 65–68, 103; NCWV conference, 148–49; suffrage parade, 143–44. *See also* Congress, U.S.
Washington, Illinois, 4–5
Washington Council of Women Voters, 154
Washington Herald, 55
Washington State Federation of Labor, 120–21, 134
Washington State Republican Committee, ESD's work: overview, 167–68; campaign activity, 174–75, 180–81, 182; leadership appointments, 167, 176–77, 182; membership organizing, 177–78, 179; national convention, 170–71, 226n23; presidential elector position, 170–71, 175–76; state conventions, 170–71, 181
Washington State Republican Committee, gender role expectations, 169–71, 225n20
Washington (territory and state), statehood bill, 26
Washington (territory and state), suffrage campaign: coalition-building approach, 120–21, 134, 214n41; eastern region activities, 121–22; ESD's leadership summarized, 113–14, 115, 118–20; ESD's Washington D.C. visit, 132–33; federal campaign, 149–50, 153–55, 157, 216n99, 224n114; high school suffrage clubs, 123, 214n52; legislative lobbying, 123–25; neighboring state support, 132–35; Nineteenth Amendment ratification, 139, 164–65,

175; organizational conflicts, 122–23, 125–30, 216n86; Pomeroy speech, 185–87; publicity-oriented tactics, 115, 130, 131–32; senate election, 155; and South Dakota's campaign, 161; train campaign, 127–28; vote outcomes, 94, 114, 134–36

Washington Times, 148

Washington Women's Cook Book, 130

Way, Amanda, 75

Weedin, Sarah, 226n23

Welch, Charles B., 171

Welch, Jim, 5, 189n2

Welch, Tom, 189n2

Wells, Emmeline B., 99

Wells, Nevada, 100

Wentworth, South Dakota, 53, 56

West Allis, Wisconsin, 113

Western region, overview of role in suffrage movement, 10–12. *See also* National Council of Women Voters (NCWV); *specific states*

Wheeler, Edwin G., 16

white ribbon bows, 198n11

Whittemore, Margaret Fay, 154–55, 157

Willard, Frances, 39, 55, 61

Willcox, Hamilton, 69–70

Williams, Clare M., 109

Wilson, John Lockwood, 136–37

Wilson, Woodrow, 144, 159, 160, 162, 168–69, 172–73, 175

Winning Plan strategy, 160

Wisconsin, 51, 74, 94, 113, 141–42, 143

Woman's Christian Temperance Union (WCTU): Baptist alliance, 16; ESD's membership, 17; finances, 40; girls school, 33–34; South Dakota suffrage campaign, 37–39, 40, 198n12; statehood activity, 26–31; suffrage advocacy style, 36; Washington campaign, 121, 214n41. *See also* temperance movement

Woman's Day events, 29, 52–53, 71, 131, 134

Woman's National Liberal Union, 61

Woman's Relief Corps, 21, 63, 111, 183, 198n15

Women's Social and Political Union (WSPU), 150

Woods, Mell, 107

Woodward, Mary Dodge, 40

Workman, Lewis E., 88

World War I period, 162–63, 172

Wright, Carroll D., 186

Wyoming, 50, 65–66, 136, 176, 186

Y

Yankton, South Dakota, 58

Yates, Elizabeth U., 88

yellow ribbon badges, 38, 198n11

Young Men's Christian Association, 17